PROJECT

Contemporary
Historical
Examination of
Current
Operations

REPORT

INTERDICTION IN SEASIA
NOVEMBER 1966 - OCTOBER 1968

30 JUNE 1969

HQ PACAF

Directorate, Tactical Evaluation
CHECO Division

PROJECT CHECO REPORTS

The counterinsurgency and unconventional warfare environment of Southeast Asia has resulted in the employment of USAF airpower to meet a multitude of requirements The varied applications of airpower have involved the full spectrum of USAF aerospace vehicles, support equipment, and manpower. As a result, there has been an accumulation of operational data and experiences that, as a priority, must be collected, documented, and analyzed as to current and future impact upon USAF policies, concepts, and doctrine.

Fortunately, the value of collecting and documenting our SEA experiences was recognized at an early date. In 1962, Hq USAF directed CINCPACAF to establish an activity that would be primarily responsive to Air Staff require- ments and direction, and would provide timely and analytical studies of USAF combat operations in SEA

Project CHECO, an acronym for Contemporary Historical Examination of Current Operations, was established to meet this Air Staff requirement Managed by Hq PACAF, with elements at Hq 7AF and 7AF/13AF, Project CHECO provides a scholarly, "on-going" historical examination, documentation, and reporting on USAF policies, concepts, and doctrine in PACOM. This CHECO report is part of the overall documentation and examination which is being accomplished. Along with the other CHECO publications, this is an authentic source for an assess- ment of the effectiveness of USAF airpower in PACOM

MILTON B ADAMS, Major General, USAF
Chief of Staff

REPLY TO
ATTN OF: DOTEC

30 June 1969

SUBJECT: Project CHECO Report, "Interdiction in SEAsia, November 1966-
October 1968" (U)

SEE DISTRIBUTION PAGE

1. Attached is a SECRET NOFORN document. It shall be transported,
stored, safeguarded, and accounted for in accordance with applicable
security directives. Each page is marked according to its contents.
SPECIAL HANDLING REQUIRED, NOT RELEASABLE TO FOREIGN NATIONALS. The
information contained in this document will not be disclosed to foreign
nationals or their representatives. Retain or destroy in accordance
with AFR 205-1. Do not return.

2. This letter does not contain classified information and may be
declassified if attachment is removed from it.

FOR THE COMMANDER IN CHIEF

WARREN H. PETERSON, Colonel, USAF   1 Atch
Chief, CHECO Division   Proj CHECO Rprt (S/NF),
Directorate, Tactical Evaluation   30 Jun 69
DCS/Operations

DISTRIBUTION LIST

1. SECRETARY OF THE AIR FORCE

   a. SAFAA 1
   b. SAFLL 1
   c. SAFOI 2

2. HEADQUARTERS USAF

   a. AFBSA 1

   b. AFCCS
      (1) AFCCSSA 1
      (2) AFCVC 1
      (3) AFCAV 1
      (4) AFCHO 2

   c. AFCSA
      (1) AFCSAG 1
      (2) AFCSAMI 1

   d. AFGOA 2

   e. AFIGO
      (1) AFISI 3
      (2) AFISP 1

   f. AFMSG 1

   g. AFNIN
      (1) AFNIE 1
      (2) AFNINA 1
      (3) AFNINCC 1
      (4) AFNINED 4

   h. AFAAC 1
      (1) AFAMAI 1

   i. AFODC
      (1) AFOAP 1
      (2) AFOAPS 1
      (3) AFOCC 1

   (4) AFOCE 1
   (5) AFOMO 1

   j. AFPDC
      (1) AFPDPSS 1
      (2) AFPMDG 1
      (3) AFPDW 1

   k. AFRDC 1
      (1) AFRDD 1
      (2) AFRDQ 1
      (3) AFRDQRC 1
      (4) AFRDR 1

   l. AFSDC
      (1) AFSLP 1
      (2) AFSME 1
      (3) AFSMS 1
      (4) AFSPD 1
      (5) AFSSS 1
      (6) AFSTP 1

   m. AFTAC 1

   n. AFXDC
      (1) AFXDO 1
      (2) AFXDOC 1
      (3) AFXDOD 1
      (4) AFXDOL 1
      (5) AFXOP 1
      (6) AFXOSL 1
      (7) AFXOSN 1
      (8) AFXOSO 1
      (9) AFXOSS 1
      (10) AFXOSV 1
      (11) AFXOTR 1
      (12) AFXOTW 1
      (13) AFXOTZ 1
      (14) AFXOXY 1
      (15) AFXPD 6
         (a) AFXPPGS 3

3. MAJOR COMMANDS

    a. TAC

        (1) HEADQUARTERS
            (a) DO 1
            (b) DPL 2
            (c) DOCC. 1
            (d) DORQ. 1
            (e) DIO 1

        (2) AIR FORCES
            (a) 12AF
                1. DORF 1
                2. DI 1
            (b) 19AF(DI). 1
            (c) USAFSOF(DO) 1

        (3) WINGS
            (a) 1SOW(DO). 1
            (b) 4TFW(DO). 1
            (c) 23TFW(DOI). 1
            (d) 27TFW(DOI). 1
            (e) 33TFW(DOI). 1
            (f) 64TAW(DOI). 1
            (g) 67TRW(C). 1
            (h) 75TRW(DO) 1
            (i) 316TAW(DOP) 1
            (j) 317TAW(EX). 1
            (k) 363TRW(DOC) 1
            (l) 464TAW(DO). 1
            (m) 474TFW(TFOX). . . . 1
            (n) 479TFW(DOF) 1
            (o) 516TAW(DOPL). . . . 1
            (p) 4410CCTW(DOTR). . . 1
            (q) 4510CCTW(DO16-I). . 1
            (r) 4554CCTW(DOI) . . . 1

        (4) TAC CENTERS, SCHOOLS

            (a) USAFTAWC(DA). . . . 2
            (b) USAFTARC(DID) . . . 2
            (c) USAFTALC(DCRL). . . 1
            (d) USAFTFWC(CRCD). . . 1

            (e) USAFAGOS(DAB-C) 1

    b. SAC

        (1) HEADQUARTERS
            (a) DOPL. 1
            (b) DPLF. 1
            (c) DM. 1
            (d) DI. 1
            (e) OA. 1
            (f) HI. 1

        (2) AIR FORCES
            (a) 2AF(DICS) 1
            (b) 15AF(DI). 1

        (3) AIR DIVISIONS
            (a) 3AD(DO) 3

    c. MAC

        (1) HEADQUARTERS
            (a) MAOID 1
            (b) MAOCO 1
            (c) MACHO 1
            (d) MACOA 1

        (2) AIR FORCES
            (a) 21AF(OCXI). 1
            (b) 22AF(OCXI). 1

        (3) WINGS
            (a) 61MAWg(OIN) 1
            (b) 62MAWg(OCXP). . . . 1
            (c) 436MAWg(OCXC) . . . 1
            (d) 437MAWg(OCXI) . . . 1
            (e) 438MAWg(OCXC) . . . 1

        (4) MAC SERVICES
            (a) AWS(AWXW) 1
            (b) ARRS(ARXLR) 1
            (c) ACGS(AGOV). 1
            (d) AAVS(AVODOD). . . . 1

TABLE OF CONTENTS

FIGURES   Follows Page

FOREWORD

The war in Southeast Asia in 1967 and 1968 comprised an astounding complexity of conventional and unconventional wars, political and geographic boundaries, Rules of Engagement, areas of operation, command responsibilities, wet and dry seasons, sanctuaries for both sides, and a terrain of mountains, jungles, and flood plains. From the Red Chinese Border to the Mekong Delta, the enemy supply lines ran this tangled natural and man-made gauntlet--attacked the whole way by the air interdiction campaign. In North Vietnam, the railroads and bridges on the Joint Chiefs of Staff (JCS) target lists were the prime interdiction targets. Interdiction operations in Laos meant attacking the trucks rolling down the Ho Chi Minh Trail, closing the roads with airstrikes, and bombing the supplies stockpiled off the Trail. Within South Vietnam, all airstrikes were nominally considered close air support for ground forces. Seventh Air Force operations against in-country enemy roads only slowly became an interdiction campaign. The Cambodian government's refusal to sanction U.S. airstrikes within its borders put U.S activities there within the scope of unconventional warfare and outside the conventional interdiction efforts.

Despite many natural and man-made variables, "air interdiction" had certain common characteristics, particular tactics, and specific munitions For instance, the Air Force experience in Korea was repeated in SEA when the enemy's heavy antiaircraft artillery (AAA) degraded accurate bombing of roads and railroads. Also, few efficient area denial weapons existed to prevent rapid enemy repair of the bomb cuts made on the roadbeds. This proved true

against roads running through Laos into South Vietnam, as well as against railroads around Hanoi.

Air Force doctrine and common usage in 1967 and 1968 left the meaning
of interdiction subject to both very broad and narrow interpretations. Air
Force and JCS usage defined "interdict" as "to prevent or hinder, by any means,
enemy use of an area or route." Air Force Manual 1-1 (14 August 1964) in
Chapter Five, concerning conventional air operations, distinguished between
counterair, close air support, and interdiction, with the latter "to reduce
enemy logistic support below the high level necessary to sustain conventional
operations." Air Force Manual 2-1 (14 June 1965), on tactical air operations,
devoted a short chapter to interdiction operations. This is a quotation from it:

> *"Tactical air force interdiction operations are designed*
> *to disrupt this flow /of personnel, supplies, and equip-*
> *ment along lines of communication/ through destruction,*
> *delay or harassment to neutralize the effectiveness of*
> *enemy reserves and compromise the position of enemy forces*
> *engaged directly in combat."*

Targets along the lines of communication (LOCs) included transportation centers,
supply depots and storage facilities, repair and modification centers, troop
staging areas, and industrial installations producing equipment and material
for combat forces.

The PACAF Manual 55-13 (1 April 1965) on joint operations elaborated
several aspects of air interdiction, especially how airpower followed the enemy
LOCs back to the source of supplies:

*"Air interdiction is that air effort designed to deny
to the enemy's deployed combat forces the supplies,
replacements, and reinforcements needed for continued
operation and to limit their freedom of movement. Air
interdiction operations are conducted to destroy or
neutralize the enemy military potential before it can
be brought to bear effectively against our own forces
and to restrict the mobility of hostile forces by disrupting enemy lines of communications throughout an
area of operations. A properly planned air interdiction
campaign can encompass the entire line of communications
system of the enemy and will seek to deny movement of
appreciable quantities of personnel and material. Major
consideration is given to the isolation of the surface
battle area so that engaged enemy forces are prevented
from continued operations. Although the effects of an
air interdiction campaign are seldom immediately observ-
able, a well-planned and executed campaign can contribute
decisively to the attainment of the joint force mission.
The overall effects of air interdiction are achieved by
destruction, neutralization, delay, and harassment."*

In line with these several thoughts, this report defines interdiction
as the destruction or disruption of enemy troops and material moving along
lines of communications supporting enemy combat operations. This definition
of interdiction is neither as broad as AFM 2-1 nor so narrow as blockading
roads. Lines of communications include air, land, and water transportation
systems. The Navy had responsibility for interdicting infiltration by sea
into South Vietnam from either North Vietnam or Cambodia, and organized operations GAME WARDEN and MARKET TIME to intercept enemy supply vessels heading
toward South Vietnamese shores. Seaborne resupply to the I and II Corps was
essentially halted. Air infiltration was negligible, though occasionally
intelligence told of high ranking enemy officials being flown south to base
camps along the South Vietnamese borders. The Air Force was concerned with
the interdiction of ground LOCs--roads, railroads, and rivers--used by the

enemy in the Indochina Peninsula.

Just how to interdict enemy LOCs was the subject of voluminous paper work and untold man-hours of 7AF alone, not to mention MACV, PACAF, PACOM, and the many interested agencies in Washington. Yet, a quick glance at actual air interdiction operations from 1966 through 1968 in SEA shows less an evolution of strategy than variations on the same themes. Basically, airstrikes achieved interdiction by three means: cutting the LOCs to prevent traffic movement; destroying the vehicles of transportation; or destroying the supplies in storage areas. New weapons, tactics, and target emphasis were introduced as the enemy reacted. Three notable 7AF innovations were the introduction of the Forward Air Controller (FAC) into Southern Laos in December 1965, the 1967 attacks against the railroad rolling stock around Hanoi, and the 1968 intensive choke point campaign in the North Vietnamese panhandle. The enemy countered. Increasing AAA and improving clandestine operations made the FAC job more difficult, while moving the boxcars into no-strike zones reduced the loss of railcars. The November 1968 bombing halt banished the choke point bottlenecks in North Vietnam.

The story of air interdiction from 1966 to 1968 was one of 7AF introducing a new tactic and the enemy attempting to circumvent that tactic. Conceivably, new weapons could achieve more effective interdiction. A new series of area denial weapons could be developed to combine delivery accuracy with relative immunity from rapid enemy clearing operations, thus permitting effective 24-hour road cuts. (Mixed "packages" of assorted antipersonnel and destruction mines achieved some area denial for road cuts in COMMANDO HUNT in the spring of 1969.)

The example of road closure tactics is useful in illustrating the hobbling effect of inadequate munitions. Area bombing with 750-lb.-3,000 lb. bombs could achieve road cuts in the absence of suitable bomb/missiles with pinpoint accuracy, but the enemy filled the bomb craters or cleared the landslides. To prevent road clearance during the night, 7AF tried maintaining presence over the choke points. Armed reconnaissance/FAC/flareship/gunship presence reduced traffic but could not prevent all trucks from getting through. Either the enemy accepted the loss of men and trucks and pushed through the choke point, or he built a bypass. Another approach was to periodically bomb the choke point throughout the night, but this was expensive considering ordnance costs, bombing and night attack accuracy, limited air resources, and the number of bypasses. Seeding with the available area denial weapons—MK36, gravel, Dragon Tooth, delayed fuze bombs—did stop traffic for varying periods, depending upon the availability of enemy explosive ordnance demolition teams. The realistic objective of air interdiction was not to strangle or absolutely stop enemy resupply. This point needs clarification because of the frequent criticism in the popular press concerning the promises of interdiction. For instance, former Ambassador John K. Galbraith was quoted as saying:[1]

> "Repeatedly, the Air Force has made these claims: 'Let us bomb this pass and we will stop all movement down to South Vietnam.' 'We're interdicting the movement along the Ho Chi Minh Trail.' 'The air attacks are all-important for stopping the movement of men and supplies out of North Vietnam into South Vietnam....' We've had dozens of these promises, all of them ending in failure."

Political analyst Stewart Alsop in a column paraphrasing off-the-record comments of top Johnson Administration advisers claimed one of the "lessons of

Vietnam was "don't overestimate what airpower can do." Alsop stated:[2]

> "I don't think any of us--or many of us, anyway--
> thought we could win the war with airpower alone.
> But some of us certainly hoped so....One thing
> we've learned--you can't interdict infiltration
> or supplies, for this kind of war, with bombs."

This use of "interdict" by critics implied stopping or halting enemy movement, but, judging by 7AF operations plans, the mission of interdiction was never stated in such absolute terms. The 7AF OPlan 483-67 for part of the Laotian panhandle gave the following mission:[3]

> "Deny NVN the use of a mechanized logistics system
> in Laos for support of its armed forces in RVN by
> destroying enemy facilities and LOCs in Laos,
> harassing, disrupting, and impeding movement of
> men and materials through Laos into RVN."

The OpOrd 100-68 for ROLLING THUNDER assigned three objectives for airstrikes in the North:[4]

- Reduce, disrupt, and harass the external assistance being provided to NVN.

- Disrupt and destroy resources that support aggression.

- Harass, disrupt, and impede movement of men and materials southward.

The 7AF OPlan 512-68 for the Northeast Monsoon Campaign gave the same three objectives, while the OpOrd 433-68 for BARREL ROLL/STEEL TIGER had two missions: "to support Royal Laotian ground operations, and disrupt the logistic flow of the Pathet Lao, Viet Cong, and NVN Forces."[5] From this spectrum of plans, it can be generalized that the purpose of interdiction was to "destroy, harass, disrupt, and impede" enemy LOCs.

To achieve this and to comply with the Rules of Engagement, the early campaigns in Laos and North Vietnam used armed reconnaissance. Both countries were divided into armed reconnaissance areas. Alpha through Golf in Laos, and Route Packages I through VI in North Vietnam. At the end of 1965, the FACs entered the lower part of the Laotian panhandle and obtained an increase in truck kills. In ROLLING THUNDER, the expansion north brought increasingly important fixed targets under attack, disrupting traffic. The increased truck kills and the destruction of major bridges and transshipment points caused the enemy to disperse his operations, build an impressive though inefficient complex of bypasses, and increase his AAA defenses. By early 1967, the initial lucrative targets were nearly gone (except around Hanoi/Haiphong) and both sides had settled down to a war of attrition along the supply lines.[6/]

"USAF Air Interdiction in SEA, November 1966 - October 1968" highlights certain areas of the evolution of interdiction strategy, concepts, and tactics employed by 7AF during two full climatic years or four monsoon seasons. It is a sequel to CHECO report "Interdiction in SEA, 1965 - 1966", and ends with the 1 November 1968 bombing halt in North Vietnam. (A new interdiction campaign called COMMANDO HUNT began on 15 November in Southern Laos; the old STEEL TIGER North and TIGER HOUND areas were abolished. In South Vietnam, the dry monsoon began about this time, thus making the end of October a logical termination date for this report.)

A two-year summary of interdiction in Southeast Asia includes a large chunk of the out-country war, plus a growing facet of the in-country war. Only the air war in northern Laos has been excluded, as it was not directly related to enemy logistical support of VC/NVN troops in South Vietnam. The 1968 interdiction campaign in Route Package I is only briefly mentioned, because another CHECO report has already been written about that area. Significant parts of the air war in Laos will be found in CHECO Report "USAF Operations from Thailand, 1 January 1967 to 1 July 1968."

Caution should be exercised concerning the statistics in this report. They are cited to indicate trends and approximations, not to establish absolutes. Obviously, visual truck sightings depend not only on the amount of enemy truck traffic, but also on the number of FACs airborne, weather conditions, and AAA in areas with volume traffic. Criteria for claiming truck kills were stringent, but the totals were estimates nonetheless. Totals for enemy personnel and trucks on the Ho Chi Minh Trail and estimates of tonnage moving through Cambodia and Laos from any source should be viewed with equal caution.

CHAPTER I

ENEMY LOCs

North Vietnam

In mid-1967 North Vietnam received one-quarter of its foreign aid from the Chinese Communists and three-quarters from the Soviet Bloc nations. [1] Of this, approximately 70 percent came by sea and 30 percent by land (mostly by rail). [2] Ammunition and military equipment entered North Vietnam almost exclusively by rail. The actual tonnage imports in 1966 totaled an estimated one million metric tons via sea, mostly into Haiphong, and 420,000 metric tons by rail. [3] In 1967, imports increased 45 percent and exports declined 50 percent. [4]

North Vietnam had only three ports capable of receiving oceangoing vessels. Cam Pha and Hon Gai, both north of Haiphong, shipped mostly coal and cement, two of the country's main exports. They handled little incoming cargo. Haiphong handled an estimated 70 percent of North Vietnam's total imports, 85 percent of all maritime shipping, and 95 percent of the imported POL. [5] Typical Soviet cargo into Haiphong included trucks, heavy construction equipment, rolled steel products, bridge building material, drugs, medical equipment, and food. In 1967, the bulk of the 188,000 tons of POL to North Vietnam came in 39 Soviet tankers, all but four from Vladivostok. [6]

Goods coming by rail from the Soviet Bloc moved over the Trans-Siberian Railroad to the vicinity of Mongolia, south to the Peking area, and south again to Nan-ning, the southern terminus for goods going to North Vietnam. From Nan-ning to the border, a train (in early 1967) normally took three and a half

1

hours. At one time, a major bottleneck existed at the border because
supplies were shifted from the Chinese standard gauge to the Vietnamese meter
gauge. But by mid-1967, a third rail laid on the Vietnamese Rail Line 2 to Kep
solved the problem.[7] The two railroads coming from China converged on Hanoi,
the traditional transportation hub of North Vietnam. The Northeast Railroad
(Line 2) carried by far the most tonnage and especially ammunition and combat
equipment. (Fig. 8.) The Northwest Railroad (Line 1), paralleling the Red
River, was used by the Chinese Communists to move bulk products and especially
POL. No definite evidence existed that the Soviets shipped supplies over this
railroad during the time frame of this report. Supplies at Haiphong in early
1967 moved to Hanoi primarily along Rail Line 3 and secondarily by road or
river. The intensified U.S. rail campaign in that year forced some shift
toward water shipments.

The cited figures and percentages on tonnage and the relative importance
of LOCs are of course rough estimates. Although they are much more definite
than the tonnage estimates of supplies moving through Laos, they are still
subject to debate. For instance, the statement that 85 percent of all maritime
shipping went through Haiphong is contrasted with a CINCPACFLT message saying
Haiphong handled 95 percent of North Vietnamese shipping during 1966.[8]

From these estimates, emerged a picture of the logistic system in the
enemy heartland. Hanoi was the transportation and redistribution hub of the
nation. Down the Northwest Railroad came the least tonnage--mainly Chinese
bulk items. Ammunition and other combat items came almost exclusively over
the Northeast Railroad. General cargo such as trucks and steel products

2

totaling about 70 percent of all North Vietnamese imports moved through Haiphong to Hanoi by rail, road, and water. To these imports were added North Vietnamese manufactures from the Hanoi-Haiphong-Thai Nguyen area and food from the Red River Delta. Much of this native imported tonnage moved into the greater Hanoi area.

From Hanoi, an intricate network of roads and waterways spread over the Red River Delta. Especially in the triangle of Hanoi, Haiphong, and Nam Dinh, the extensive waterways carried heavy traffic and provided a bypass for roads in the area. However, the long railroad and highway bridges spanning the rivers were vulnerable interdiction targets. During the dry season, their use was restricted. New road construction went on during the U.S. bombing of the North, some of it to increase the alternate routes south. In the panhandle of North Vietnam, the roads were built through dense forests to take advantage of concealment and to hide truck parks and storage areas; right of way clearance was minimal. Road surfaces were of dirt, generally four to five meters on primary roads and two and a half to three meters on secondary roads, and of a limited all-weather capability. Materials for base and surface construction were locally obtained and not hauled far. Roads followed the terrain to avoid steep grades and cut-and-fill. Ferries crossed the major streams--no long bridges--and small bridges had bypass fords.[9] In short, the North Vietnamese built well, with an eye to counterinterdiction attacks.

Supplies destined for South Vietnam via land LOCs moved south to Thanh Hoa, site of the famous railroad bridge upon which U.S. fighter-bombers repeatedly scored direct hits, but were unable to drop into the river because

3

of the uniquely hard construction of the bridge. Rail Line 4 from Hanoi to Thanh Hoa carried considerable tonnage. According to a 7AF DI summary of enemy LOCs, the dense population and the economic and military significance of the Red River Delta area probably account to a large degree for the higher use rate in the area north of Thanh Hoa. [10/]

The North Vietnamese panhandle began south of Thanh Hoa. The major LOCs ran north-south with Route 1A following the coastal lowlands and Route 15 running through the western mountains. These routes and Rail Line 6 converged at Vinh, the logistics hub of the panhandle, while the Song Ca (Water Route 11) opened the town to coastal water traffic. [11/] Vinh was also notable as the gateway to Nape Pass only 40 miles to the southwest. In 1965, the major infiltration into Laos went through Nape Pass over Route 8, but by 1967 the heavy tonnage had shifted south to the Mu Gia Pass.

Below Vinh, the railroad left the coast and paralleled mountain Route 15, ending just below 18° North. From here, Route 15 cut through the Mu Gia Pass to Laos, and Route 101 ran southeast toward the Phuong Chay Ferry junction where Route 137 headed southwest through the Ban Karai Pass. These routes became targets for the highly successful Summer Interdiction Campaign of 1968. Below Dong Hoi, the military supply area for the region north of the DMZ, the several roads and trails leading to the DMZ branched off the coastal network of roads. Thus, the panhandle had one railroad two-thirds of its length, a complex road system on the coastal plain, certain important but isolated mountain roads, and four primary infiltration areas to enter Laos or South Vietnam: the DMZ and the Nape, Mu Gia, and Ban Karai Passes.

4

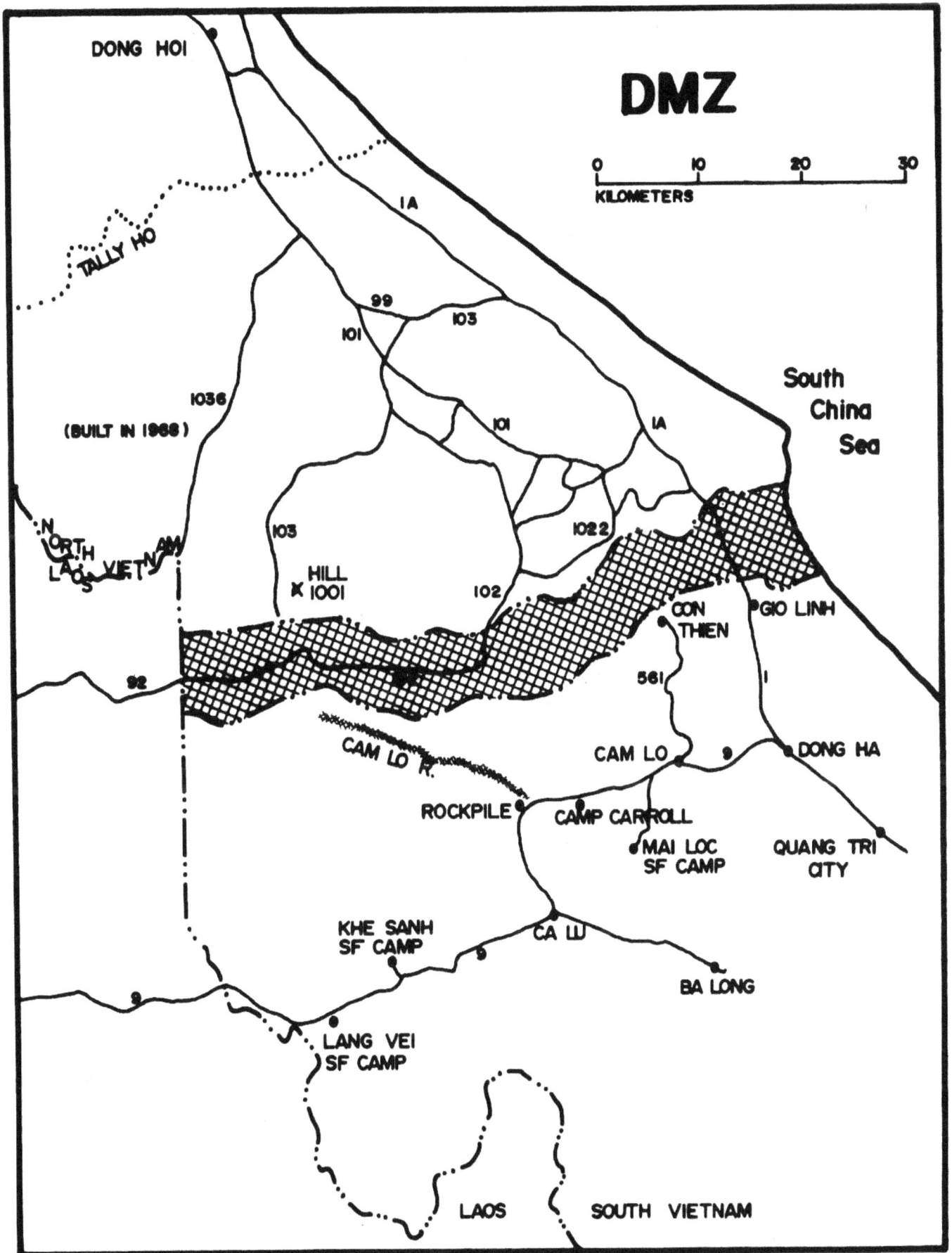

DMZ

DONG HOI

TALLY HO

1A

99

101   103

1036

(BUILT IN 1968)

101

South
China
Sea

103

HILL
× 1001

102

1022

NORTH
LAOS   VIETNAM

CON
THIEN

GIO LINH

9 2

561

1

CAM LO R.

CAM LO

9

DONG HA

ROCKPILE

CAMP CARROLL

MAI LOC
SF CAMP

QUANG TRI
CITY

KHE SANH
SF CAMP

9

CA LU

BA LONG

9

LANG VEI
SF CAMP

LAOS   SOUTH VIETNAM

0   10   20   30

KILOMETERS

FIG. 1

Demilitarized Zone

North Vietnamese road siting and construction in southern Route Package I sought to cope with the DMZ and the partial strong point barrier built by the U.S. Marines. The old coastal Route 1A over the Ben Hai River was supplemented by many roads to the west that ran toward the zone and narrowed to trails and footpaths in the DMZ. Route 103 angled southwest toward the Laotian end of the DMZ, and Route 1036, built in 1968, provided another road even farther west in the mountains. (Fig. 1.) Enemy infiltration of troops into South Vietnam traditionally included an end run around most of the DMZ. Prior to the intensified bombing of the panhandle, the infiltrating troops arrived by truck down Route 103, walked past Hill 1001 into Laos, and then cut back south of the DMZ into the Cam Lo Valley north of Khe Sanh.[12/] In October 1966, PACAF reported 95 percent of the captured NVA troops as saying they came into South Vietnam past Hill 1001.[13/]

In 1966, the Marines moved into Khe Sanh and took over the camps of Ca Lu and Ba Long to prevent troop infiltrations from the North. However, in June 1966, three regiments of the 432B NVA Division crossed through the center of the DMZ and, later, units of two other divisions followed. The U.S. responded by strengthening its line of camps, increasing ground operations south of the DMZ, and stepping up the bombing inside the DMZ. The antiinfiltration system was formalized in 1967 by Secretary of Defense, Robert S. McNamara, as the Strong Point Obstacle Subsystem along the eastern DMZ, and the DUMP TRUCK Antipersonnel Subsystem using sensors along the western end of the DMZ.

The heavy U.S. bombing in the panhandle of North Vietnam disrupted the

NVA pattern of infiltration to the extent of forcing the troops to walk south from Thanh Hoa to the western DMZ for the end run around the zone or down the Ho Chi Minh Trail through Laos. By the same token, U.S. vigilance along the DMZ precluded sizable enemy supplies from being carried across the DMZ.

Laos

The alternating wet and dry seasons in Laos acted much like a traffic light for both enemy trucking and U.S. air operations--go during the dry season and stop during the wet. From November to May, the enemy pushed through the large amounts of military supplies to keep the war going in South Vietnam. Without the Ho Chi Minh Trail, the enemy could not sustain the troops necessary to maintain their aggression in SVN. Keeping the Trail open was imperative for the enemy.

During the 1964/1965 dry season, the truck route from North Vietnam ran through the Nape Pass (Route 8) and the Mu Gia Pass (Route 12) and then west to the Mekong riverport of Thakhek, and south and east by the Laotian road network to trails leading east into South Vietnam. This was unsatisfactory for the NVA. Movement of heavy supplies had to pass through the Thakhek area held by Royal Laotian forces. Further, the road system was not usable during the heavy summer rains. [14/] However, there were jungle trails running southwest from the DMZ into Laos. It was down these primitive trails, the NVA troops moved under severe hardships, suffering especially from malaria, malnutrition, and often a shortage of water. Since the trails ran through the thinly populated and unpopulated eastern portion of the Laotian panhandle, they provided the obvious solution to avoiding Royal Laotian surveillance. This network became

6

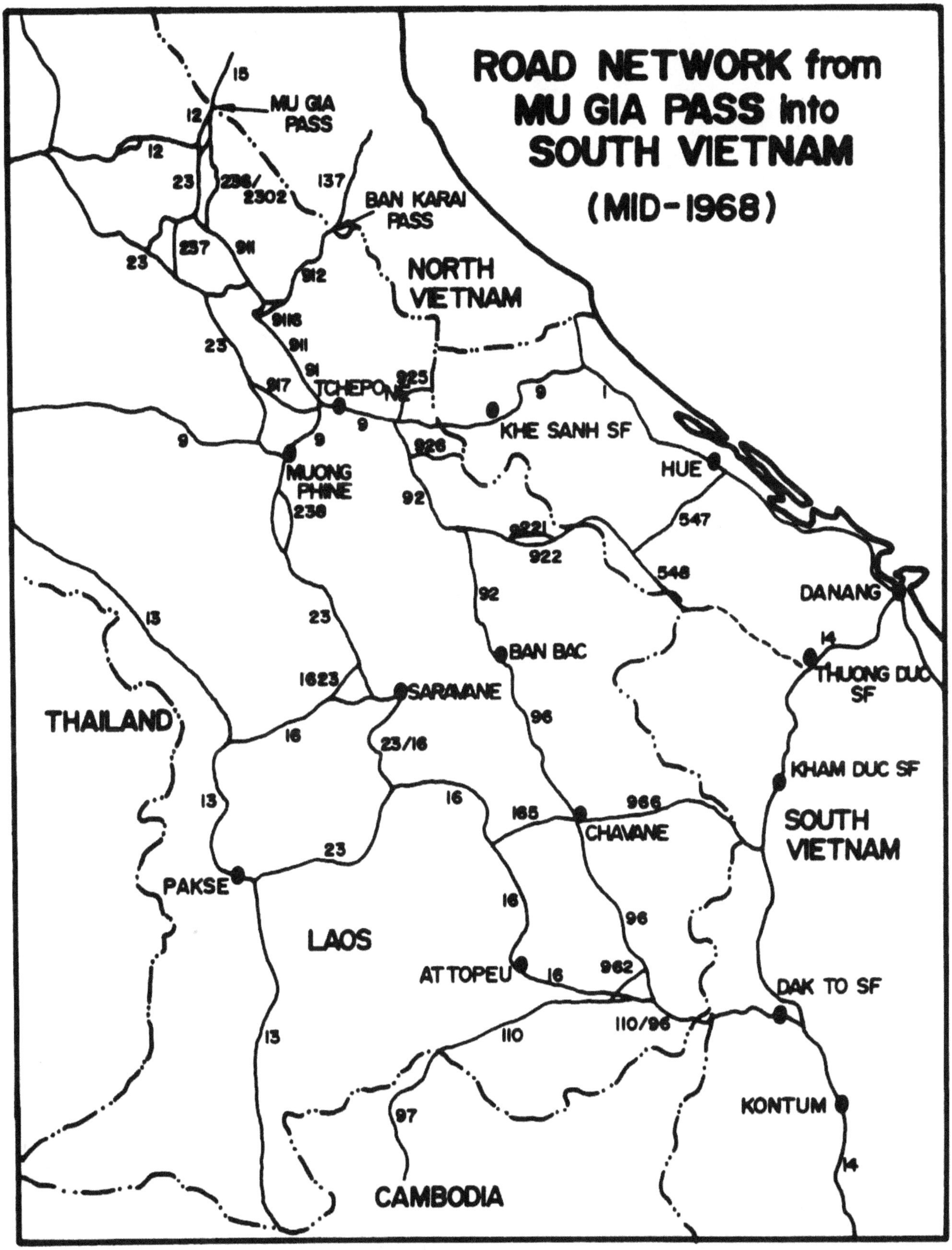
ROAD NETWORK from
MU GIA PASS into
SOUTH VIETNAM
(MID-1968)
15
MU GIA PASS
12
23
137
BAN KARAI PASS
237
911
912
NORTH VIETNAM
23
917
TCHEPONE
925
9
1
KHE SANH SF
MUONG PHINE
926
92
HUE
922
547
548
DANANG
13
23
BAN BAC
14
THUONG DUC SF
1623
SARAVANE
THAILAND
16
96
23/16
KHAM DUC SF
13
16
165
966
CHAVANE
SOUTH VIETNAM
PAKSE
LAOS
ATTOPEU
962
DAK TO SF
110
110/96
KONTUM
97
CAMBODIA

FIG. 2

the true Ho Chi Minh Trail.

Through constant use, many of the trails widened into roads; others were reconstructed and improved. By the efforts of many thousands of laborers stationed along the trails and by the wearing action of hundreds of trucks, the trails became rutted roads and the roads became all-weather truck routes. Under the cover of tropical nights and thick jungle cover, the enemy built a LOC system capable of sustaining a large volume of logistics to his forces in South Vietnam.

In late 1965, an estimated 4,500 enemy troops and 300 tons of supplies a month were entering South Vietnam via the Trail.[15] Extensive construction had opened Route 911 east of Route 23, thus providing direct access to Tchepone without the wide detour to Thakhek. Also, Route 92/96 was being extended south to Chavane on Route 165, which ran east into several trails that entered South Vietnam in the Kham Duc area. However, in 1965, Route 23 remained the primary logistics route to the south.

By 1967, the enemy had shifted operations to the eastern corridor down Route 911/92 and improved the Ban Karai Pass, which had been opened in 1966 Just as the Mu Gia Pass was nearer to the DMZ than Nape Pass, so Ban Karai was half again closer than Mu Gia. During this year, an estimated 40,000 laborers and 25,000 NVA troops--kept the trucks rolling and manned the antiaircraft defenses.[16] By sheer manpower, the enemy kept the Ho Chi Minh Trail open despite the costly price exacted by American airstrikes. During the two year period of this report, the enemy, when the weather was favorable, pushed through supplies into South Vietnam. How much was not known and could be only very roughly estimated.

The jungle covered much of the trail and spread its double and triple canopy over the truck parks and storage areas. Pictures taken by guerrilla teams showed well-used dirt roads, little wider than truck width, deeply rutted and worn, and improved major routes wider and in good shape. Other stretches of road ran through open areas where the enemy was especially vulnerable to airstrikes.[17/] Supplies were trucked at night and kept in storage areas during daylight hours. Generally, the trucks moved between shelters 10 to 30 kilometers apart, with the NVA officer at each shelter determining if a truck convoy could reach the next shelter before dawn so as not to be caught in daylight on the road. The presence of fighters during daylight effectively kept the enemy off the road 12 to 14 hours out of 24. One common shelter design was to have 30 to 50 hillside excavations with dirt roofs, each big enough for one truck. Nearby were strengthened supply shelters where the cargo could be stored each night. Such truck parks usually lay 500 to 1,000 meters off the main roads in thick canopied forests. From 30 to 60 NVA soldiers manned each shelter and the surrounding area. Road repair crews were strategically stationed at vulnerable points along the roads with the necessary tools and repair materials ready to be used.[18/]

Only every third to fifth shelter had refueling facilities but every shelter was linked to the others by a wire phone system. Normally, a truck convoy traveled between three to seven shelter areas and then returned to its original shelter to complete the circuit. A shuttle system made every driver

8

familiar with his run, permitted servicing of the trucks by mechanics familiar with the individual vehicles, and eliminated the threat of a large number of trucks piling up around one good choke point closed by airstrikes.[19]

Elaborate precautions were taken to counter the air interdiction campaign. Among the systems reported in use to warn of approaching aircraft were lookouts on the truck cabs, red warning beacons turned off during danger periods, a single or series of single shots, and movable road barriers put up when air attacks were expected. Truck lights were shielded and beams reduced to slits. Trucks in convoy often followed small red lights on the trucks ahead. Numerous intelligence reports in 1967 told of infrared driving aids to further reduce reliance on visable light.[20]

Other active and passive countermeasures along the Ho Chi Minh Trail included foxholes all along the routes; road repair crews and prepositioned repair materials such as wood, bamboo, rock, and earth-fill ready for anticipated airstrikes, especially at fords; construction of bypasses around troublesome interdicted segments of road; and most importantly, deployment of antiaircraft weapons.

Thus there emerges a picture of enemy operations along the Ho Chi Minh Trail. During the summer dry season in the panhandle of North Vietnam, the enemy moved supplies through the Mu Gia and Ban Karai Passes and had them poised for the October-November return of the dry season in Laos. Crews tried to keep the roads in good shape and toward the end of the rainy season began reconditioning and improving the Trail. When the roads dried out, the supplies moved

9

south--not over broad highways but down narrow dirt roads snaking through tunnels of trees and crossing scattered open areas. To the American aircrews orbiting the black night sky over the Trail, the trucks came at irregular intervals, running from one concealed area to another, always alert to shut off their lights and turn into the trees.

In the opinion of one intelligence analysis of the Trail in early 1967: [21]

> "The system owes its success to the vast number /of men/ that are devoted to keeping the road open and the trucks moving. The trucks are backed up by bicycles, pack animals and coolies capable of by-passing the most severe interdiction. As long as this vast pool of labor exists and continues to persist in its efforts to move men and supplies south, our task of countering these operations will be extremely difficult."

During each Laotian dry season, the enemy expanded and improved the Trail to speed shipments and bypass road segments vulnerable to flooding and U.S. air-strikes. An estimated 80 kilometers of new road were built in the panhandle in the 1966/1967 dry season. In the next dry season, an estimated 306 kilometers of road were constructed, including four links that crossed into South Vietnam. [22] New roads in the 1967/1968 season included Route 236/2302, east of Route 23 out of the Mu Gia Pass, thus providing an alternate to that heavily used route and better access to storage areas hidden in karst to the east. Route 9116 detoured south around the heavily interdicted 911/912 junction. Another typical addition was Route 9221, an 11 kilometer bypass around a bottleneck on the road to the A Shau Valley. Interestingly enough, this new construction and other extensive rehabilitation were reportedly done while reducing manpower an

10

estimated 11,000 and adding heavy road equipment. One report estimated three-quarters of the following equipment were operated in the Laotian panhandle in the 1967/1968 dry season: 20 bulldozers, 11 road graders, three rock crushers, and two steamrollers.[23/]

In May 1968, a wealth of enemy documents were captured in the A Shau Valley by U.S. 1st Cavalry and ARVN troopers in Operation DELAWARE. More than 90,000 pages of documents revealed for the first time details of the 559th Transportation Group and its management of the Ho Chi Minh Trail from Tchepone to northern II Corps. The description given here comes from an analysis of 7,000 pages by the Combined Document Exploitation Center (CDEC)--the MACV-Vietnamese Joint General Staff intelligence center. The depth of insight into enemy supply operations given in these captured documents remains unparalleled to date.[24/]

The 559th Group took its name from its activation date of May 1959. Its headquarters at Ha Tinh, south of Vinh in the North Vietnamese panhandle, commanded several divisions and 40 battalions, including engineers, ordnance, anti-aircraft, infantry, medical, signal, rear service, civilian laborers, and voluntary youths.

According to the captured documents, the 559th Group controlled the transportation system in the Mu Gia, Ban Karai, and Hill 1001 areas, as well as the Ho Chi Minh Trail down to Tchepone, to Chavane, and east into all of I Corps and northern Kontum Province. However, the captured documents dealt with the area from Hill 1001 through the A Shau Valley to southern I Corps. This main route south was called the "Axis". Responsibility for particular lengths and

11

areas of the Trail lay with the military stations placed along the Trail. Seven large stations of known location were #1 at Hill 1001, #2 at Tchepone, #3 west of Lao Bao in Laos, #4 possibly in the Arum secret zone in Laos, west of A Shau, #7 near a Luoi in the A Shau Valley, #8 on Route 547 toward Hue, and #21 near Thuong Duc Special Forces Camp on Route 14 in central Quang Nam Province.

During the 1967/1968 dry season, the 559th Group directed that four times the tonnage of the previous season should be moved to support the general offensive. Trucks would operate 26 nights a month at near capacity loads, covering 60 kilometers per night in the dry season. Actual captured records claimed truckers drove 90 to 132 kilometers per night, to support the Tet Offensive. Truckers were expected to drive 12 hours a night, while road crews and other laborers worked even longer hours--up to 16-18 hours a day. According to the documents, the 559th Group in 1966 and 1967 built 353 kilometers of road and widened 359 kilometers for two-way truck traffic and 277 kilometers for one-way traffic.

According to the CDEC intelligence report, the A Shau Valley was "the most important VC War Zone in South Vietnam," because it had roads and trails fanning out from a massive logistics center to all populated areas of I Corps. Military Station 7 near A Luoi had four Transportation Truck Battalions and two "bulldozer" companies, plus AAA units that claimed 143 aircraft shot down. During the 1967/1968 dry season, the station made a maximum effort to supply the battlefields around Hue and Da Nang. If unit records were correct, one company alone moved 400 tons in January and 1,000 tons the next month.[25/] Operation

12

DELAWARE wreaked havoc on Military Station 7 in late April and early May 1968, significantly impeding enemy offensive actions in I Corps in May.

Cambodia

Supplies coming through Cambodian ports or procured locally in that country for use by the VC/NVA constituted the least known aspect of infiltration into South Vietnam. A glance at a map of the Indochina Peninsula shows that two-thirds of the western border of South Vietnam adjoins Cambodia and that III and IV Corps are a long way from any part of Laos. Therefore, as Free World/ U.S. forces pressed the VC hard in the years after the 1965 troop buildup, the enemy responded by sending NVA regular units farther and farther south, until eventually large numbers fought in III and parts of IV Corps. These regulars required sizable logistical support and could not forage as did indigenous VC units. Thus supply lines from North Vietnam had to reach very far south following the troops. Naturally, Cambodian neutrality was exploited.

In the Laotian civil war, the NVA fought with the Pathet Lao, causing the Royal Laotian Government to seek aid from the U.S. and to permit American air-strikes against the NVA along the Ho Chi Minh Trail. No such circumstances led the Cambodian government to acquiesce to U.S. operations inside its borders. Rather, Head of State, Prince Norodom Sihanouk showed the traditional Cambodian suspicion of the neighboring Vietnamese and Thais--both U.S. Allies--and their claims on Cambodian territory. Both countries provided money to anti-Sihanouk rebels--the Khmer Serai or Free Cambodians.[26] Further, the Prince disliked the U.S. and seemed to believe the North Vietnamese would win the war and he naturally sought an accommodation with them. For instance, in June 1967, the

Cambodian government recognized the National Liberation Front in return for North Vietnamese recognition of Cambodia's existing boundaries.[27/] "Neutralism" led to ignoring the VC/NVA troops on Cambodian soil and strict insistence that the U.S. had no justification for air operations in the country because Cambodia did not harbor any VC/NVA.

Cambodian reactions to the VC/NVA ran hot and cold depending upon how much the communists disrupted the economy, how the Khmer Rouge (Cambodian Reds) fared, and the prospects for victory by the Allies in South Vietnam. The Geneva Accords fragmented Indochina, duplicating the tortuous politics of the pre-World War II Balkans. To illustrate this with respect to enemy resupply and Cambodian attitudes, several intelligence reports are cited here from the 7AF "Weekly Air Intelligence Summary" (WAIS) over a two-year period. In December 1966, the WAIS reported Sihanouk ordered the Army to stop VC supplies and to use road blocks to reduce the flow to "token amounts."[28/] The following April, it reported the VC still operating in Phnom Penh and Sihanoukville with the government-controlled news media supporting the Hanoi/Peking position on the war.[29/] At about the same time, the WAIS related a report that Cambodian Army officials were helping the VC obtain rice.[30/] In January 1968, the WAIS reported the replacement of northeast provincial and military authorities, who were cooperating in delivering food to the VC/NVA at the expense of inflating the rice prices in Cambodia.[31/] In late August, Prince Sihanouk announced over the radio that the communists controlled one-third of Cambodia's far northeast province in the Tri-Border area.[32/] In September, Sihanouk said there were no permanent VC camps in Cambodia, and therefore he withdrew authorization for

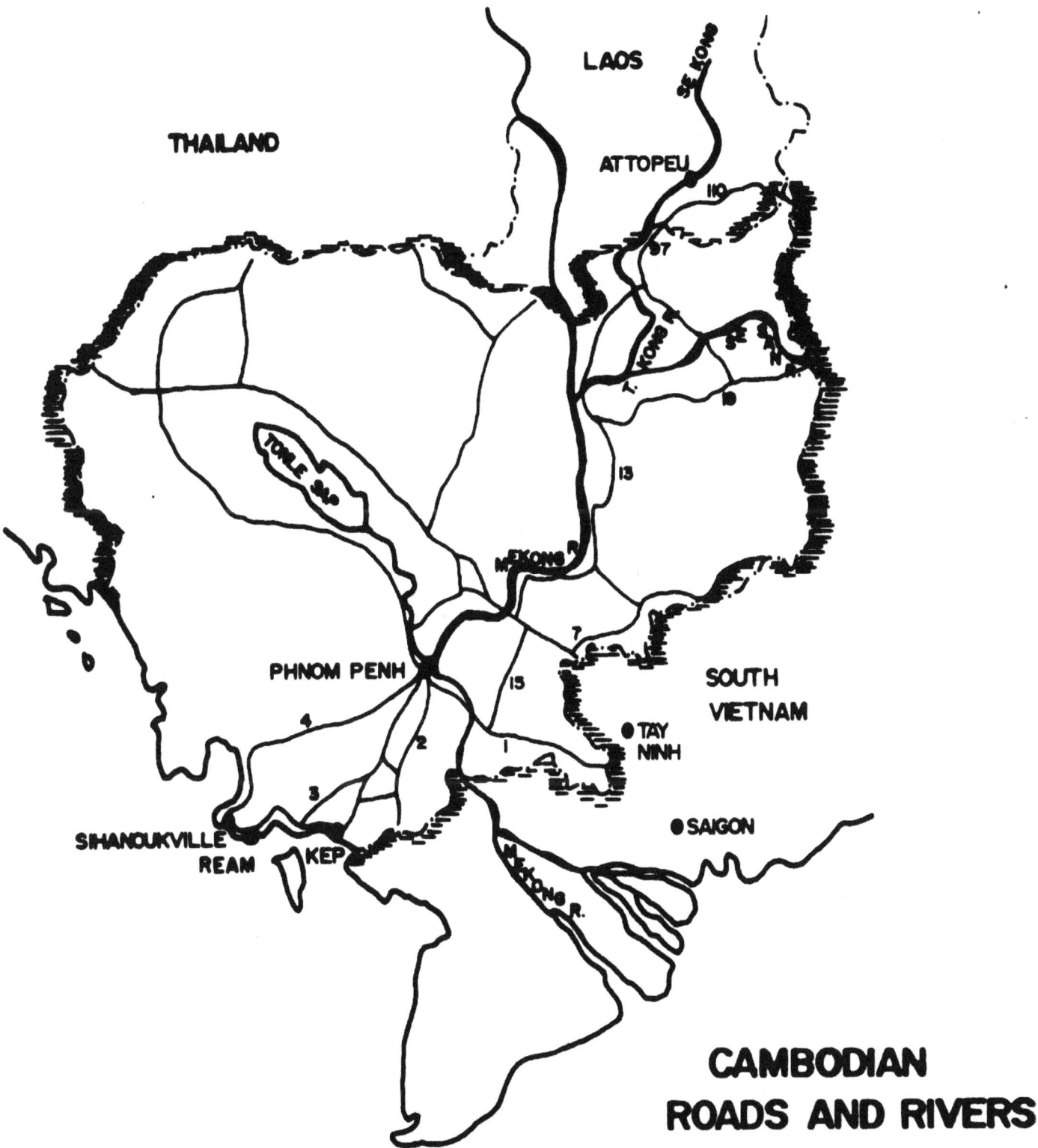

THAILAND

LAOS

SEKONG

ATTOPEU

110

TONLE SAP

MEKONG

MEKONG

PHNOM PENH

15

SOUTH
VIETNAM

4

2

1

TAY
NINH

3

SAIGON

SIHANOUKVILLE
REAM

KEP

MEKONG R.

CAMBODIAN
ROADS AND RIVERS

FIG. 3

the International Control Commission to investigate "alleged" VC camps. He

further accused the U.S. of interference in internal Cambodian affairs by mak-

ing such charges.[33/]

In actual fact, the U.S. knew the VC/NVA used Cambodia as a sanctuary and

rice source, but was unsure of the amounts of military equipment coming through

Cambodian ports. Intelligence suggested both legal and illegal 1966 rice

sales in Cambodia to the VC may have exceeded 55,000 metric tons, while the

1967 total was slightly lower.[34/] The rice went to northern III Corps or north

via Route 97 into Laos for shipment into the Tri-Border area. Since Cambodia

manufactured no munitions, military supplies for either the Royal Khmer Army or

the VC/NVA had to be imported or smuggled into the country. A mid-1967 analysis

by CINCUSARPAC of Cambodian military aid to the VC concluded that there "was no

large-scale Cambodian program to supply the Viet Cong with military equipment...."[35/]

However, certain corrupt Cambodian commanders were renting their Army trucks

to move VC/NVA supplies, and by 1968 were probably reaching into the government

stocks for salable weapons and ammunition.[36/] Drugs and pharmaceuticals were

imported through normal trade channels and later smuggled into South Vietnam.

The actual LOCs used to move food and materiel included roads and rivers.

Munitions might be unloaded at Sihanoukville or Kep and then trucked east to

IV Corps for infiltration along rivers and canals, or they could be trucked

north to Phnom Penh and redistributed. One VC related how his C-7 Transporta-

tion Company received arms trucked from Sihanoukville--machine guns, carbines,

rocket and grenade launchers, mortars, mines, and ammunition--and moved them

by canal sampans into IV Corps.[37/]

15

Major supply links included Route 1 through the Parrot's Beak to Tay Ninh or within 30 miles of Saigon, Route 2 to Seven Mountains Area of southwestern IV Corps, or north to Route 7, which serviced the major enemy base areas bordering northern III Corps. Supplies destined for the Tri-Border area moved north to the Siem Pang area, where they could be trucked into Laos on Route 97 to join Laotian Route 110, or transported on the Kong River (Tongle Kong in Cambodia and Se Kong in Laos). This Sihanouk Trail allowed supplies to move into southern Laos, especially in the rainy season when the rivers were high and the Ho Chi Minh Trail was washed out.[38]

The actual tons of military equipment sent through Cambodia remain at this writing very uncertain. PACAF reported the following supplies may have been sent into South Vietnam from Cambodia in the one month of October 1968: 70 crates of arms, 102.75 tons of ammunition, 802.75 tons of rice, 1,400 tins of milk, unidentified quantities of medical supplies, and 1,048 tons of unidentified material. According to this report, "Transportation for the operation supposedly involved 186 trucks, 177 sampans, and 44 pirogues. The volume of supplies and the number of vehicles used to transit probably represent only a small percentage of the true total for October."[39]

From July to October 1968, the Air Force and Navy conducted an intensified interdiction of the North Vietnamese panhandle, and by October reduced truck traffic over the Mu Gia and Ban Karai Passes to very low numbers. Based on this, the DCS/Intelligence, 7AF, drew the following conclusion:[40]

> *"Successful blockade of the North now resolves beyond all reasonable doubt the enemy's enormous dependence*

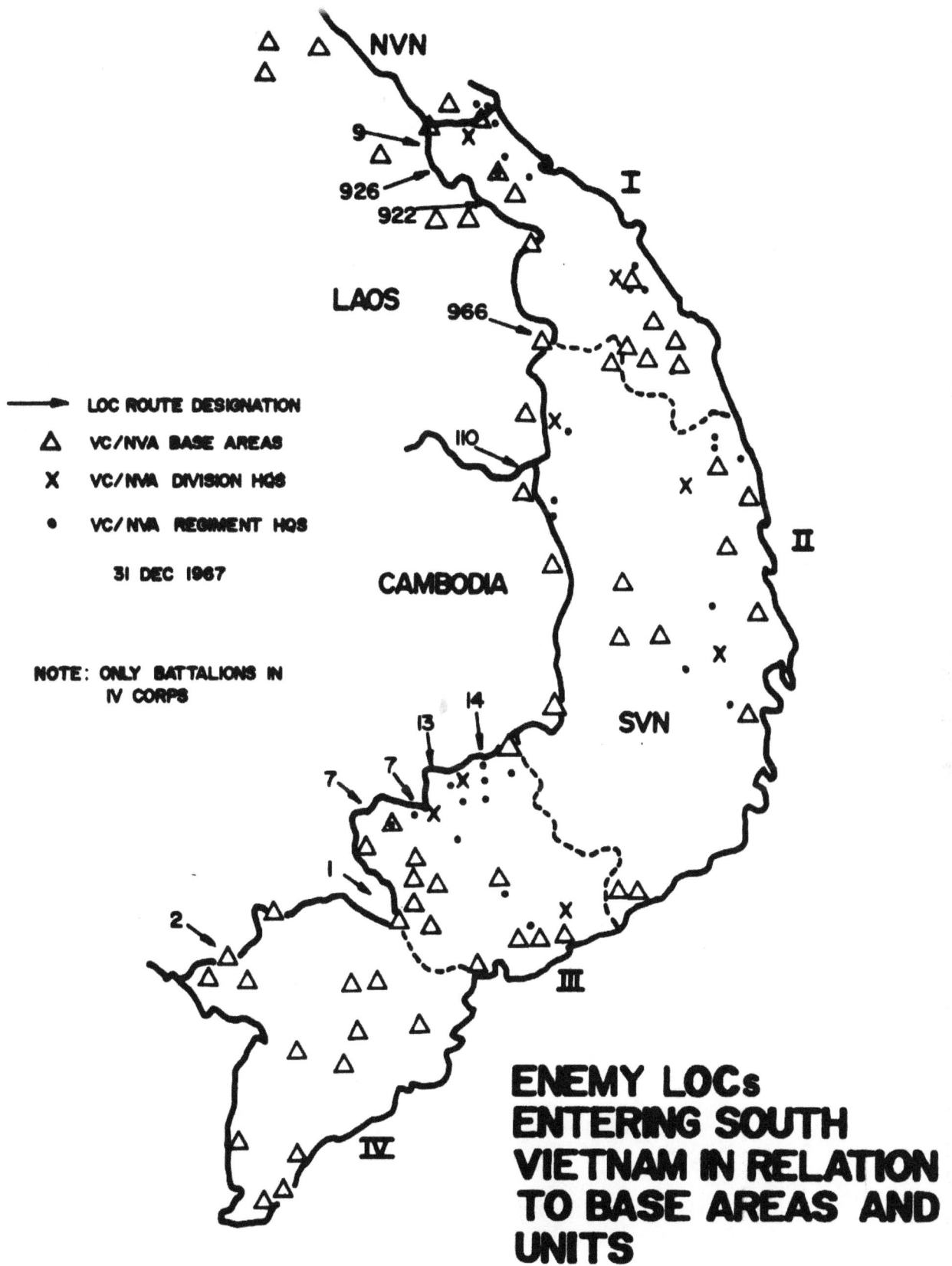

NVN

9

926

922

LAOS

966

110

CAMBODIA

SVN

LOC ROUTE DESIGNATION

△ VC/NVA BASE AREAS

X VC/NVA DIVISION HQS

• VC/NVA REGIMENT HQS

31 DEC 1967

NOTE: ONLY BATTALIONS IN
IV CORPS

I

II

13

14

7

7

1

2

III

IV

ENEMY LOCs
ENTERING SOUTH
VIETNAM IN RELATION
TO BASE AREAS AND
UNITS

SOURCE: MACV HIST. 1967   FIG. 4

upon the Port of Sihanoukville and Cambodia for
most of his munitions and supplies in III and
IV Corps areas of South Vietnam. With the
complete closure of the routes from the North
and through Laos during the summer of 1968,
Cambodia became the sole source of support for
the enemy's extensive combat operations in the
South."

South Vietnam

The location of enemy LOCs inside South Vietnam obviously depended upon
suitable political and geographical conditions, and on where the main force
VC/NVA units were located. Figure 4 shows how the LOCs entering from Laos and
Cambodia centered on the enemy troop concentrations in I and II Corps and the
Tri-Border area.

All through the 1960s the enemy had resupplied his guerrilla and regular
forces via trails crossing the border. In III Corps, the old French road
system to the plantations of Tay Ninh and Binh Long Provinces connected with
those in neighboring Cambodia. In I Corps, the more primitive road system
in southern Laos did not often connect with the Vietnamese system, except for
Route 9 below the DMZ. There were trails into the A Shau Valley, the Kham Duc
area on the I/II Corps Border, and the Tri-Border area. However, in all these
areas, in late 1967, a major road construction effort along the border areas
linked Routes 922, 966, and 110 to the South Vietnamese National Highway
system. (Fig. 2.)

The VC/NVA supply system centered on rear service groups acting as area
support commands, responsible for the units operating in their areas. For
instance, should the 9th VC Division in 1967 move from its Tay Ninh base area

17

into Binh Duong Province, the Division would leave Rear Service Group 82 and now draw supplies from Rear Service Group 83. Coolie labor--both sympathetic and kidnapped--and regular transport units carried the supplies from Laotian and Cambodian sanctuaries by trails, waterways, and roads to the base camps of the units. There the supplies were stockpiled, distributed to subordinate units, or cached at the site of future operations. Combat units operating in agricultural areas supplemented their rations by raising rice, vegetables, chickens, and pigs or by buying or taxing food from the local farmers.[41/]

Disrupting such clandestine supply channels obviously required ground troops to closely supervise arable lands and local populations; it was not an Air Force responsibility. Even the movement of porters and supplies down jungle trails in isolated mountain jungles far from major Allied Forces was not very vulnerable to an air interdiction campaign. Only when the enemy began building improved roads and trucking supplies into and around South Vietnam, beginning in early 1968, did the Air Force begin a formal interdiction campaign in-country.

CHAPTER II

EVOLUTION OF INTERDICTION, 1964-1966

Beginning of Air War in Laos

Interdiction in Southeast Asia was not significant in the very early years
of American assistance to South Vietnam. U.S. restraint prohibited attacks
against North Vietnam, while American observance of Laotian neutrality kept the
Ho Chi Minh Trail off limits. Events soon widened the war.

In May 1964, the Pathet Lao attacked neutralist forces in the Plaine des
Jarres, and on 19 May, USAF flew the first YANKEE TEAM photo reconnaissance
mission in Laos. The first Air Force jet attack of the war (F-100s from Da
Nang) occurred on 9 June 1964 against an antiaircraft site in northern Laos.[1/]
Two months later the Gulf of Tonkin incident evoked U.S. Navy retaliatory strikes
against North Vietnamese naval bases and POL storage sites. In the following
months, several more retaliatory raids were flown in both Laos and North Vietnam in response to enemy attacks.

Planning for American airstrikes in an interdiction role was initiated
by JCS in July 1964, with the object of cutting Route 7, the enemy entrance
into the Plaine des Jarres in northern Laos. In the following months, very
high-level diplomatic negotiations were conducted among the U.S. and the
Royal Lao and Thai governments over this sensitive proposal and the use of
Thai-based aircraft in Laos. On 14 December, the first armed recon strike was
flown, fragged against targets of opportunity on Routes 8 and 12 in the Laotian
panhandle. This first U.S. interdiction strike in the Vietnam war initiated

19

BARREL ROLL, the armed recon operation in Laos.[2/]   (Fig. 5.)

At first, the Rules of Engagement stipulated that only targets of opportunity of unmistakable military activity would be struck. Further, these rules forbade missions not separated by 72-hour standdowns and banned the use of Thai-based aircraft and napalm. Later, the requirement for three-day waiting periods was reduced to 48 hours.[3/]   On 7 April 1965, Thai-based U.S. aircraft flew their first strike against Laotian targets.[4/]   Through 1965, other restrictions were gradually lifted, such as the December relief from Washington-required approval of preplanned missions.

The limitations of armed recon in BARREL ROLL were apparent from the start, and there could be no delusions about "interdicting" 91,500 square miles of Laos with a maximum of one day mission and one night mission. BARREL ROLL had originated to counter the Pathet Lao offensive in the Plaine des Jarres, and to provide airstrikes in support of the Royal Lao and Neutralist forces. Interdicting the Ho Chi Minh Trail was secondary. To place more emphasis on the latter, JCS directed the creation of Project STEEL TIGER, to begin on 3 April 1965. This separated close air support/interdiction operations in BARREL ROLL from the fledgling interdiction program in the Laotian panhandle.[5/]

To maximize damage to the enemy LOCs, several techniques were proposed. One was armed night recon in conjunction with long-range aircraft equipped with detection equipment such as flares, infrared (IR), and side-looking airborne radar (SLAR). Another technique proposed closing choke points, periodically reseeding them with mines and delay-fuzed bombs, and using armed reconnaissance

20

BARREL ROLL
14 DEC 1964

BR

BARREL ROLL

STEEL TIGER
3 APR 1965

BR

SL

BR

CRICKET
21 JAN 1966

TALLY HO
17 JUL 1966

TIGER HOUND
6 DEC 1965

SL

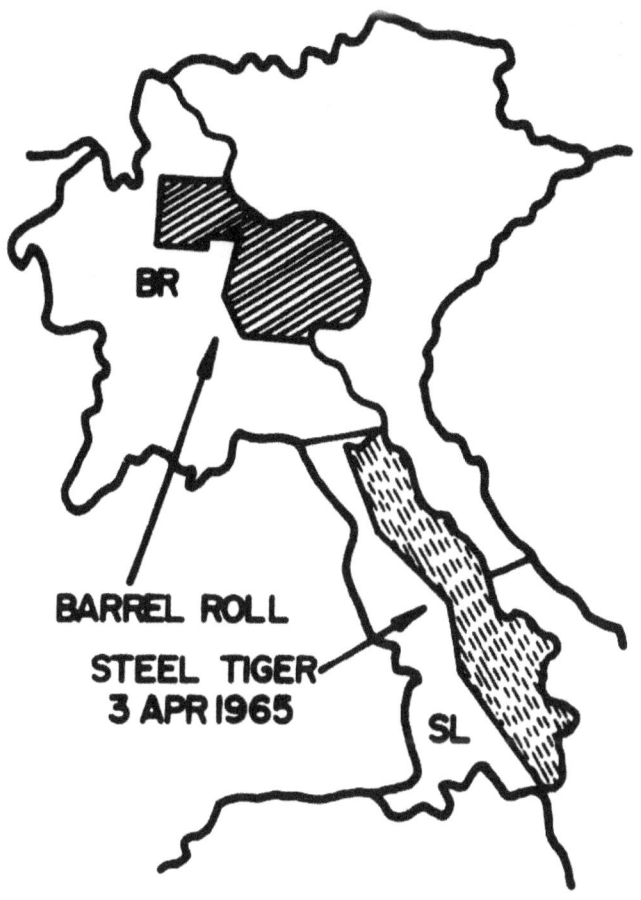

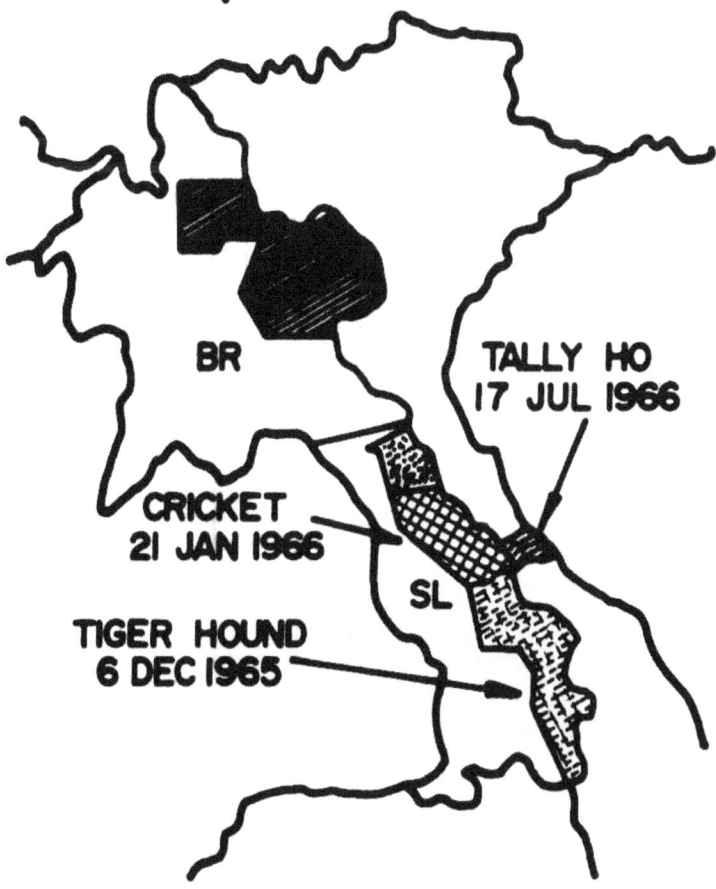

EVOLUTION of
BARREL ROLL
STEEL TIGER
TIGER HOUND
TALLY HO, &
CRICKET

1964-1966

FIG. 5

against the resulting enemy traffic backlogged behind the choke points. [6/]

Thus, within the first months of BARREL ROLL and STEEL TIGER operations, the interdiction program was being examined for the appropriate roles of such techniques as armed recon, choke points, backlogged enemy traffic, and night interdiction using visual/electronic improvements and innovations.

Impact of the Monsoons

By mid-1965, the climatic differences between Laos and North Vietnam were imposing the patterns of the seasonal monsoon conditions on out-country air operations. Once a sizable number of daily sorties were being fragged in-to Laos and North Vietnam, the air operations were shifted among geographical areas to take advantage of good weather and to avoid bad weather conditions. Figure 6 plots the total strike sorties (less B-52 strikes) in both Laos and North Vietnam from September 1966 to September 1968 and shows this seasonal allocation of strike forces. Since the enemy dirt roads deteriorated badly in heavy rains (especially in Laos), the enemy logistics system in the different areas also had seasonal peaks of activity followed by troughs of inactivity. Thus, in the Southeast Asian interdiction campaign there soon evolved the pattern of a Southwest Monsoon Campaign (May to October) when the weather was "good" over North Vietnam, and a Northeast Monsoon Campaign (November to April) when the skies were clear and dry--though hazy--over Laos and South Vietnam. By 1967, Seventh Air Force was publishing campaign plans to coordinate maximum efforts in the "good weather" regions and to minimize disruptions in the "bad weather" areas.

A brief and highly-simplified look at the monsoon seasons is necessary for

an understanding of interdiction in Southeast Asia. In the summer, the southwest wind blows off the Indian Ocean, bringing towering thunderstorms and monsoon rains to Thailand, Cambodia, Laos, and the Mekong Delta of South Vietnam.
North Vietnam has hot summer weather with good visibility, because the Annam
Cordillera blocks much of the southwest winds. But so deep is the warm air
over Laos that some spills across to the east bringing thunderstorms to the
Red River Delta. Hanoi's heaviest rain comes in August. [7]

In the winter, the cold continental high over Siberia and northern China
causes northeast winds to blow across the South China Sea and the Gulf of Tonkin
and into northern and central Vietnam. The mean onset of the Northeast Monsoon
in SEA comes on 20 October, with 5 October the earliest and 15 November the
latest on record. There was a 95 percent probability that the Northeast Monsoon would begin from 4-24 October in southern Laos and northern South Vietnam.
Low overcast, fog, and drizzle blanket North Vietnam much of the winter, but
the wind flow is generally too shallow to spread very far across the western
mountains except in parts of northeastern Laos. However, in the mountains, the
clouds and haze definitely reduce visibility and hamper air operations on the
Laotian mountains. Thailand, Cambodia, Laos, and the Mekong Delta have dry,
relatively clear weather in the winters, permitting the heavy seasonal surge
of enemy infiltration and trucks to move down the Ho Chi Minh Trail. [8]

Beginning of Air War in North Vietnam

As the air war in Laos expanded, the sustained bombing of North Vietnam
began. From November 1964 through February 1965, the Viet Cong made several
attacks on American billets in South Vietnam. In response, several FLAMING

22

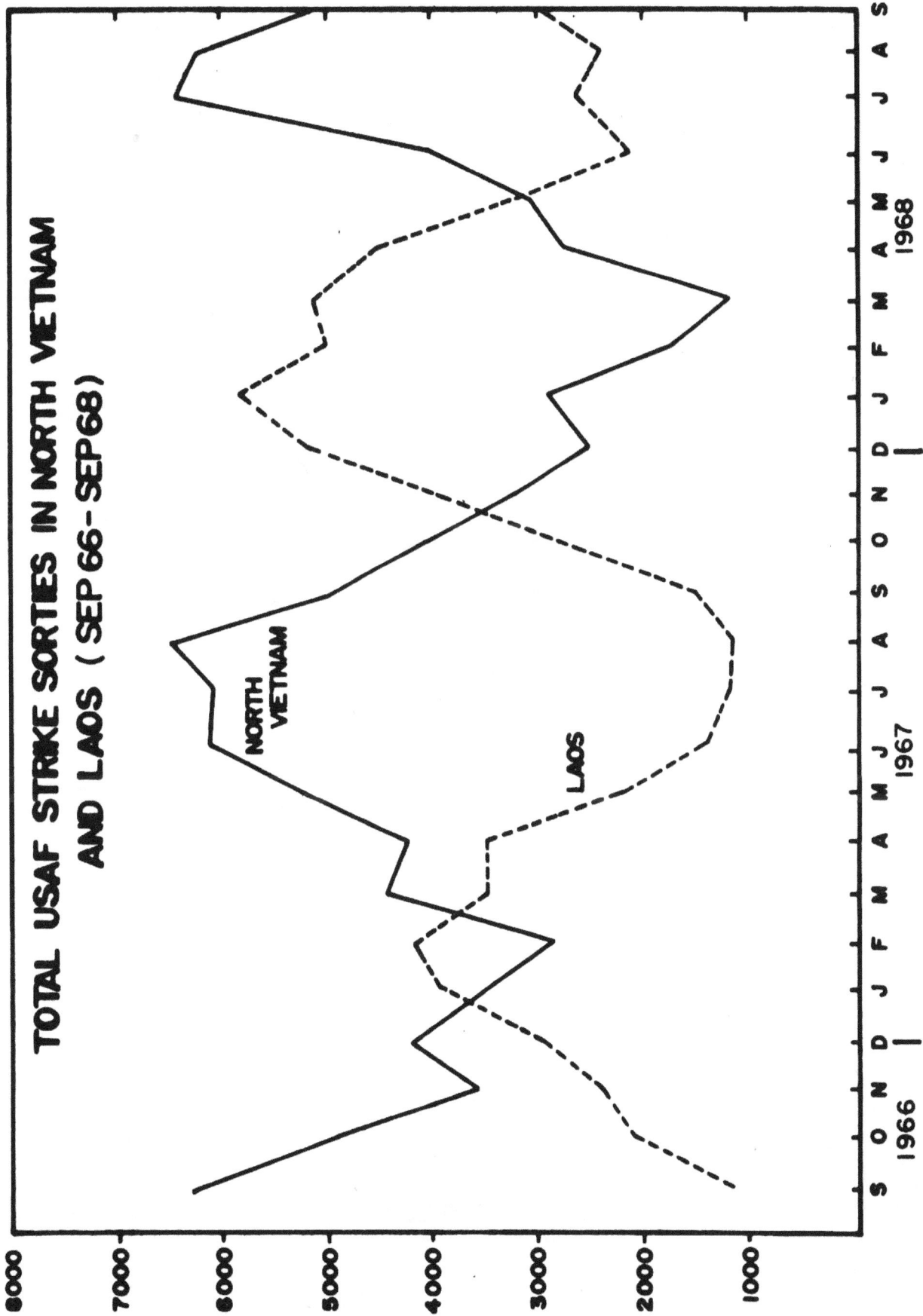

TOTAL USAF STRIKE SORTIES IN NORTH VIETNAM
AND LAOS (SEP 66 - SEP 68)

NORTH VIETNAM

LAOS

FIG. 6

DART raids attacked North Vietnamese Army (NVA) barracks just north of the DMZ, with the last raid occurring in response to a 10 February VC attack on a U.S. billet in Qui Nhon. This period of escalation by both sides culminated with a JCS recommendation on 12 February for an eight-week program of sustained bombing of North Vietnam. The first ROLLING THUNDER mission was flown on 2 March 1965, initiating a three-year period of increasing pressure.[9/]

At first, ROLLING THUNDER was limited to the area south of the 20th parallel and concentrated on bridges, ferries, choke points, ammo and supply depots, army barracks (used for troop infiltration), and power plants. Armed recon attacked the LOCs. However, airfields and radar sites were also attacked and, according to Air Force doctrine, these were counter-air targets. Thus, from the beginning in ROLLING THUNDER "strategic", "counter-air", and "interdiction" targets appeared on the same target lists.

In the usual pattern, in mid-1965, the Ho Chi Minh Trail was not usable due to summer rains and the major air effort was concentrated on North Vietnam. As the summer months passed, the American attacks on North Vietnam widened. Of special note was the intensified air effort in May and June to isolate the town of Vinh and curtail its capacity as a logistics center in the North Vietnamese panhandle.[10/]

ROLLING THUNDER 18 authorized strikes against targets above 20 degrees with the first occurring on 11 June 1965. By ROLLING THUNDER 33 at the end of September, an estimated 91 percent of the JCS targets below 20 degrees were damaged (85 of 93) and 24 percent were damaged above 20 degrees (30 of 125). No industrial targets except thermal power plants had been attacked.[11/]

23

On 24 December 1965, the beginning of a 37-day bombing pause gave the enemy a breathing spell and provided the U.S. with a chance to reevaluate the effects of ROLLING THUNDER. In 1965, 23,194 strike sorties were expended over North Vietnam: USAF 10,975, USN 11,656, and VNAF 563. In the judgment of CINCPAC, all major LOCs in North Vietnam were in extensive use at the beginning of the bombing pause, and an estimated 80 percent of the enemy traffic was moving at night.[12/]

CINCPAC also told the Senate Armed Services Committee that the VC found their rice in South Vietnam and thus relied on North Vietnam logistics mainly for weapons and ammunition. He noted that guerrilla needs for ammunition did not run too high and "they would almost carry everything they needed down [from North Vietnam] on their backs, if they had to. That's what they did, of course, in Korea."[13/]

First Winter Campaign in Laos - TIGER HOUND

By October 1965, the shifting monsoon brought drier weather to Laos and permitted the characteristic surge of enemy infiltration down the Ho Chi Minh Trail. By then, the term "Trail" was already a misnomer that understated and minimized the capacity of the truck routes through Laos. Judged by Southeast Asian standards, "Ho Chi Minh Highway" would have been a more accurate term.

This activity did not go unnoticed. In response to a JCS request for a review of the NVA infiltration, CINCPAC stated that air harassment of the infiltration lines could not effectively deter enemy efforts unless the distribution points and Haiphong in North Vietnam were heavily attacked. COMUSMACV responded to the surge of infiltration by increasing Air Force sorties and requesting an increase in Navy sorties in the panhandle. In late November, the U.S. Ambassador to Laos approved the use of ARC LIGHT B-52s along the Laos/South Vietnam border.[14]

On 6 December, the TIGER HOUND Task Force was created under the command of an Air Force Colonel with control of significant FAC O-1 resources to perform visual reconnaissance and to direct airstrikes. The introduction of FACs into Laos was the major innovation of TIGER HOUND. The TIGER HOUND headquarters was located at Tan Son Nhut, the forward operating site at Da Nang, and the O-1s at four forward operating locations: Dong Ha near the DMZ and the three Special Forces camps of Khe Sanh, Kham Duc, and Kontum along the Laotian Border. The Rules of Engagement permitted unlimited armed recon within 200 yards of all motorable roads in TIGER HOUND. Beyond 200 yards of the motorable roads, the Rules of Engagement remained restrictive.[15]

TIGER HOUND marked the first integrated interdiction program in Laos, integrated in the sense of combining a C-130 Airborne Battlefield Command and Control Center (ABCCC) called HILLSBORO, FACs, Army Mohawks (OV-1s with IR and SLAR), fighter aircraft, B-52s, flareships, and defoliation aircraft. At first, the results did not seem to justify the effort, but by February the intensified reconnaissance and night operations achieved mounting truck kills. According to the Commander of the TIGER HOUND Task Force, the key to success was the FAC, who sought out the trucks, truck parks, and supply dumps, and the ABCCC, which provided the highly responsive control of tac air. In May and June, the truck kills and the number of secondary explosions declined to negligible levels when the Southwest Monsoon rains closed the Trail.[16]

At about the same time as the TIGER HOUND program was begun, an area of operation was created north from TIGER HOUND to the Nape Pass and designated CRICKET. Initially, it had five O-1s operating out of Nakhon Phanom. Also, within its area of operation were Controlled American Sourse (CAS) road watch teams providing intelligence. By teaming up (even though hampered by incompatible radio nets), the road watch teams and the FACs made CRICKET an immediate success despite the significantly fewer tac air sorties given it compared to TIGER HOUND.[17/] The effectiveness of the road watch teams so impressed the Commander, 7AF, that he suggested to COMUSMACV that CAS road watch teams be put into TIGER HOUND. He thought the highly effective ABCCC should also be used in CRICKET.

In June 1966, the sortie rate in STEEL TIGER/TIGER HOUND fell to the lowest level since December 1965, and the Laotian 1965/1966 dry season was clearly over. Before recounting the summer campaign in North Vietnam, it would be well to clarify the terms used to describe the Laotian areas of operation. All northern Laos was technically in BARREL ROLL, though only an eastern portion had Rules of Engagement permitting relatively free armed recon strikes. All southern Laos--the panhandle--was in STEEL TIGER, though the term applied mostly to the eastern armed recon portion. The northern half of the armed recon area was termed STEEL TIGER North and it included CRICKET. The southern half of the armed recon area of STEEL TIGER was TIGER HOUND.

First Summer Campaign in NVN-GATE GUARD and TALLY HO

At the approach of the 1966 summer season in North Vietnam, extensive plans and revisions of the Rules of Engagement were made. This was the first

extensive "good weather" campaign against North Vietnam. At the Honolulu
Conference in late January, three objectives were defined for the total Southeast Asian interdiction effort:[18]

1. Reduce/restrict NVN assistance from external sources.

2. Destroy in depth those resources already in NVN contri-
buting most to the support of aggression; destroy or
deny use of all known permanent military facilities; and
harass and disrupt dispersed military operations.

3. Harass, disrupt, and impede movement of men and materials
through southern NVN into Laos and SVN.

On 31 January, the 37-day bombing pause ended with a resumption of attacks
against the North. In March, extensive correspondence passed between the
various U.S. Headquarters in Saigon, Honolulu, and Washington over the Rules of
Engagement in the recently assigned Route Packages (RP). COMUSMACV especially
wanted operations in RPs I and II patterned after the successful TIGER HOUND
operations then nearly at the peak of success. On 1 April 1966, CINCPAC issued
the operations order permanently assigning responsibilities for recon and strike
forces in North Vietnam. COMUSMACV had RP I (which meant using USAF, VNAF, and
USMC aircraft). CINCPACFLT had RPs II, III, IV, and VIB, the coastal areas
most accessible to his Task Force-77 fleet. CINCPACAF had RP V and VIA. Thus,
Seventh Air Force had primary interest in RP I from COMUSMACV and RP V and VIA
from CINCPACAF.[19]

The summer air campaign in North Vietnam began with an integrated attempt
to interdict the LOCs in RP I. This was actually the first full season interdiction campaign in the North deserving the name. In 1965, the sustained air

27

war against the North began in March and the extremely sensitive politics of escalation had held center stage and governed U.S. planning and target selection. By April 1966, a year of bombing had brought a certain routine aspect to the operations in the North that freed planners to concentrate on maximizing interdiction efforts.

GATE GUARD in May 1966 sought to simultaneously interdict the LOCs in RP I on several east-west lines from the sea to the mountains. As the southernmost "gate" backed up traffic (which was then destroyed), the next "gate" north would be closed. The traffic would be trapped by day cuts and destroyed by night strikes. In two months, 318 trucks were destroyed (half at night) and 411 damaged (two-thirds at night).[20]

Circumstances were dissimilar between GATE GUARD and TIGER HOUND. AAA defenses in RP I were too intense for the O-1 and thus the outstanding visual recon accomplishment in TIGER HOUND and CRICKET was missing in GATE GUARD. Also, the flat coastal plain permitted rapid repair of cratered roads.

Even as airpower attempted to roll back enemy supply lines in RP I, the NVA made its first sizable violation of the DMZ and sent a division directly across to threaten Quang Tri Province. In response, COMUSMACV ordered the Marines to conduct Operation HASTINGS to drive the enemy back across the DMZ. For longer term operations, he established TALLY HO, modeled after TIGER HOUND and, indeed, tied directly to TIGER HOUND, since the two would share assets and shift them as the seasons demanded. TALLY HO was created on 17 July 1966 under control of the TIGER HOUND Task Force to cover the area from Dong Hoi

28

in the north to the Demarcation Line in the south (including the North Vietnamese half of the DMZ).

The impact on TALLY HO was uncertain. Not many trucks were discovered or destroyed, but there were 806 secondary explosions in just 40 days. Since the O-1 was confined to the western half of the area--TALLY HO WEST--intensified air surveillance was not available in the heavily traveled coastal plain. In the opinion of the U.S. Director of the Tactical Air Control Center (TACC), the campaign had helped, along with HASTINGS, in blunting the much anticipated 1966 NVA offensive in northern I Corps.[21]

Summary: 1964-1966

By late fall, the rains had turned many of the RP I roads into mud and brought an end to the summer campaign. In Laos, its now routine seasonal rise in sorties was begun. At this point, it would be useful to evaluate the interdiction program up to the end of 1966. The CHECO report, "Interdiction in SEA, 1965-1966," preceding this present report ended with the first TALLY HO campaign. In a brief summary of the total interdiction effort, it stated:[22]

> *"Admittedly, with the open-end logistics system allowed North Vietnam through /U.S./ self-imposed constraints, no interdiction program could cut off the flow completely, but a well-planned and executed one could raise the cost to the enemy, disrupt his time-table, and thwart his plans."*

The doubtful success of the interdiction efforts, however, was also noted:[23]

> *"From the first few ill-prepared and uncoordinated*

interdiction efforts in December of 1964, the
overall interdiction campaign had grown to
massive proportions by early 1967. Intergrated,
sophisticated, and unquestionably a factor in
the conduct of the war /sic/. However, the
prime question, 'Did interdiction succeed?'
remained quantitatively unanswered. A wealth
of evidence--prisoner reports, photographs,
statistical data--indicated its undeniable
impact at specific times and places. Yet, by
spring of 1967, the enemy order of battle had
grown from the estimated (Nov 65) 83 Viet Cong
and 27 NVA battalions to 190 VC battalions and
95 battalions of North Vietnamese (1 Apr 67).
These were combat units that were receiving the
bulk of their weapons and ammunition, medicine,
and other supplies directly or indirectly from
North Vietnam. Uncounted sorties, from A-1s
to B-52s, unloaded hundreds of thousands of
pounds of bombs in Mu Gia Pass alone, yet week
after week the road watch teams reported 'road
open and motorable.' Every bridge worthy of
the name in the southern portion of North Vietnam (with one notable exception--Thanh Hoa) had
been dropped at least once, yet the LOCs remained
viable. By the criterion of 'Reduce the enemy's
logistical flow below the level needed to sustain
him in battle,' the interdiction programs were
not 'successful.'"

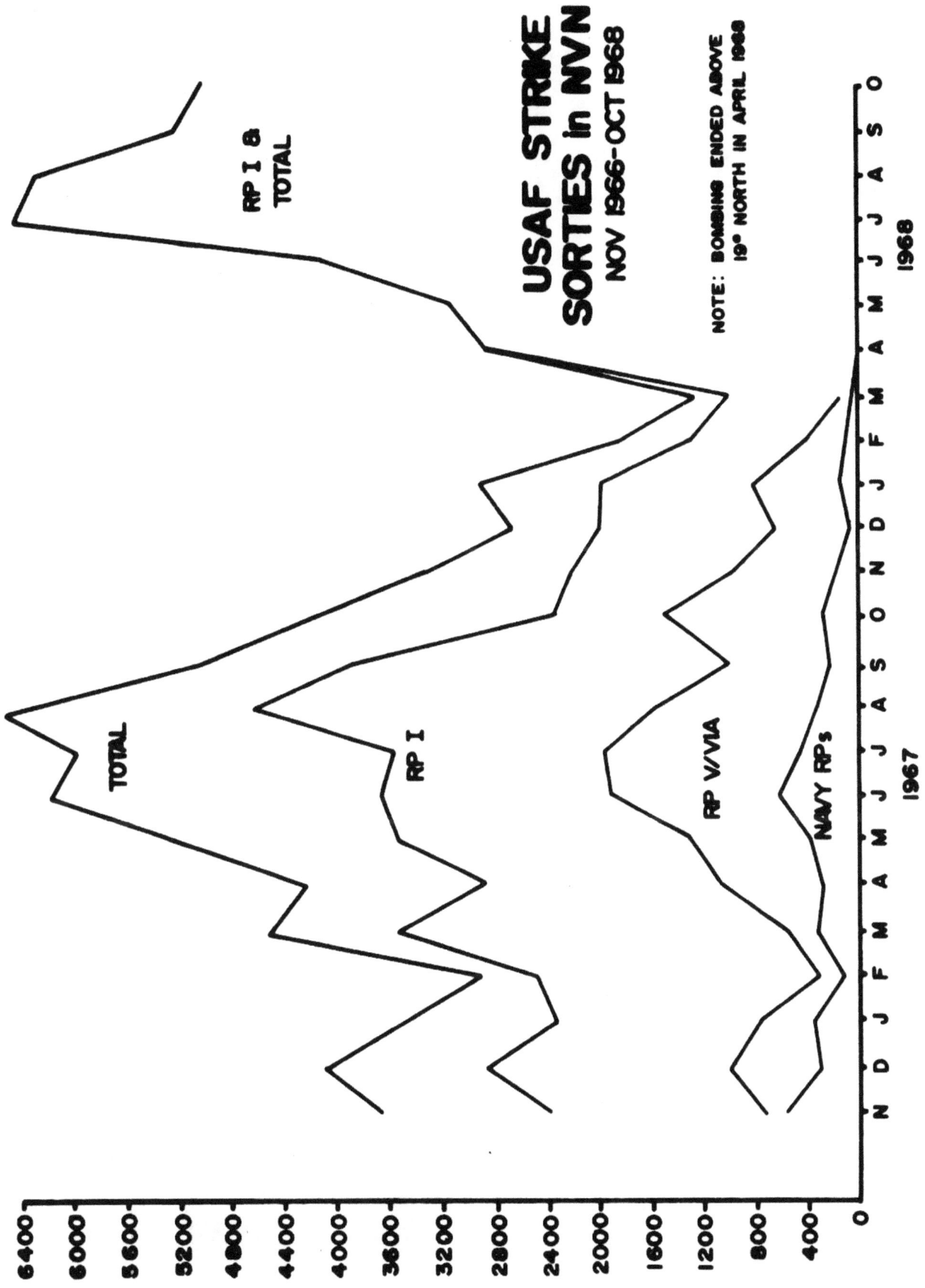

USAF STRIKE
SORTIES in NVN
NOV 1966-OCT 1968

RP I & TOTAL

TOTAL

RP I

RP V/VIA

NAVY RPs

NOTE: BOMBING ENDED ABOVE
19° NORTH IN APRIL 1968

1967   1968

FIG. 7

6400
6000
5600
5200
4800
4400
4000
3600
3200
2800
2400
2000
1600
1200
800
400
0

N D J F M A M J J A S O N D J F M A M J J A S O

CHAPTER III

INTERDICTION IN NORTH VIETNAM

ROLLING THUNDER

In the 17 months before the April 1968 bombing halt, the Air Force flew 68,137 attack sorties in North Vietnam and another 33,298 from April to October 1968.[1] Figure 7 shows how the total sorties in North Vietnam fell to very low levels in the two months before the April bombing halt. This period when 7AF was devoting large resources to the defense of Khe Sanh marked a transition between two decidedly different air campaigns against the North. The first was a broad campaign within constraints against North Vietnamese industry and transportation in the heartland and, to a lesser degree, in the panhandles; the second was an intensive highly specific interdiction campaign in RP I employing the choke point concept.

The objective of bombing North Vietnam, as expressed by Secretary of Defense McNamara to the Senate Preparedness Subcommittee in August 1967, was to "reduce the flow and/or to increase the cost of the continued infiltration of men and supplies from North to South Vietnam," to raise the morale of the South Vietnamese people, and to make the North Vietnamese "pay a price" for continuing aggression in the South.[2] The Secretary noted the agrarian nature of the North Vietnamese economy, the highly diversified transportation system, and the minimal number of war-making industrial targets. Commenting on the selective bombing campaign by the U.S. and the achievement of the first objective--reduction of supplies reaching the South--McNamara noted that:[3]

> *"The capacity of the lines of communication and of
> the outside sources of supply so far exceeds the
> minimal flow necessary to support the present level
> of North Vietnamese military effort in South Vietnam
> that the enemy operations in the South cannot, on
> the basis of any reports I have seen, be stopped by
> air bombardment—short, that is, of the virtual anni-
> hilation of North Vietnam and its people."*

At the same Senate hearing, Gen. Earle G. Wheeler, CJCS, stated that the major objectives of the air campaign were "to obstruct, reduce, and harass the flow of war supporting material within North Vietnam, and from North Vietnam to South Vietnam," to destroy the war-supporting facilities, and to impress upon the North Vietnamese the "heavy price" of aggression. 4/

In January 1967, a message from CINCPAC to his subordinate commands outlined the "1967 Goals for Evaluation of Progress in SEASIA":

> *"Take the war to the enemy by unremitting but selective
> application of United States air and naval power thus
> reducing Hanoi's capability to support and direct military
> operations in South Vietnam:*
>
> *(1) Goal—Achieve and maintain a level of damage to war
>   supporting targets which will render those targets
>   unusable for their intended purpose.*
>
> *(2) Goal—Reduce capability of NVN to move men and material
>   within NVN and into SVN along all land and water lines
>   of communication.*
>
> *(3) Goal—As authorized, progressively reduce monthly military
>   imports into NVN.*
>
> *(4) Goal—Reduce capability of NVN to interfere with our air
>   operations over NVN, as measured by enemy aircraft inven-
>   tory, SAM inventory and the friendly aircraft loss rate."*

These broad goals of the Secretary of Defense, CJCS, and CINCPAC were

32

translated into armed reconnaissance sorties and attacks on fixed targets. As of mid-1967, the CJCS estimated there were "some 9,000 separate entities" in North Vietnam, with "entity" being anything from a pagoda to a steel mill. Military or military-associated targets totaled 5,200 on the Basic Target List. Of these, the JCS had identified 242 of major importance and assigned them JCS target numbers. For instance, the Paul Doumer Hanoi Highway-Railroad Bridge was JCS 12.00 and the Canale de Rapids Bridge was JCS 13.00. CINCPAC recommended an additional 185 targets. In early August 1967, the two lists were consolidated into the Operations Target List with a total of 427 targets. 5/

One main purpose of the Senate Preparedness Subcommittee hearings was to learn how many targets had been struck and why some targets recommended by JCS/CINCPAC were not authorized for strike. As of 9 August 1967, 289 of these had not been attacked. Another 27 were considered inactive or insignificant targets and 111 were not authorized for strike. The latter included targets in the following categories (with the number of JCS targets given in parenthesis): 6/

Within Chinese Buffer Zone	22	(9)
Within Hanoi-10 Mile Radius	53	(12)
Within Haiphong-4 Mile Radius	21	(3)
Ports	3	(3)
Mining Operations	5	(5)
Locks	7	(7)
Total Targets Not Authorized	111	(39)

In addition to the 159 JCS/CINCPAC targets struck, 1,625 other targets on the Basic Target List had been attacked, meaning that by 9 August 1967 a calculated 1,784 fixed targets had been attacked out of the 5,200 targets in North Vietnam considered military or military-associated. By late August, these struck targets included 57 significant bridges and 50 major rail yards. 7/ A great

33

number of fixed targets in North Vietnam were not lucrative enough to warrant strikes.

This brief summary of the status of fixed targets in North Vietnam provides the necessary background to place the interdiction campaign in perspective. Many of the lucrative fixed targets of the interdiction efforts were major bridges and railroad marshaling yards and required specific JCS authorization to strike. Other non-JCS/CINCPAC fixed targets could be struck at the field commander's discretion. But it should be borne in mind that while the lucrative and spectacular JCS targets received great emphasis by 7AF and Seventh Fleet regarding targeting, strike tactics, and BDAs, only 10 percent of the attack sorties in North Vietnam by August 1967 had been directed against fixed targets. According to the Secretary of Defense, fully 90 percent of the sorties flew against LOCs and vehicles.[8/]

In terms of total attack sorties, the greater effort went into armed reconnaissance and for this the North was divided into the Armed Reconnaissance Route Packages (RPs) shown in Figure 8. Air campaigns in North Vietnam were authorized by ROLLING THUNDER (RT) execute orders. ROLLING THUNDER 52, issued on 12 November 1966, added 13 JCS targets to the four approved in the July RT 51, making a total of 17. The Air Force RT 52 targets included the following:[9/]

       Thai Nguyen Steel Plant (Area G, K & RR Rolling Stock)
       Thai Nguyen Steel Plant (Area Q)
       Ha Gia POL Storage Area
       Ha Gia RR Bridge and Ha Gia Highway Bridge
       Yen Vien RR Classification Yard
       Kinh No SAM Storage Area
       Hanoi SAM Storage NE
       Dap Cau RR/Highway Bridge

VI A

THAI
NGUYEN

2

V

VI B

5

9

HANOI

3

HAIPHONG

AIR FORCE MAY STRIKE
IN WESTERN NAVY
RP II, III, AND IV
WITH PRIOR
COORDINATION

4

IV

THANH HOA

III

VINH

17

II

ARMED RECONNAISSANCE
ROUTE PACKAGES

8

I

TALLY HO

DMZ

AIR FORCE
  I (COMUSMACV)
  V-VI A (CINCPACAF)

NAVY
  II, III, IV, VI B (CINCPACFLT) ←•←•←•→ RAILROADS

FIG. 8

RT 52 also authorized 10,100 attack sorties a month, with 5,000 sorties from the Seventh Fleet and 5,100 from 7AF bases in Thailand. The Navy flew in RPs II, III, IV, and VIB, while 7AF was authorized 2,500 sorties to RP I and Laos; 1,100 to RPs V and VIA, and 1,500 to the western portions of the Navy packages II, III, and IV.[10/] The Air Force received authorization on 26 August 1966 to use the sectors west of Route 15 in those three packages to provide secondary targets for attack sorties weathered out of RPs V and VIA. Previously, such weather diverts created a saturation situation by flooding into RP I in excessive numbers.[11/] Although authorized 1,500 sorties in the western portion of RPs II-IV, 7AF after October 1966 never put more than 604 sorties into the Navy areas (including VIB) in any one month and averaged 302 a month in 1967. From November 1966 to the bombing halt above 19°, the actual distribution of total Air Force attack sorties into North Vietnam was 4,784 (7.0%) into the Navy armed reconnaissance packages, 16,696 (24.5%) into RPs V and VIA, and 46,667 (68.5%) into RP I (Laos not included).[12/] Relative to RP I, it should be noted that 21,707 of those sorties came from bases in South Vietnam; in-country based aircraft rarely flew north of RP I and thus could not be diverts from the north.

Winter Campaign of 1966/1967

In the winter air campaign, the main emphasis turned to Laos and RP I, because the low overcast of the Red River Delta precluded most airstrikes. Thus, in November 1966, only two of the authorized JCS targets were struck. Also, RT 52 had stipulated that 5 of the 13 new JCS targets should be attacked before 18 November; the time limit lapsed before any strike aircraft could reach through the weather to attack.[13/] Total USAF sorties into RP V and VIA declined to 205 in February 1967, rose to 1,990 in July, and fell to 41C in February 1968.

However, sorties in RP I remained much higher, because of the less impenetrable weather in the lower panhandle, because strikes weathered out of the Red River Delta often diverted to RP I, and because radar control sites in I Corps could direct COMBAT SKYSPOT sorties into RP I. During the winter campaign, the lowest number of sorties into RP I in one month was 2,336.

The air campaign in the North during the winter of 1966/1967 placed heavy emphasis on reaching JCS targets and generally reducing the transportation system to serve inefficiently. Most strikes went into RP I where few lucrative fixed targets existed and armed reconnaissance prevailed. The impact of a general campaign of attrition against a widely dispersed LOC system of such large capacity as RP I was very difficult to measure. One firm piece of evidence indicating disruption of panhandle LOCs was that three enemy work camps in the lower panhandle reported POL shortages from September through November despite "more than sufficient" POL stocks in North Vietnam. One of these camps by December had received only four of the 22 metric tons of POL programmed for it in the last quarter of 1966.[14/]

A month by month description of airstrikes and BDAs is available in the PACAF "Effects of Air Operations--Southeast Asia." Some notable or representative interdiction efforts are included here to illustrate aspects of this general campaign of attrition.

Road watch teams on the North Vietnamese side of the Mu Gia Pass counted 235 trucks from 9-29 January 1967, mostly an estimated 40 trucks shuttling between the Nuy Caay seeding area where 7AF maintained round-the-clock attacks and the border to the west. On 26 January, road watch personnel estimated 200 yards of road at Nuy Caay were under repair by 70 men. However, airstrikes kept ahead of repairs, causing a definite drop in truck traffic through the Mu Gia Pass.[15/]

In the same period of January, the Northwest Railroad was struck on seven days by 94 sorties causing an estimated 11 rail cuts, 9 rail bridges destroyed or damaged (D/D), and damaging 6 rail yards. Meanwhile, the Northeast Railroad was attacked by 56 sorties on 6 different days with a BDA of 5 rail yards interdicted and 2 bridges D/D.[16/]

On 20 February, a break in the weather in the Mu Gia Pass allowed strike aircraft to locate a large convoy during daylight--something very unusual--and 74 sorties directed to the pass attacked an estimated 108 trucks with a BDA of 42 trucks D/D, 8 large fires, a 200-foot fireball, and three violent secondary explosions.[17/]

From 20 February to 19 March 1967, the Air Force and Marines put most of their 427 sorties in RP I into the TALLY HO area in support of MACV operations in I Corps. In light of the bad weather, most of the strikes were controlled by COMBAT SKYSPOT. During this period, attacks against the Northwest Railroad continued in RP V, but in RP VIA, the major effort was against the Thai Nguyen Iron and Steel Plant during a period of favorable weather.[18/]

The general bad weather in RP V and VIA precluded sustained interdiction in the heartland, but in RP I, the magnitude of strike sorties could at least be termed intensive, though much of it was by radar bombing under MSQ-77 COMBAT

SKYSPOT. During some weeks in March up to 80 percent of the Air Force strikes in North Vietnam were SKYSPOT sorties.[19] The monthly RP I total sorties from November through April ran 2,369, 2,861, 2,487, 3,599, and 2,926. The LOCs in RP I were not severely crippled despite the heavy armed reconnaissance. During the 8-12 February Tet Truce, the enemy moved a staggering amount of tonnage. The CJCS estimated 23,000 tons of supplies moved down toward the DMZ in the four days that bombing was halted.[20] PACAF reported 2,499 vehicles sighted during the truce in RP I. Clearly, then, the complex system of road and water LOCs, when not subject to attack, could be rapidly repaired or the interdicted portions quickly bypassed.[21]

Summer Campaign of 1967

The Summer Campaign of 1967 in North Vietnam was the most massive ever directed against the enemy heartland, the most free from restrictive Rules of Engagement, and, as it turned out, the last good-weather campaign flown north of 19°. In the Red River Delta, the weight of effort sought to destroy North Vietnam military/industrial facilities and to paralyze the railroads. Fragmentary evidence suggests that the cumulative effect of the summer campaign severely disrupted North Vietnam's economy, though the impact on the war in the South could not be quantified.

How best to exploit the opportunities of the coming summer and to maximize disruption was the concern of CINCPACAF and CINCPACAFLT in their January summary of concepts of targeting for 1967. CINCPACAF called for "no circles around Hanoi and Haiphong," so that "every significant military supply target" could be attacked. CINCPACAF outlined his generalized concept as follows:[22]

*"Considering our capabilities and practical realities,
we must strive for target mix that is attainable and
will give maximum return for effort. Our targeting
concept should therefore:*

A. *Be bold and broad enough to demonstrate national
determination and create untolerable spectre of
long war. For example, strikes on thermal power
plants, selected industrial targets, and Hanoi
RR and Bridge in rapid succession would show
determination and produce series of immediate
shock effects and lasting psychological impact.*

B. *Maximize attrition of war supporting material in
prime distribution centers. Large supply and
storage facilities in vicinity of Hanoi and Haiphong must be brought under attack. We must
attrit supplies before they are dispersed in
small units throughout country. Forces should be
concentrated when striking this target system to
compound effects. Continuing coordinated strike
campaign by both Navy and Air Force on supply and
storage facilities is required to produce maximum
attrition of war supporting materials.*

C. *Continue attrition of war supporting goods and
facilities at dispersed locations along the LOCs
south of Hanoi/Haiphong. This attrition in depth
should provide profitable opportunities to further
diminish war-making capability. This effort will
therefore range from dispersed storage areas in
southern NVN to industrial installations in north.*

D. *Although no extensive interdiction effort anticipated, occasional selective strikes at key bridges
required to impede traffic, permit attrition of
vehicles and restrict redeployment of labor force
occupied in repair activities."*

Worthy of special note from this message was the statement that "no extensive interdiction effort anticipated," though some bridges should be dropped to
impede traffic.

The CINCPACFLT thoughts in ROLLING THUNDER target concepts sprang from a

tightly reasoned analysis based on the interrelationship of targets within
target groupings and what type of targets created the most lasting impact. Thus,
where a major route crossed a river, a particular bridge would be far more
lucrative if no bypass existed or if the bypass bridges were down. Also,
CINCPACFLT valued long term effects and had definite suggestions on which interdiction targets had more lasting impact:[23/]

> *"An important tenet of the targeting concept is that
> the enemy can often be hurt more seriously by the
> destruction of a less easily replaceable item such
> as a truck or locomotive, than by cratering a road,
> the interdiction of a rail line, or the destruction
> of a bridge. Destroyed transports and supplies are
> a total loss and require replacement, whereas, damaged
> rail lines and sidings are quickly bypassed or a single
> thru line constructed.*
>
> *"Empty rail yards are normally poor targets whereas rail
> cars in yards are prime targets that often produce bonus
> effects from secondary explosions. The same is true for
> transshipment points and other areas. Unless they are
> being utilized, they do not justify strike efforts. It
> is through the maintenance of a severed LOC system to
> cause logistics backlog that these areas become lucrative.
> Fleeting targets of a lucrative nature occur more often
> as a result of the destruction of grouped targets, and
> will have the highest priority in the interdiction program."*

CINCPACFLT also emphasized the inefficiency of dispersing forces and the
value of concentrating airstrikes to achieve maximum effort at minimum cost.
Inherent in this thinking when added to the long-term impact of destroying
fleeting targets was the desirability of striking transient targets when they
collected in truck parks, rail yards, and water transshipment points. Attacking LOC choke points--bridges, causeways, tunnels, canal locks, passes, and
other vulnerable road and rail segments--sought to immobilize or concentrate

vehicles. The worth of the choke point lay with the difficulty of repair or
bypass and the amount of traffic it could disrupt.[24/]

Seventh Air Force formalized its thinking on interdiction in a plan called
Operation COBRA. In March 1967, the 7AF Commander directed his staff to prepare
a unified campaign plan for out-country air operations in the coming Southwest
Monsoon season. Since 1965, many operational plans (OPlans) and operational
orders (OpOrds) had been published on various regional operations such as STEEL
TIGER and ROLLING THUNDER and on special projects such as COMMANDO NAIL and
SLAM. The 7AF Commander wanted a combined campaign plan to interrelate the
various out-country operations.[25/]

Under Operation COBRA, the enemy heartland had the highest priority to
exert maximum military and psychological pressure on North Vietnam. Along
with the JCS targets, the Northeast and Northwest Railroads would be attacked to
keep them interdicted as much as possible. Armed reconnaissance day and night
would attack rolling stock and transportation facilities. In the Northwest
Mountains (RP V), primary strikes would not normally be scheduled, but the area
did have adequate divert targets such as radar sites, storage areas, and LOC
interdiction points. Armed reconnaissance and route interdiction were the
lowest priority in the mountains, just as in the Delta.[26/]

However, 7AF did propose to favor LOC interdiction. It proposed that
"interdiction belts" be established around Thanh Hoa and Vinh to slow "through-
put flow," i.e., cut the LOCs to impede traffic and maintain pressure to prevent
repairs. The backed up traffic would then be struck. Intensive SAM and AAA

suppression would be used to keep the belts permissive. The Bai Thuong/Thanh Hoa Canal/River complex would be the best "interdiction belt," because the mountains to the west and the U.S. naval blockade to the east funneled enemy logistics through this narrow area. Additionally, the Red River Delta water network did not extend to the south and thus could not provide potential bypasses. The Vinh belt would center on the Song Ca River where the panhandle LOCs converged at Vinh. South of Vinh, 7AF proposed that armed reconnaissance attack logistic concentrations and not attempt to interdict the myriad of LOCs. However, "temporary movement bottlenecks" might be made with divert air-strikes coming into RP I, if no better targets could be found.[27/]

Clearly then, Operation COBRA proposed to center LOC interdiction in the northern panhandle, make RP I an "adjunct" to interdiction farther north, and de-emphasize interdiction in the heartland. In the words of the Chief of the 7AF Combat Plans Division:[28/]

> "The plan recognizes that a timely effective program of interdiction against logistics movement in NVN cannot be conducted in Route Packages V, VIA, and VIB. This is true for two primary reasons. These are: (a) the maze of inter-connecting routes make bypass possible under al- most any circumstances; and (b) lack of clearance to close the port of Haiphong. However, the plan also recognizes that there are valid reasons for continuing operations in the enemy 'heartland.'"

Operation COBRA was briefed to CINCPACAF in April. He agreed with the concept of publishing a combined campaign plan for the Southwest Monsoon, but objected to the interdiction belts because they would detract other missions. According to a 7AF memo for record, "General [John D.] Ryan [CINCPACAF] wanted

42

the interdiction emphasis placed on destroying trucks and rolling stock and not on interdicting lines of communications."[29] When the plan went to the Pacific Fleet and Task Force 77, the Navy objected to the portion on Air Force operations in a Navy area, and made it clear that the plan was not satisfactory.[30] Operation COBRA was never approved and never published.

Air Force interdiction in the summer campaign stressed destroying trucks and rolling stock and de-emphasized choke points except for bridges. Not only did CINCPACAF desire this, but RT 55/56 emphasized it. RT 53/54 centered on army barracks, depots, thermal power plants, and iron and steel works. But on 23 April 1967, CINCPAC issued RT 55 on orders from JCS to authorize the Air Force five JCS targets, of which three concerned transportation. ROLLING THUNDER 56 superseded RT 55 in May by authorizing seven Air Force targets with four relating to LOCs. ROLLING THUNDER 56 continued until 21 July, thus encompassing, along with RT 55 the height of the railroad interdiction campaign.

Seven of 12 Air Force authorized Alpha targets in RT 55/56 concerned LOCs or vehicles:[31]

> RT 55 Hanoi RR/Highway Bridge - 4.6 miles north of Hanoi;
>   738' long, 20' wide; only connection of RR#1 and #2
>   to Hanoi.
>
> RT 55 Hanoi RR Car Repair Shop - 2.3 miles north of Hanoi
>   on RR #2; had five repair shops, repair yard, and
>   110 warehouse support buildings.
>
> RT 55 Dan Phuong Highway Causeway - 11 miles west of Hanoi;
>   600' long, 40' wide, and about 20' above marshy ground.
>
> RT 56 Kinh No Motor Vehicle Repair Area - north of Hanoi.
>
> RT 56 Bac Mai Motor Pool Facility - 3.1 miles north of Hanoi;

a major maintenance and repair facility.

RT 56 Yen Vien RR Classification Yard - north of Hanoi
        at RR #1/#2 junction; largest rail classification
        yard in North Vietnam. (This target approved in
        previous RT list and later deferred.)

RT 56 Nguyen Khe Storage Area - on Rt 3 just north of
        Yen Vien RR Classification Yard; a major trans-
        shipment point.

Some comparative statistics on freight performance in North Vietnam in
1963 (the last year available and representative of the early 1960s) show the
paramount importance of the railroads. The first column gives the percentage
total of metric tons moved by the various types of LOCs and the second column
shows the percentage of tons moved per kilometer:[32]

	% Total Metric Tons	% Total Tons/Kilometers
Inland waterways	38	28
Coastal waterways	2	9
Railroads	22	53
Highways	38	10
	100	100

These figures show that in 1963, the North Vietnamese roads were used for short-
haul and the railroads for longhaul. Since nearly all ammunition and military
equipment imported into North Vietnam came over the Northeast Railroad, the
lucrativeness of the railroads becomes readily apparent.

The Air Force did not need JCS/CINCPAC authorization to strike many of
the bridges and railyards outside the Hanoi/Haiphong restricted areas and away

44

18 AUG 67   SPAN DOWN

21 OCT. 67 SPAN REPAIRED

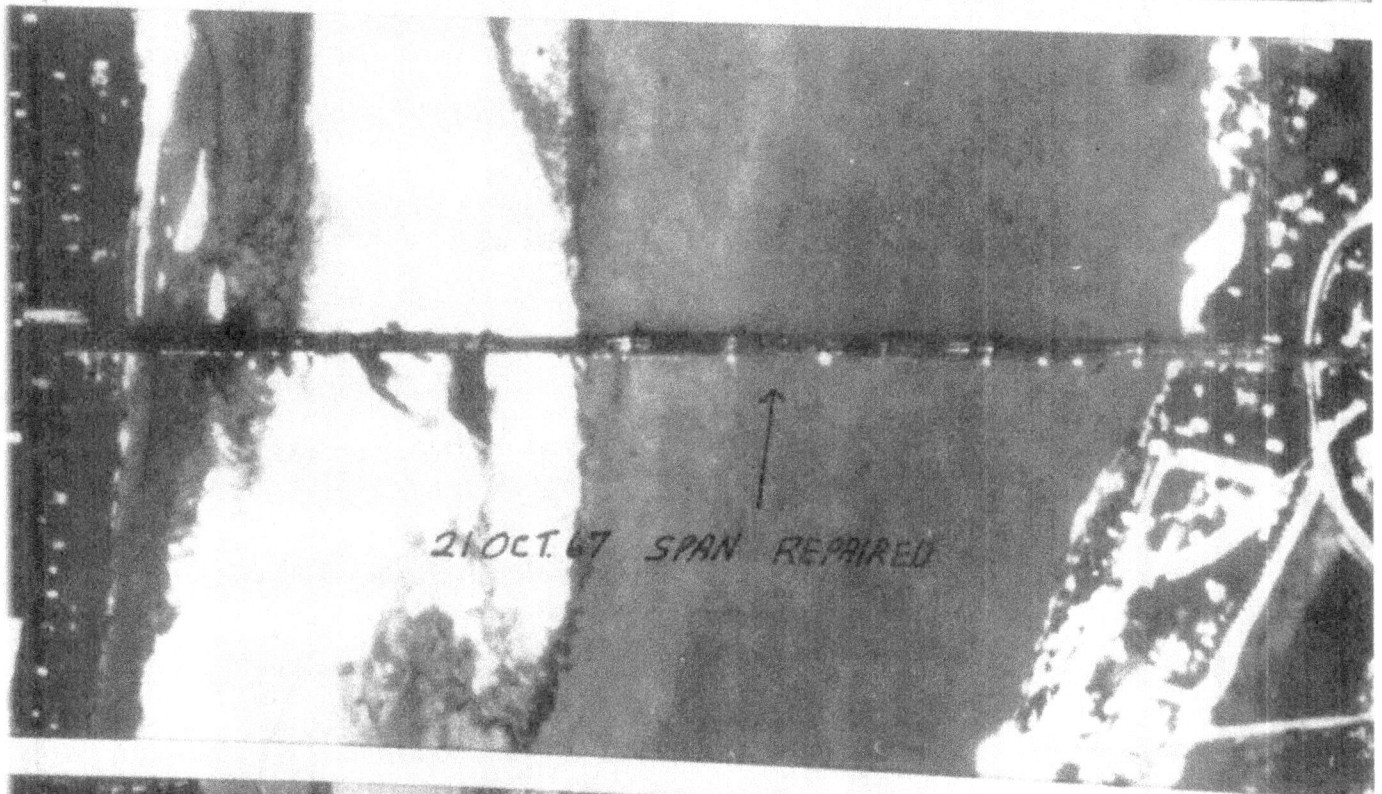

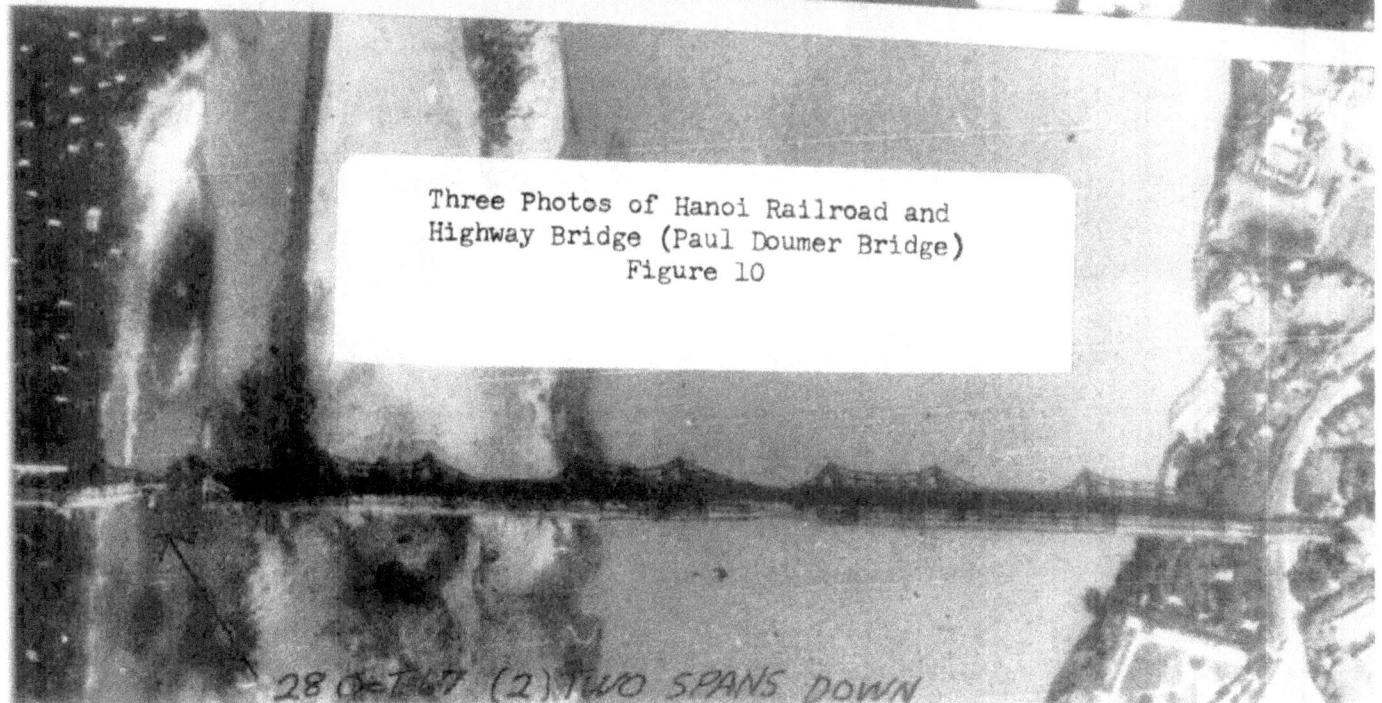

Three Photos of Hanoi Railroad and
Highway Bridge (Paul Doumer Bridge)
Figure 10

28 OCT 67 (2) TWO SPANS DOWN

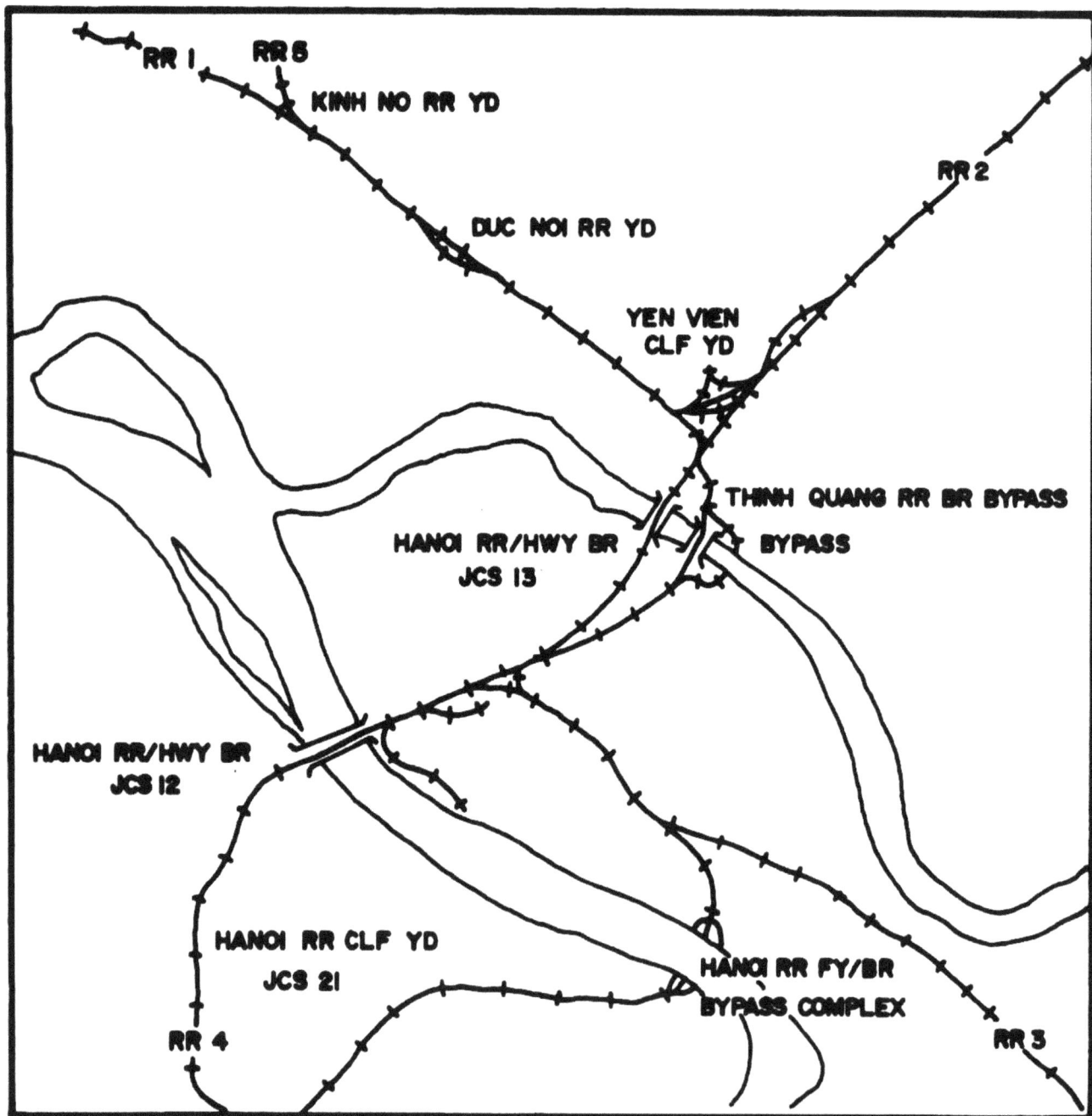

RR 1
RR 5
KINH NO RR YD
DUC NOI RR YD
RR 2
YEN VIEN
CLF YD
THINH QUANG RR BR BYPASS
HANOI RR/HWY BR
JCS 13
BYPASS
HANOI RR/HWY BR
JCS 12
HANOI RR CLF YD
JCS 21
HANOI RR FY/BR
BYPASS COMPLEX
RR 4
RR 3

HANOI RAIL NETWORK
JULY 1968

FIG. II

from population centers. Therefore, on 20-22 April, three rail yards on the Northeast Railroad (RR #2) were attacked, with approximately 170 pieces of rolling stock D/D, including three locomotives. However, on 24 April, three trains were sighted traveling RR #2 in daylight.[33]

As authorized by RT 55, on 25 and 28 April, F-105s attacked the Hanoi RR Car Repair Shop using 500, 750, and 3,000-pound bombs. A photo BDA of the April attack showed 48 buildings destroyed, 26 damaged, six pieces of rolling stock destroyed, and two locomotives damaged. The Hanoi RR/Highway Bridge was first attacked on 26 and 29 April and two spans dropped apparently due to a direct hit on one concrete pier. On 5 May, the Yen Vien RR Classification Yard was struck, but smoke prevented a BDA. Photos taken on 20 May showed 12 pieces of rolling stock destroyed and four tracks still interdicted. Due to these heavy strikes and attacks on three other rail yards and two other bridges, PACAF estimated the Northeast Railroad was unserviceable for 9 of the first 14 days of RT 55.[34]

The Nguyen Khe Storage Area was bombed on 12, 14, and 22 May with the building complex completely destroyed and the open storage area heavily damaged. The Kinh No Motor Vehicle Repair facility sustained two buildings destroyed and three extensively damaged in a 24 May attack using 3,000 pound-bombs and CBU-24s. Twelve F-105s attacked the Bac Mai Motor Pool facility on 21 May, damaging 9 buildings "to some extent." During the period 8-21 May, the Air Force also struck four rail yards on the Northeast Railroad, destroying 48 of 73 pieces of rolling stock.[35]

In late May, the interdiction campaign against the northern railroads intensified to the point where it dominated Air Force operations in the heart-

land. Imposition of a ten-mile prohibited circle around Hanoi on 23 May

reinforced the shift from JCS targets to railroad interdiction. From 22 May to

4 June, 289 strike sorties dropped 872 tons of bombs on 35 separate targets on

the northern railroads. (Fig. 12.) Results included 39 rail yards interdicted,

one major rail bridge destroyed, four rail bridges damaged, and 25 other rail

cuts made. Bottling rail cars between the cuts helped achieve the 171 cars

D/D.[36/]

This rail interdiction campaign continued through June and at a lesser

pace through July. In June, an estimated 34 percent of the rolling stock

capacity on the Northeast Railroad (RR #2, #5, and #9) was destroyed--about

34,000 metric tons.[37/] During the generally favorable weather of June and July,

the cumulative impact of the bombing crippled the two rail routes from China

to Hanoi. According to PACAF: "Repair teams cannot cope with the level of

destruction imposed by airpower."[38/] Downed bridges were repaired or bypassed,

but at the price of costly manpower levies needed for the army and the fields.

In the face of severe rail car losses--over 900 D/D in June and nearly 500 in

July--the North Vietnamese countered keeping the trains and rolling stock in

the Chinese Border and Hanoi buffer zones and "shooting the gap" between

sanctuaries whenever the lines were open.[39/] A PACAF article assessed the

results of the campaign in June:[40/]

> "A concentrated effort against the northern rail lines
> was launched in June. Railroad #5, Hanoi-Thai Nguyen,
> was unserviceable 23 days. The Northwest line was
> struck on eight separate days. Pilots reported inter-
> diction of six rail yards, damage to four rail bridges,

46

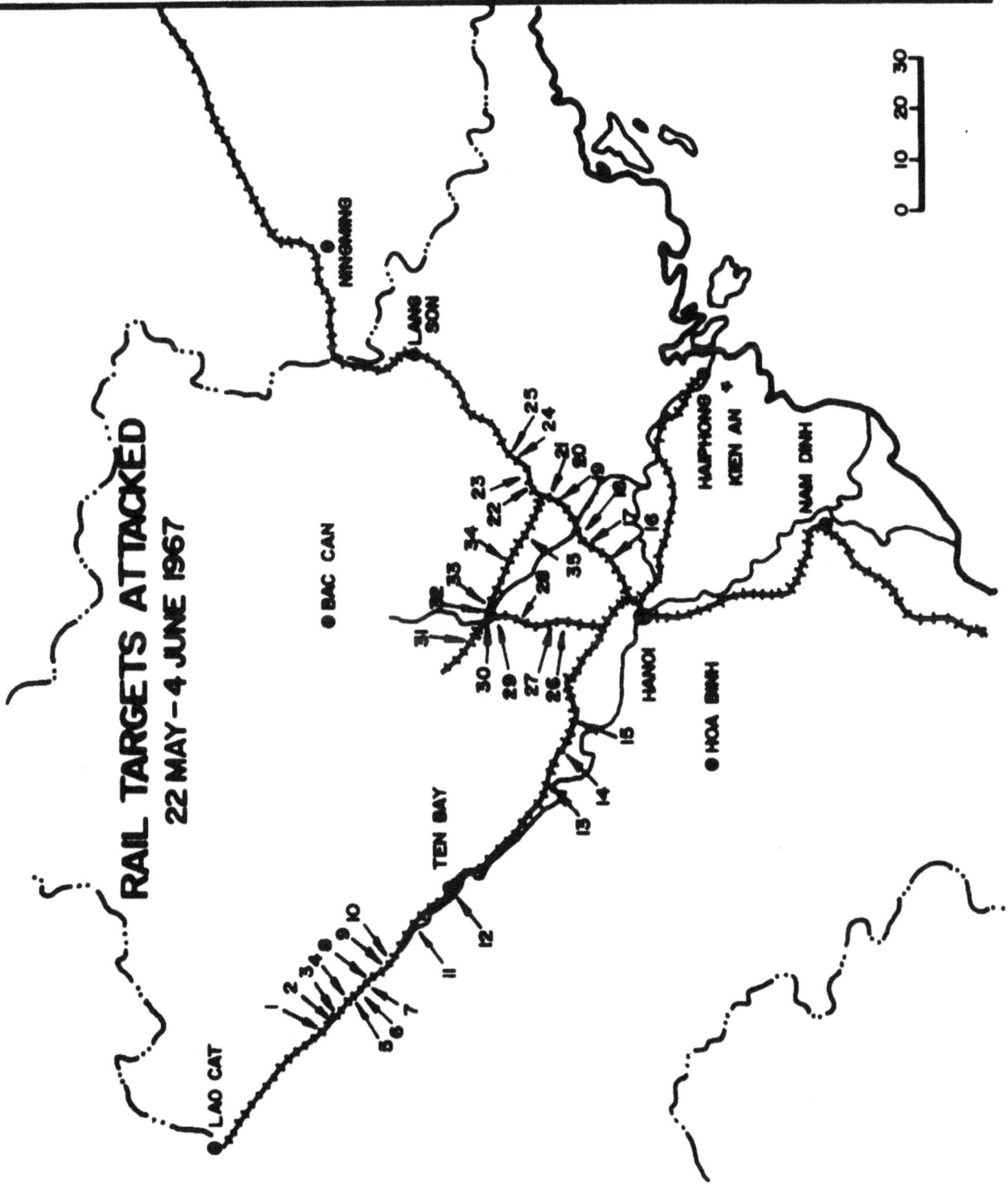

RAIL TARGETS ATTACKED
22 MAY – 4 JUNE 1967

289 SORTIES

872 BOMB TONS

LAO CAI

1
2 3 4
5 9
6
7 8
10
11
TEN BAY
12
13
14
15
HANOI
HOA BINH
BAC CAN
33
34
32
31
30
29
27
28
35
23
22
26
21
20
18
24
25
19
17
16
NINGMING
LANG SON
HAIPHONG
KIEN AN
NAM DINH

0 10 20 30

FIG. 12

> and 14 other rail cuts. The Northeast line was
> closed to through traffic eight days, and probably
> interdicted an additional 17 days. USAF strikes
> destroyed/damaged 956 pieces of rolling stock in
> the northern areas. Rail traffic from China toward
> Hanoi has been severely hampered."

What was the enemy's reaction to an interdiction campaign of attrition? CINCUSARPAC published two short articles in the PACOM "Intelligence Digest," one on the regeneration of destroyed rail yards and the other on construction of multiple bypasses around major bridges. The former was based on a detailed study of seven rail yards--two in Air Force packages. It was found that the rapid repair of classification yards in the panhandle took second place to reopening through traffic. Apparently, classification yards in the panhandle were not vital because the small amount of tonnage going north had little need for classification and the large tonnage moving south was apparently classified near points of origin. Based on photo interpretation of bomb craters, the article concluded that a work force of 50 men working under good conditions could repair a single track interdiction in less than five hours and under the worst conditions in less than ten. Further, the enemy sought to offset the bombing of rail yards by "reaction activities" and "preplanned activity," which meant making repairs or bypasses or new lines in anticipation of attacks. [41/]

An analysis of 11 major bridges (six in Air Force packages) emphasized the detailed care the North Vietnamese took in anticipating strikes and reducing the dependence on a few major bridges. By July 1967, the Hanoi RR/Highway Bridge had two bypasses, while the Ninh Binh RR/Highway Bridge in RP IV had the original bridge (destroyed), three bypass bridges, and one railroad ferry which could transport rail cars. Further, the newest railroad bridge had very short spans to lessen bomb damage and facilitate repair. On 10 June, the Viet Tri RR/Highway Bridge on the Northwest Railroad had the original bridge (destroyed), two highway pontoon bridges (one unserviceable), two RR ferry sites requiring offloading of rail cars, and one vehicle ferry. These dispersed crossings probably did not have the capacity of the original bridge.42/

The summary of conclusions was that the enemy could repair his LOCs:43/

> "The foregoing examples depict some reconstruction methods of deception, and techniques of repair which enable the North Vietnamese to keep important river crossings in operation. Vital river crossings in North Vietnam, such as major rail bridges, are replaced or repaired almost immediately after they are struck. Bridges of lesser importance may not be replaced or repaired until such time as the need arises. The time required to repair the damaged bridges or to build an additional fixed bridge at the site varies according to the type structure, length of crossing, and the relative importance to the line of communications. Since these factors vary from one structure to another, a general statement of time cannot be made for replacement or regeneration.

> "In most cases, however, a float bridge or ferry operation will be placed at the site either permanently or until the bridge is repaired or replaced with another of equal capacity. Since the float bridges and the ferries used in North Vietnam are somewhat standard and can be related to US-type equipment, an estimate of the time necessary to construct them can be made. In the case of ferried, they can be operational one hour after the bridge is knocked out, provided the approaches are available. Improved earth approaches could be constructed in approximately four hours. Float bridges could be constructed within one day regardless of the length, but the use of float bridges is limited by stream velocities and availability of equipment.

> "When a railroad bridge is struck and damaged, the reaction generally is to rebuild the original structure. If this

fails, a new railroad bridge is constructed of approx-
imately the same or larger capacity. If the area is
too vulnerable, such as in the southern portion of the
country, the North Vietnamese are either forced to use
other methods of crossing the river or abandon the line.
For a combination railroad and highway bridge, the high-
way traffic is diverted to other types of crossings,
such as fords, ferries, and floating bridges. When a
bridge is built, such as in the case of the Ninh Dinh by-
pass, many short spans are used to reduce the effects of
bombing.

"Types of deception techniques found have been removable
floating and sliding spans and cable bridges which give
the impression of unserviceability. Construction tech-
niques such as fabrication of the deck on the banks speed
the replacement of bridges because more than one operation
can be accomplished at the same time (there have been
incidents of material positioned at the bridge sites be-
fore the bridges are hit). It should be pointed out that
most river-crossing sites in North Vietnam already have
one or more alternate crossings available. All these
conditions enable the North Vietnamese to keep their im-
portant lines of communications open."

As with the multiple bypass, the enemy developed an effective counter to
attacks on his railroad cars. Attrition from the June intensive rail interdiction campaign caused the marshaling of rolling stock in rail yards and sidings
off limits to U.S. airstrikes--primarily in the Hanoi and Chinese Border buffer
zones. The following statistics (totals vary slightly from others in this
chapter) for both services illustrate an important trend between units sighted
and units D/D: [44]

	RR Rolling Stock Sighted	RR Rolling Stock D/D	% Sighted TO D/D
MAY	1,366	135	9.9
JUNE	3,920	1,135	31.3
JULY	2,743	493	18.0

	RR Rolling Stock Sighted	RR Rolling Stock D/D	% Sighted TO D/D
AUGUST	2,243	332	14.8
SEPTEMBER	2,072	90	4.3

These statistics clearly illustrate the initial impact of the intensive June campaign and the adoption by the North Vietnamese of counter tactics. To substantiate the subjective impression that the enemy was exploiting sanctuaries, the PACAF Target Development Center examined the period from 11 September to 10 October 1967. This study revealed that of 2,202 pieces of rolling stock, 1,306 were in areas unauthorized to airstrikes and 896 in authorized areas. This ratio contrasted sharply with the fact that of the 84 rail yards and sidings in North Vietnam, 62 were authorized and only 22 not authorized for airstrikes. In other words, 27 percent of the yards had 59 percent of the sighted rolling stock. The authorized yards had a density of 14 units compared to 59 for the unauthorized. In conclusion, the PACAF analysis noted that while initial attacks on these lucrative authorized yards would be high and then decline, without "protected areas" the rail system would suffer from the inefficiency of necessary dispersion.[45/]

Interdiction in Route Package I

While the rail interdiction campaign ran in the heartland, 200 miles to the south a war of attrition was concentrated in RP I, with twice the total strike sorties used in RP V and VIA. Nearly all of the sorties struck fixed LOC targets such as fords, bridges, truck parks, ferry complexes, and POL storage areas. Route Package I never had lucrative targets comparable to the Hanoi-Haiphong area, and its few military-industrial targets had already been destroyed or heavily damaged. When armed reconnaissance patrols could not locate "movers"--trucks or watercraft--they attacked the fixed targets. From 8-21 May, 60 percent of the strikes against highways in RP I attacked fixed LOCs and from 5-25 June, the percentage rose to 67 percent.[46/]

Destruction resulted in RP I when air attacks were brought to bear against a rather small area such as the southern panhandle. The railroad remained unserviceable, all major bridges were down, and army barracks and storage transshipment areas absorbed repeated strikes. For instance, Air Force pilots on 12 days attacked the Giap Nhat Petroleum Products Storage Transshipment area 20 times, causing a reported 19 secondary explosions and 14 secondary fires.[47/]

Attacks on trucks played an important part in the RP I campaign. According to PACAF calculations, the ratio of trucks destroyed to trucks attacked ran 34 percent in June and 36 percent in July.[48/] The following statistics from the 7AF "Weekly Air Intelligence Summary" (Route 15 leads into the Mu Gia Pass) give an indication of the success of the program:

1967		Trucks Sighted	Trucks D/D
	RT 15	All RP I	All RP I
15-21 June	44	497	73
22-28	75	452	45
29-5 Jul	118	743	88
6-12	532	1,018	213
13-19	471	946	111
20-26	230	697	166
27-2 Aug	149	820	166
3-9	342	1,226	316
10-16	395	1,071	209
17-23	43	379	103
24-30	43	457	142

1967		Trucks Sighted	Trucks D/D
	RT 15	All RP I	All RP I
31-6 Sep	616	1,741	204
7-13	124	379	62
14-20	73	142	22
21-27	97	176	17
28-4 Oct	257	486	6
5-11	350	427	17

Based on these totals, there were 10,568 truck sightings (many of the same trucks sighted more than once) to 20 September and 1,920 trucks were destroyed or damaged.

On 21 July, RT 57, as issued by CINCPAC, authorized nine Alpha JCS targets and also eliminated the sortie allocations (2,500 Air Force sorties in RP I), and authorized the relevant commanders "to conduct attack sorties against NVN and Laos as necessary to accomplish assigned missions."[49] RT 57 continued until the April bombing halt because JCS had not removed struck targets and issued new execute orders. Rather, the list of authorized targets was expanded nearly every month with new additions. Through August, RT 57 grew from the original nine JCS targets to 51.[50] Strikes in the Hanoi and Chinese Border Buffer Zones were flown. By February, there were 93 authorized JCS targets.[51] At the same time, weather deteriorated and sorties declined. (Thailand and South Vietnam sorties in RP I declined at about the same pace.) The Air Force maintained a presence in the heartland but the consistently poor weather precluded constant pressure. In February and March 1968, the Tet Offensive and the battle for Khe Sanh absorbed heavy air resources even from Thailand. In the month before the April bombing halt, the Air Force put 223 sorties into all of North Vietnam, north of RP I.

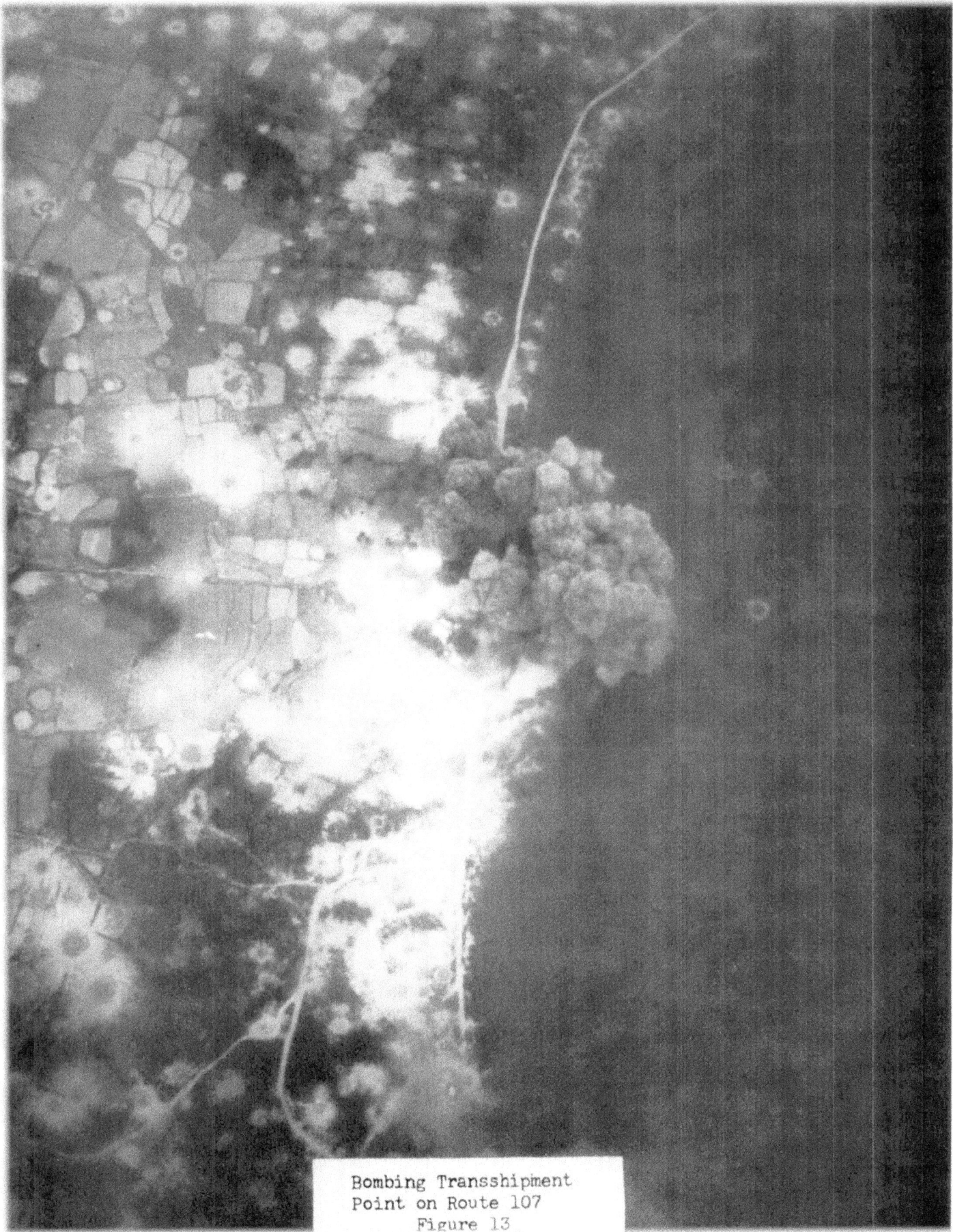

Bombing Transshipment
Point on Route 107
Figure 13

The 1 April 1968 bombing halt restricted Air Force ROLLING THUNDER operations to RP I, with an occasional sortie into RP II and III. However, in early April, 64 of the 69 RT targets in RP I were "unserviceable, abandoned, or not considered worthy to strike."[52] Armed reconnaissance continued to dominate RP I operations.

Mid-June intelligence predicted an enemy offensive within two months in South Vietnam, causing COMUSMACV to request from 7AF an interdiction campaign in RP I to disrupt the anticipated offensive. At the direction of the 7AF Commander, the operations and intelligence sections developed a plan to isolate northern RP I from the southern half. This would channel truck traffic away from the mountain passes and toward the coastal plain, where theoretically the open lowlands would permit more trucks to be attacked and destroyed.

A 30-day interdiction plan proposed establishing choke points on the mountain roads leading to the Mu Gia and Ban Karai Passes. These choke points would be kept closed by heavy bombing, mining operations, armed reconnaissance, and intensive surveillance "presence" over the choke points. At the same time, fords and ferry crossings would be mined with the MK-36.[53] The Navy at this time was trying the same thing in RPs II and III against what were called Traffic Control Points.[54] Due to prohibitions against B-52 strikes above 17°10', only four strikes per day were used instead of the planned 24 per day and these sorties expended ordnance over storage areas just north of the DMZ.[55]

As implemented, the 30-day interdiction campaign had three major choke points: one on Rt 15 to the Mu Gia Pass, one on Rt 137 to the Ban Karai Pass, and one on Rt 101, which linked Rt 15 and 137. Two of the choke points were

53

mountain switchbacks and one a road along a karst cliff undercut by a

river cave. In the first 30 days, 12 percent of the strike force in RP I went
against these three points.[56/] The 7AF Directorate of Intelligence estimated

that the choke points were closed to through traffic, respectively 30 percent,

60 percent, and 23 percent of the time. Later in the campaign, three other

points joined the list and in September, a total of 27 percent of 5,200 sorties

were used against the six choke points. From late September until the bombing

halt, 7AF Intelligence reported Rts 15 and 137 closed nearly the entire time.[57/]

The results were impressive. By the end of the first 30 days, truck

sightings fell from 400 a week to less than 100 or lower. Comparing ten-week

periods before and after mid-July for 1967 and 1968 revealed that truck sight-

ings in all of RP I rose between the 1967 before and after periods from 5,458

to 7,088, but fell in 1968 from 6,444 to 5,048.[58/] Figure 14 plots truck sight-

ings on Rts 15 and 137 for 1967 and 1968.

The causes for this significant curtailment of enemy truck traffic were

several. The choke points cut the main routes to Laos for a significant number

of days. During August and September, two typhoons flooded the roads, turning

the bombed areas into mudholes. Also, the bombing halt made available one-

third more aircraft to RP I than ever before, allowed the full weight of 7AF

efforts to concentrate on RP I, and permitted the fragging and arming of air-

craft to be tailored for operations in RP I.

Although the impact of the 1968 summer campaign in RP I on enemy combat

operations in-country cannot be precisely quantified, it is clear that concen-

trated air operations achieved a reduction in enemy truck movement--a notable

54

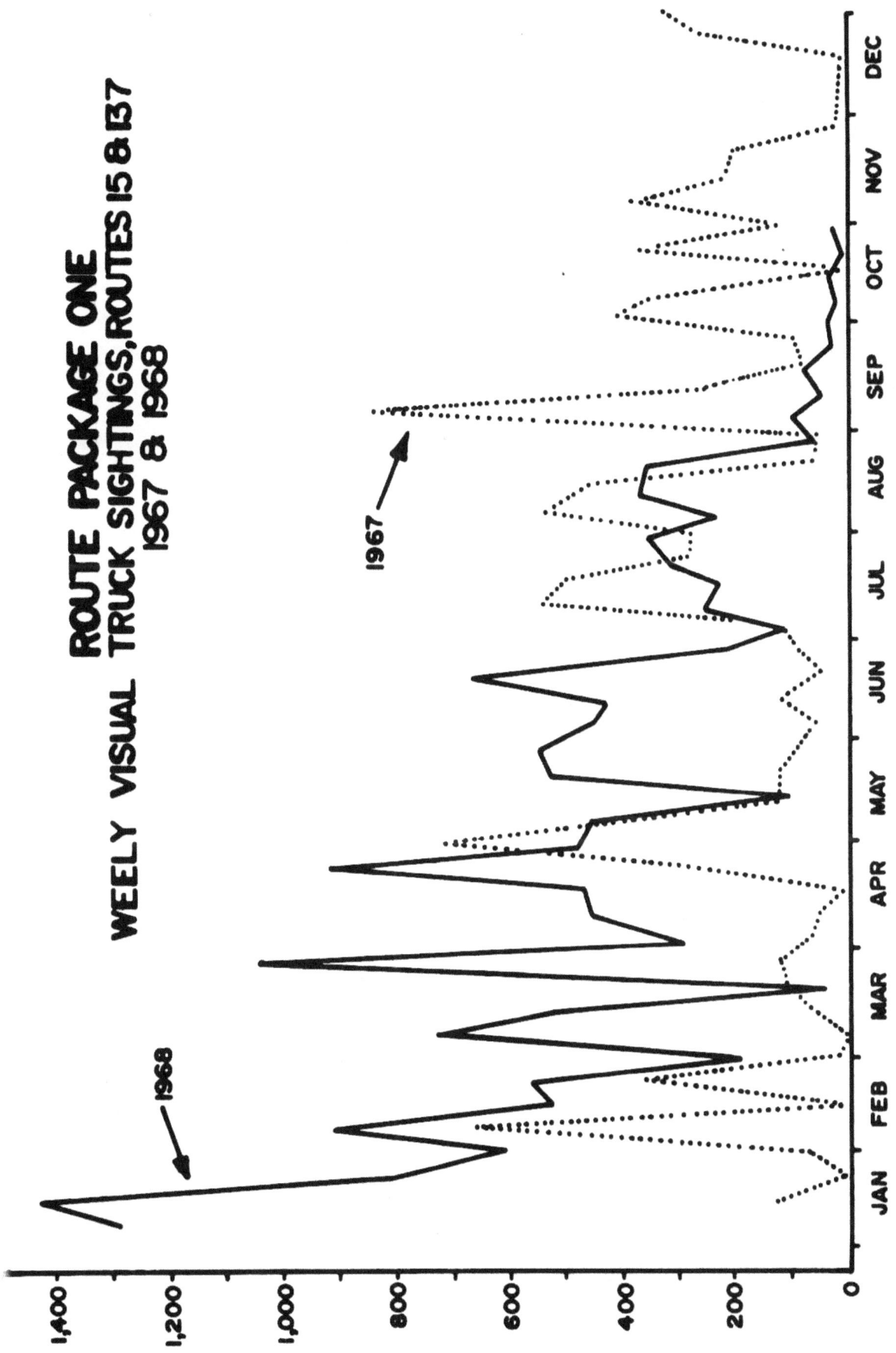

ROUTE PACKAGE ONE
WEELY VISUAL TRUCK SIGHTINGS, ROUTES 15 & 137
1967 & 1968

SOURCE: 7AF WAIS
FIG. 14

achievement considering increasing truck traffic trends of previous years. Whether the choke point concept could have continued to keep Routes 15 and 137 effectively closed during the traditional November to April logistics surge through Laos was not tested because on 1 November 1968 all bombing of the North stopped.

CHAPTER IV

INTERDICTION IN LAOS, 1966 - 1968

Rules of Engagement

The basic Rules of Engagement in STEEL TIGER at the start of the 1966/1967 winter interdiction campaign permitted airstrikes within the armed reconnaissance area on motorable trails and roads out to 200 yards. Fixed targets inside 200 yards could be struck only if validated as Royal Laotian Air Force (RLAF) targets Beyond 200 yards, targets of opportunity and fixed targets could be struck only if one of the following conditions were met:

- Target was a validated RLAF target.

- AA/AW weapons were firing on friendly aircraft.

- Approval was obtained from an authorized Air Attache representative in Laos.

- Military boat/barge was located on any river within the armed recon area, if the strikes were controlled by a FAC.

FACs were also required for close air support for strikes when requested by the American Embassy at Vientiane, and for all targets within five kilometers of the Cambodian Border.[1]/

Other restrictions required U.S. aircraft to avoid five Laotian towns in STEEL TIGER by ten nautical miles distance and 15,000 feet altitude: Savannakhet, Saravane, Attopeu, Pakse, and Thakhet. In the Laotian special road watch area (the Elephant Area) on Route 9 over the border from Khe Sanh, FAC control and radio contact were required. Napalm was prohibited in Laos, except under authorization by the American Embassy at Vientiane, or when under FAC control if the target were a validated RLAF target, a motorized vehicle within the armed recon area, or an AA/AW position firing on friendly aircraft. Night attacks on fixed targets were forbidden, as were attacks on camp fires and civilian houses. Yet another restriction forbade flights within five nautical miles of the DMZ, unless directed by frag orders or when FAC controlled.[2]

In November 1966, an armed recon "Special Operating Area" was designated in the eastern part of TIGER HOUND bordering South Vietnam. The Rules of Engagement permitted airstrikes without FAC control on all enemy activity on all roads, trails, and rivers, and on all RLAF validated targets. Aircraft positions had to be confirmed by radar or tactical air navigation (TACAN) before attacking without FAC control. This relaxation of the rules in the sparsely populated eastern panhandle was in recognition of the need to accommodate diverted aircraft from North Vietnam. These diverts often arrived over STEEL TIGER low on fuel with no FACs immediately available. The new rule permitted those aircraft to attack any enemy activity in the Special Operating Area.[3]

Short Rounds on Laotian villages had always been a very sensitive issue because of injuries and damages caused, and because such strikes exposed the U.S. to criticism concerning the 1962 Geneva Accords on Laotian neutrality.[4] Therefore, the Rules of Engagement were very strict and included such prohibitions as no night strikes on fixed targets and no attacks on camp fires. Further, 7AF laid increasing emphasis on FAC control of airstrikes, something that had not existed in the very early BARREL ROLL and STEEL TIGER programs. In January 1967, 7AF ordered all jet strike aircraft in STEEL TIGER to be under positive FAC or MSQ-77 control, the only exceptions being the A-37s, and F-100Fs,

both capable of FACing for themselves. [5/] According to PACAF, this FAC requirement forced the FACs to spend more time controlling airstrikes and degraded
the visual reconnaissance program by reducing the time available to search for
targets of opportunity. [6/]

The Short Rounds continued and on 18 March the basic Rules of Engagement
in STEEL TIGER were amended to create four strike zones increasingly restrictive
as they approached the populated Mekong River plain in the west. By observing
the old boundaries of the Special Operating Area and the armed recon portion of
STEEL TIGER, the new rules did not drastically change the Rules of Engagement.
Figure 15 shows the Special Operating Area permitting attacks without FAC
control as the new Zone I. Zones II and III did differ from each other in that
armed recon was allowed in Zone II inside 200 yards of motorable roads, while
in Zone III, all strikes had to be FAC/MSQ-77-controlled. However, Zones I, II,
and III made up the old armed recon area of STEEL TIGER. [7/]

Zone IV included the remainder of STEEL TIGER and continued the requirement for Air Attache approval, as well as FAC control for all strikes. The
prohibition against overflights within 10 nautical miles below 15,000 feet AGL
continued for the five major panhandle towns with Muong Phalane added. Other
special areas with restrictions were the Elephant Area on Route 9 and the CAS
road watch area around the Mu Gia Pass.

On 1 May 1967, a ten-nautical-mile buffer zone was created in North Vietnam bordering Laos to guard against uncontrolled airstrikes in Laos. From the
DMZ north to 19°30', the Radar Control Zone required positive radar control for

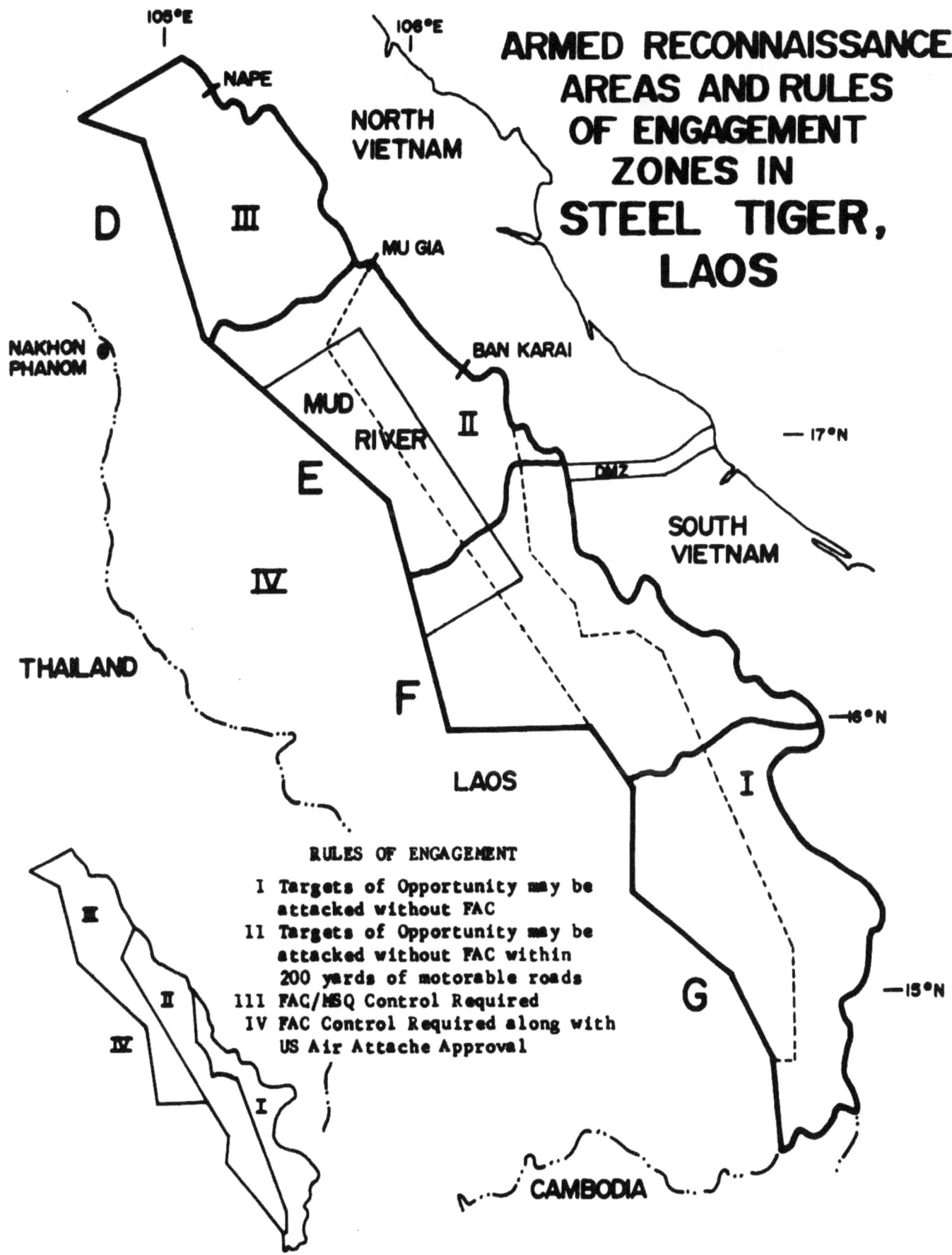

ARMED RECONNAISSANCE
AREAS AND RULES
OF ENGAGEMENT
ZONES IN
STEEL TIGER,
LAOS

105°E

106°E

NAPE

NORTH
VIETNAM

D

III

MU GIA

NAKHON
PHANOM

BAN KARAI

MUD

RIVER

II

— 17°N

E

DMZ

SOUTH
VIETNAM

IV

— 16°N

THAILAND

F

I

LAOS

RULES OF ENGAGEMENT

I Targets of Opportunity may be
   attacked without FAC
II Targets of Opportunity may be
   attacked without FAC within
   200 yards of motorable roads
III FAC/MSQ Control Required
IV FAC Control Required along with
   US Air Attache Approval

G

— 15°N

III

II

IV

I

CAMBODIA

FIG. 15

strikes in North Vietnam. From 19°30' north to 22°, the Laotian Buffer Zone required the exercise of extreme caution in delivering airstrikes. [8]

Campaign Against Interdiction Points

By October 1966, the winter air interdiction campaign in Laos had definitely begun. As total monthly Air Force strike sorties into North Vietnam declined, they rose in Laos. In January and February 1967, more strikes went into Laos than into North Vietnam, and then the trend made a seasonal reversal and strike sorties into Laos began declining to a 1967 low in July and August. It is interesting to note that in the next Laotian dry season--that of 1967/1968-- the Laotian monthly Air Force sortie totals exceeded those directed into North Vietnam for seven months rather than just two months as happened in the 1966/ 1967 dry season. (Fig. 6.)

Behind these seasonal fluctuations in total sorties lay a far more significant story of the varying target emphasis of the interdiction campaign. Many potential combinations of targets and tactics were available: concentrating the air effort against truck parks and storage areas; flying armed reconnaissance to destroy moving trucks, or putting round-the-clock airstrikes and reconnaissance into interdiction points to cut and close roads. Sometimes the STEEL TIGER program concentrated on a particular technique, but usually pressure was maintained against the total interdiction target system rather than a single target category. In the view of some individuals, this approach was viewed as diffused and wasteful. The tendency was to look for a panacea to targeting that would achieve dramatic results. The Commander-in-Chief, U.S. Pacific Fleet, (CINCPACFLT) made this point in January 1967 in regard to North Vietnam

59

by calling for tactics that forced the enemy to concentrate his logistics
resources:[9/]

> "The broad dispersion of important targets in NVN
> had greatly reduced the value of striking fixed
> targets on a random basis. It has been demonstrated
> that targets must be developed by the tactical com-
> mander in order that fleeting targets will be forced
> to collect in the multitude of transshipment points
> and rail yards."

In the same vein, a report published by the Operations Analysis Section of
7AF in February 1967 stated:[10/]

> "The current method of road interdiction to a large
> degree has reacted to the observed actions of the
> enemy. As intelligence information is developed,
> strikes are generated to interdict a road that shows
> recent usage, hit a truck convoy which was recently
> observed, strike a truck park recently discovered,
> strike recently discovered troop concentrations,
> etc. The many new targets and target folders gener-
> ated each month and/or target folders updated reflect
> favorably upon our Intelligence Directorate and the
> enemy's capabilities and energies, but had contrib-
> uted to a dilution of our attempts to cover the many
> targets generated and has suppressed our utilization
> of offensive initiative."

According to this analysis, fragging against lucrative targets resulted
in a "dilution" of effort and a loss in "offensive initiative." If the U.S.
had had a far greater number of daily strike sorties available in STEEL TIGER,
perhaps the total effort would have disrupted the enemy logistics system to
the point where it could no longer function. This probably happened in Route
Package I from August through October 1968. However, the sorties available
daily in STEEL TIGER were far below such a level. To increase the impact of
airstrikes available, several intensive special operations were conducted

60

in Laos.

During the last quarter of 1966, the interdiction program placed primary emphasis on interdiction points. This campaign against the Route 911/912 complex between the Mu Gia Pass and Tchepone resulted in the enemy rehabilitating Route 23 to the west of Route 911 as a dry season alternate route. Route 23 in this area ran over level ground impassible in the wet season but lacking choke points in the dry season. Aircraft struck small bridges and seeded the route with delayed fuze bombs.[11/]

Another problem was that many STEEL TIGER strikes were weather diverts from North Vietnam and had a time over target (TOT) characteristic of Route Packages V and VI. Of the 2,546 Air Force strike sorties flown in STEEL TIGER in December 1966, 940 were known diverts from ROLLING THUNDER and 221 were diverts from BARREL ROLL.[12/] In the six months from December 1966 to May 1967, 29 percent of the Air Force strike sorties into Laos were diverts from North Vietnam (5,418 of 18,513). When bad weather conditions caused Air Force and Navy diverts into STEEL TIGER, the FACs were swamped with flights and forced to put the strikes in near where they--the FACs--were caught by the deluge of diverts. Aside from causing a mal-distrubution of strikes in STEEL TIGER (wherever FACs were available), the diverts disrupted the FAC VR program.[13/]

In October 1966, as shown in Figure 16, a detailed record was kept of an interdiction campaign against five points in CRICKET. Only Charlie point was observed to have been cut for more than one day at a time.[14/]

In TIGER HOUND, a visual recon/photo recon survey was made to assist in the selection of 18 choke points with the intention of keeping them closed by airstrikes that interdict the road and drive off road crews attempting repairs. Of special note was interdiction point Foxtrot on Route 91 north of Tchepone. (About halfway between the Route 911/912 junction and Tchepone, the road designation became Route 91.) Being near the Nam Kok River, Foxtrot was easily located by pilots and subject to river flooding. In late November, this choke-point was struck, causing a 400-meter-wide landslide on the road. One weekly report in late December reported Foxtrot closed all week. However, by the end of the winter campaign, the enemy had a bypass around Foxtrot, though in the wet season the bypass flooded easily.[15]

Notable in this STEEL TIGER campaign were the December accomplishments of the A-26. Though they flew only seven percent of the Air Force strike sorties (175--all at night), they claimed 60 percent of the trucks destroyed or damaged (99 of 163). The December STEEL TIGER statistics were:[16]

	Total Sorties	Trucks Sighted	Trucks Destroyed	Trucks Damaged
A-26	175	148	52	47
A-1E	326	47	19	16
AF Jets	2,045	138	10	19
	2,546	333	81	82

A partial explanation for these accomplishments included the basing of the A-26 at Nakhon Phanom, where the collocated CRICKET FACs provided daily intelligence and where the proximity to the target areas increased loiter times.

Another factor was a tactic called by PACAF "an especially effective and

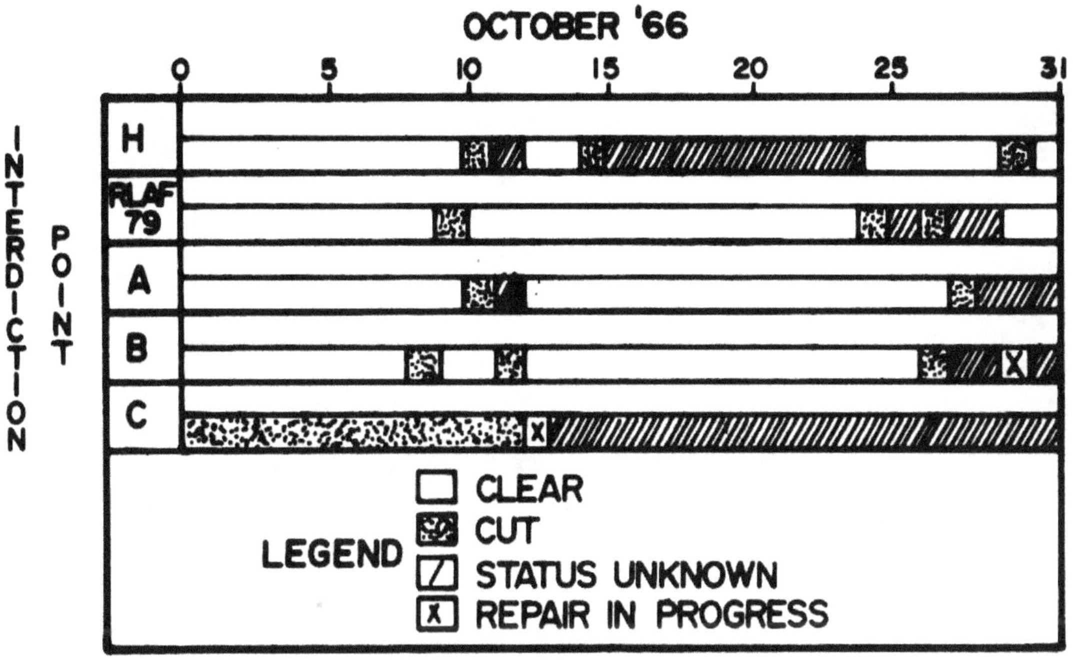

OCTOBER '66
0
5
10
15
20
25
31
INTERDICTION POINT
H
RLAF 79
A
B
C
LEGEND
CLEAR
CUT
STATUS UNKNOWN
REPAIR IN PROGRESS

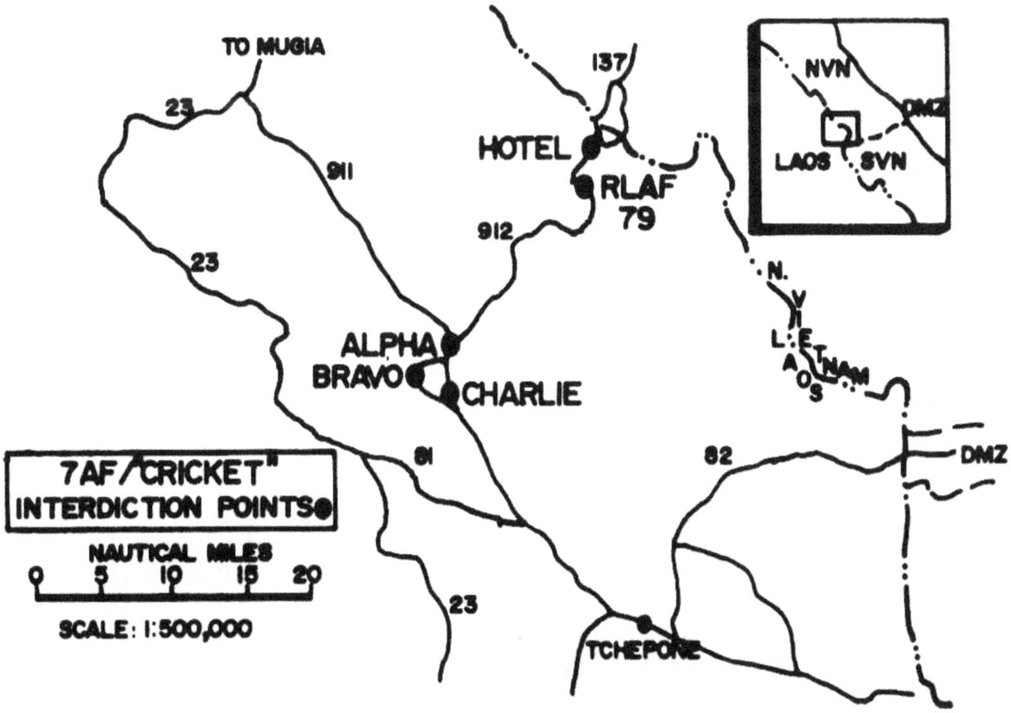

TO MUGIA
23
911
137
HOTEL
RLAF 79
912
NVN
DMZ
LAOS
SVN
N.
V
L
E
T
NAM
A
O
S
ALPHA
BRAVO
CHARLIE
7AF/"CRICKET" INTERDICTION POINTS
91
92
DMZ
NAUTICAL MILES
0 5 10 15 20
SCALE: 1:500,000
23
TCHEPONE

FIG. 16

new harassment technique." It was described as follows: 17/

> "At dusk, one good road cut is made near one of the
> selected interdiction points. 'Foxtrot' is used
> often, as its position between a karst ridge and
> the Nam Kok River requires immediate repair. Follow-
> ing this cut, the A-26 retires from the scene and
> loiters nearby at 8-10,000 feet in low cruise. The
> flareship then drops two USN six-candle-power marker
> flares at an equal distance on both sides of the cut.
> These flares burn for 45 minutes. The flareship now
> departs from the target area and as a rule, dispenses
> standard MK-24 parachute flares as though accompanied
> by attack aircraft. Prior to burnout of the ground
> flares, the A-26 rolls in, blacked out, using the
> flares to establish the attack heading and aiming
> point. Backed up trucks and road repair crews have
> been repeatedly surprised by this tactic. The 120-lb.
> frag cluster and CBU-14 appear to be the most suitable
> ordnance for this work; however, the necessity to carry
> 2 x 1,000-lb. GPs for road cuts plus a LAU-32 for FAC
> marking rounds results in less optimum ordnance. When
> trucks are discovered, the .50 cal. guns have proved
> to be the best weapon."

From 1 September through 29 December 1966 in STEEL TIGER, 24.3 percent of the truck sightings resulted in trucks destroyed or damaged (139 destroyed and 110 damaged; 1,024 sightings). Figure 17 shows how many trucks were sighted and destroyed in STEEL TIGER in December 1966 and January 1967. The PACAF Summary of Air Operations for January 1967 contained the following comment:

> "Results in the STEEL TIGER area have been less than
> desired, but continued harassment of the LOCs is a
> result of a high level of air presence. However,
> this has not permitted the damage normally expected,
> due to saturation of FACs, low fuel after diversions,
> fewer validated targets, limited interdiction points,
> and weather."

SLAMs

Many airstrikes in TIGER HOUND were part of coordinated efforts against

enemy base areas. In mid-1966 in response to the NVA invasion of the DMZ
the 7AF Commander proposed a coordinated Air Force/Navy/Marine saturation of
the DMZ with tac air, artillery, and naval gun fire. Though his concept, which
he called GRAND SLAM,[21] was not then implemented, it became the inspiration
for SLAM operations in Laos.[22]

Eventually "SLAM" came to mean Search-Locate-Annihilate-Monitor. This
acronym conveyed the interrelationship between intelligence and strike forces
that lay at the heart of the operation. In theory, the SLAM concept in Laos
had four steps:[23]

- . ARC LIGHT strikes.
- . Tac air strikes for 3-5 days.
- . PRAIRIE FIRE ground teams.
- . Psywar leaflet drops.

All available intelligence sources such as FACs and long-range reconnaissance
patrols (LRRPs) made special efforts to generate lucrative targets, especially
in known enemy storage areas.

The first two SLAMs were small and lasted only a few days. Both were in
the Route 92 area just west of the DMZ. As with the later and larger SLAMs,
allied troops were infiltrated into the area to generate targets and later to
conduct BDAs. In SLAM II, a Hornet Force platoon saw 85 enemy troops and
active bunker networks, but found no enemy casualties after heavy bomb coverage
from ARC LIGHT.[24]

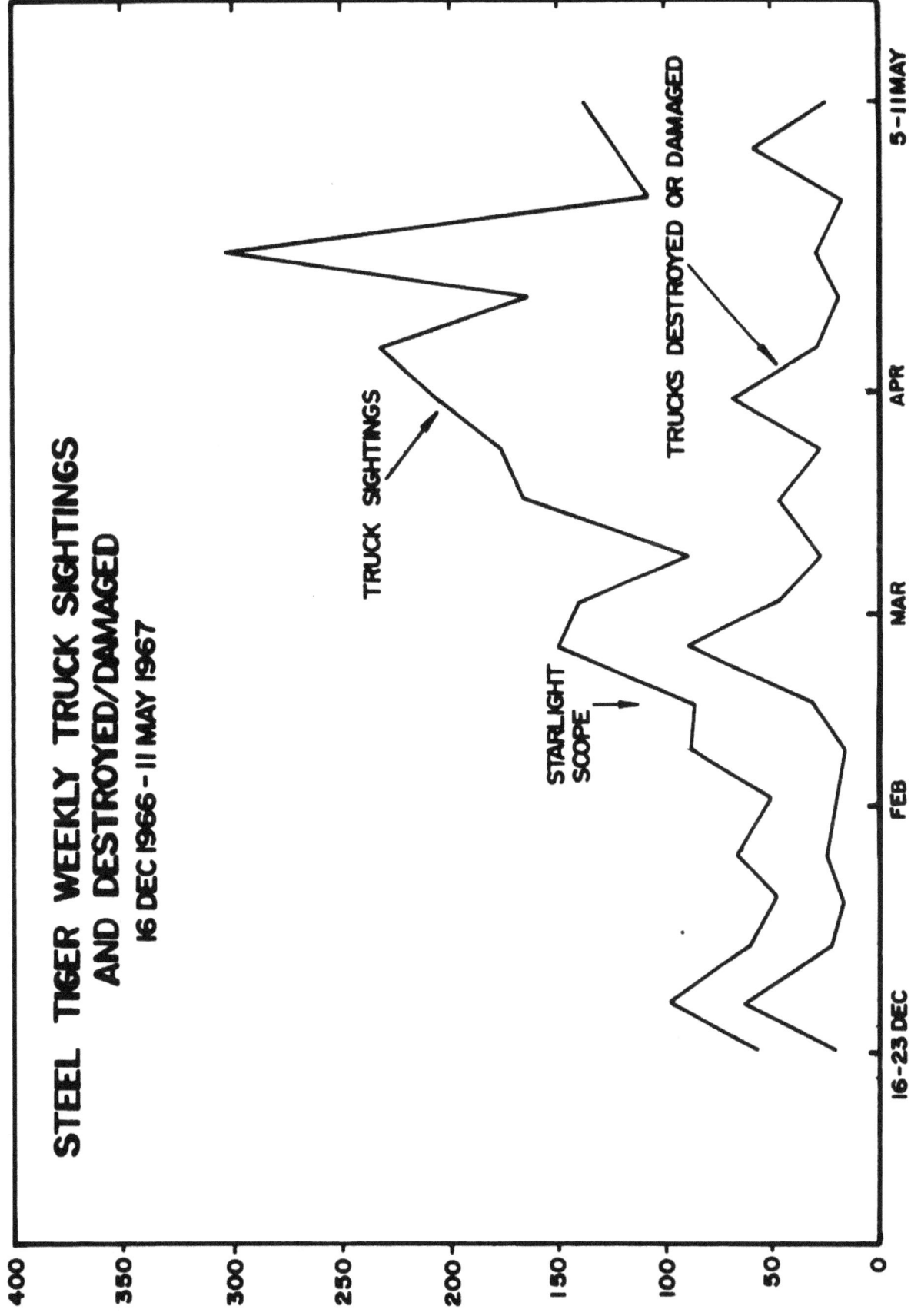

STEEL TIGER WEEKLY TRUCK SIGHTINGS
AND DESTROYED/DAMAGED
16 DEC 1966 – 11 MAY 1967

FIG.17

SLAM III was a classic example of such an operation. Lasting from 30 January to 13 March 1967, SLAM III coordinated an air campaign against enemy Base Area 609 in the Tri-Border area west of Dak To. Since BA 609 lay over the border in Laos, it was an enemy sanctuary that necessitated unconventional warfare tactics on the part of the United States. During February, eleven Shining Brass Teams (ST) and Hornet Force (HF) teams infiltrated the SLAM III area. For instance, ST Maine infiltrated on 2 February to establish a trail watch which soon spotted 85 uniformed enemy armed with AK-47s and 60-mm mortars. The team directed five tac air strikes on the enemy and reported 15 secondary explosions[25/].

On 5 February, HF Echo infiltrated the SLAM III area and two days later made contact with an estimated two companies. The HF established a hilltop perimeter defense that withstood a three-sided attack. Airstrikes put napalm within ten meters of the perimeter. Under this air cover, the HF team was evacuated with total casualties of three dead (one U.S. and two Vietnamese) and ten wounded (one U.S. and nine Vietnamese). Enemy casualties were unknown[26/].

Illustrative of the teamwork of air and ground forces in an interdiction role was the work of two HF teams. On 18 February, HF Juliet and HF Kilo entered the vicinity of SLAM III to destroy enemy supplies discovered the previous day by a FAC. The teams found an estimated 250,000 kilos of rice, 7,000 pounds of rock salt, 1,500 rounds of 82-mm mortars, and other supplies in such large quantities that they were unable to destroy all of them. After their exfiltration, tac air was put in to destroy the remaining caches[27/].

So successful was SLAM III that COMUSMACV proposed to expand the SLAM concept using a South Vietnamese Airborne or Ranger battalion with American advisers in an operation in TIGER HOUND to be termed SOUTHPAW in Phase I and HIGHPORT in Phase II. The latter phase projected using even larger South Vietnamese units for sustained ground operations in Laos beginning about January 1968. The tentative plans were never approved.[28/]

Three more SLAMs followed SLAM III, all concerned with the road into and out of the A Shau Valley. SLAM IV (9 April - 5 June) on Route 922 in BA 611 received 32 ARC LIGHT and 499 tac air sorties, causing 138 secondary explosions, 34 secondary fires, and 40 confirmed enemy KBA. SLAM V (17 June - 16 August) farther west on Route 922, had two secondary explosions, three secondary fires, and five KBA. SLAM VI, the last of the series, centered on BA 607, south of the A Shau Valley.[29/]

ARC LIGHT

Use of ARC LIGHT in SLAM operations was just one application of the B-52 in Laos. From the first ARC LIGHT strikes in Laos in December 1965 (just over the border near Kham Duc) to early 1967, the B-52s were used against enemy troops and supply concentrations. The Rules of Engagement required a nearby cover strike in North Vietnam, the DMZ, or South Vietnam for each strike in Laos. This early deception to mask B-52 strikes in Laos was later ended.

Also limiting the flexibility of scheduling ARC LIGHT missions was the guidance against using B-52s in Laos during daylight and against Thailand-based B-52s striking in Laos. Coordination requirements lessened responsiveness to tactical situations. In a message on 2 March 1967, the Secretary of Defense reviewed the basic guidance concerning which strikes in Laos the JCS were authorized to approve:<u>30/</u>

1. Strikes against targets wholly or partly in SVN (including that portion of the DMZ south of the demarcation line) require prior concurrence of GVN and Embassy Saigon.

2. Strikes against targets wholly or partly in Laos required prior concurrence by positive message response to strike nominations of Embassy Vientiane.

3. Targets are a minimum distance of one kilometer from the nearest noncombatants and do not contain monuments, temples, and other landmarks, the destruction of which cause serious political problems.

A 24-hour waiting period was required after the JCS nominated strikes to allow review of the targets by "appropriate Washington authority." However, the JCS could waive the 24-hour provision, if COMUSMACV designated the target as fleeting or an immediate threat to Allied Forces. In summary, B-52s going into Laos flew from Guam to strike only during the night hours in conjunction with cover strikes in North or South Vietnam. Depending upon the target location, approval was required of COMUSMACV, the U.S. Embassy in Vientiane, the U.S. Embassy in Saigon, and the JCS, and was subject to possible review within 24 hours by appropriate Washington authority.<u>31/</u>

Gen. William Westmoreland, COMUSMACV, personally pressed for more flexible scheduling of ARC LIGHT in Laos, and for revisions in clearance procedures corresponding more closely to tactical airstrikes authorizations. Further, he favored more attention to transitory targets and less to static targets.<u>32/</u>

In response to his wish to incorporate B-52 operations more closely into LOC interdiction in STEEL TIGER, 7AF developed OpOrd 479-56. Six choke points were chosen: three north of Tchepone on Route 9 (one of which was inter- diction point Foxtrot), one each on Routes 912 and 911 to the north, and one far to the south on Route 92. During the six-day operation (3-9 March) two of the points were to be struck three times each night by pairs of B-52s at four-hour intervals beginning at dusk. Between the TOTs of these 12 sorties would be fragged F-4s, under C-123 flareship control, seeding the points with CBU-2s (low-level delivery anti-material bomblets) or general purpose bombs. [33/]

To evaluate the concept of B-52/tac air strikes on interdiction points, extensive use was made of visual and photo reconnaissance and of the Army OV-1 SLAR. The collected data, along with other intelligence, were plotted on maps and time graphs to provide chronological breakouts of the impact of the program on enemy traffic patterns. The following conclusions are quoted from a Directorate of Intelligence, 7AF, report: [34/]

. Overall results were good. Strikes were flown as planned where results and latest intelligence directed a shift of effort, or weather caused cancellation of TAC AIR.

. TAC AIR follow-up at night and pressure during the day enhanced mission success by helping to close the gap between B-52 strikes and taking advantage of fleeting targets. Adverse weather unfortunately limited TAC AIR sorties to some extent.

. The significant shifts in traffic pattern as shown by SLAR and truck sightings indicate probably disruption of the enemy's infiltration plans.

. Instances of enemy truck movement during daylight hours on the 6th were possibly indicative of the success of the con- centrated night efforts.

. The enemy's utilization of Route 23 as a bypass to 911 as shown by traffic patterns during the period points to the need for validation of additional targets along that route.

. In summary, a seven-day evaluation period, although
extremely short for target/operation analysis, gave
excellent promise by showing vehicle movement at a
minimum through B-52/TAC AIR strikes against a relatively small interdiction grid.

COMUSMACV reported to CINCPAC that the intensive B-52/tac air concentration on

a "relatively small interdiction grid" warrented more such operations. [35]

However, as is always the case when applying limited resources, emphasis

on one accomplishment is at the expense of another. Thus, in the March

campaign, mainly against the roads, there were secondaries on only 13 percent

of the 90 ARC LIGHT sorties. Later, from 1 June to 31 August, 61 strikes

against truck parks and storage areas achieved secondaries in 72 percent of the

sorties. [36]

1966/1967 Dry Season Surge

During the early months of 1967, enemy traffic and AAA made their seasonal

increases. By the end of January, the CRICKET FACs were flying above 6,000

feet on most of Route 911 due to AAA. As of January 1967, PACAF considered

the interdiction results less than expected. [37]

> *"Results in the STEEL TIGER area have been less than
> desired, but continued harassment of the LOCs is a
> result of a high level of air presence. However,
> this has not permitted the damage normally expected,
> due to saturation of FACs, low fuel after diversions,
> fewer validated targets, limited interdiction points,
> and weather."*

In March 1967, a special task force opened at Nakhon Phanom to increase on-the-

spot supervision of the program in STEEL TIGER.

69

Just which tactics should be followed to counter the enemy traffic increases was open to differing viewpoints. The two suggestions from units at Nakhon Phanom were an example of this concerning Routes 23 and 911, the parallel routes south from the Mu Gia Pass. One favored forcing the trucks to Routes 911, where they would be easier to spot.[38/] The other proposed to close Route 911 at its junctions with Route 239, thereby forcing the traffic onto Route 23.[39/]

Despite the publicity given truck kills as a measure of success, attacks on moving vehicles were rather a small percentage of the total STEEL TIGER strike sorties.[40/] A truck killing operation called COMMANDO BASES did operate in the Mu Gia Pass and once destroyed or damaged 94 trucks in a single night, an extraordinary event.[41/] Aside from FACs, road watch teams also supplied truck sightings which were reported on a near real-time basis as Peacock Reports to Air Force personnel for action. The following summary of actions are quoted directly from daily resumes of Peacock reports for 16-20 April 1967 for the Armed Reconnaissance area Delta in the Mu Gia to Tchepone area:[42/]

> 15 Apr - At 1810Z, CAS reported 8 trucks moving from T-22 toward T-59 at 1800Z. Wx: partly cloudy. Passed to CRICKET III [STEEL TIGER Task Force] at 1817Z. Action: Alleycat [ABCCC] passed to Nimrod 36 [FAC]. Negative results.
>
> 16 Apr - At 1212Z, CAS reported 9 trucks moving from T-47 to T-28 at 1153Z. Wx: overcast. Passed to CRICKET III at 1216Z. Action: Not reported by Alleycat 01 OpRep-4.
>
> 17 Apr - No significant sighting.
>
> 18 Apr - At 1210Z, CAS reported an unknown number of trucks parked 2 NM south of T-28 at 1153Z. Wx: partly cloudy. Passed to CRICKET III at 1214Z. Action: none. Alleycat reported no resources available.

19 Apr - At 1205, CAS reported 8 trucks moving from T-25 to
T-53 at 1150Z. Wx: not reported. Passed to
CRICKET at 1209Z. Action: none. Nonpermissive
area.

The Peacock report of 1 May in the southernmost part of STEEL TIGER--GOLF--
illustrates the complexities of truck killing operations: 43/

1 May - At 1300Z, CAS reported 62 trucks moving from T-47
to T-28 at 1250Z. Wx: Clear. Passed to CRICKET
III at 1304Z. Action: at 1310Z Nathan Flight of
one RF-4C discovered a line of headlights 3 miles
long moving north after one photo recon flight
(Apache) was unable to acquire targets. Alleycat
sent Opal, Coyote 62, Hurricane and Leotard Flights
into the area. Leotard Flight (2 Ubon F-4Cs) reported
2 trucks destroyed from strikes. Other flights into
the area reported a lack of flares, RTB [return to
base] with remaining ordnance after running out of
flares, or reported no visible results.

Figure 18 shows strike and armed recon sorties distribution in STEEL TIGER
for March and April as compared to truck sightings. 44/

In March and April 1967, the sightings of trucks greatly increased, both
because of the spring truck surge and the introduction on 14 February of the
Starlight Scope, a hand-held, light-gathering aid for night vision. The
results were spectacular. For instance, from 1-12 March in STEEL TIGER nearly
half the truck sightings were made with the scope. The actual percentage
breakout of all sightings was: Starlight Scope, 47.5 percent; road watch teams,
45 percent, and pilot (naked eye) sightings, 7.5 percent. There was a ratio
of six scope sightings for every pilot sighting, though one of every ten trucks
seen with the scope had its lights on and might have been seen without the
scope. 45/

The 56th Air Commando Wing at Nakhon Phanom was enthusiastic enough later

71

to compare three-day periods of 30 November-2 December for 1966 and 1967:[46]

	Trucks Sighted (3 Days)	
	1966	1967
Visually	20	30
Starlight Scope	--	597
Trucks Destroyed	8	83

Seventh Air Force OPlan 483-67 (9 March 1967) noted "the enemy has attained a high degree of success" in his Laotian supply network; road cuts were being repaired more rapidly; AAA had increased "at an exponential rate"; and the permissiveness of low-level air operations was "questionable on all of the major LOCs."[47] By March, the increasing truck traffic without a corresponding rise in trucks D/D (Fig. 17) caused 7AF to take two significant steps: initiation of an intensified effort in STEEL TIGER North until the rainy season began, and creation of STEEL TIGER Task Force (SLTF).

In the search for more effective tactics, some personnel in 7AF favored the intensive choke point concept. In February, the 7AF Directorate of Operations Analysis published "Some Thoughts on Road Interdiction Strategy," which advocated a "closed road system" reminiscent of GATE GUARD. It showed that in the last four months of 1966, the number of trucks destroyed and damaged was not good. In RP I, 29.7 percent of the truck sightings were D/D, while in STEEL TIGER, the D/D ran 24.3 percent.[48] This study also noted that the then current method of road interdiction "reacted to the observed actions of the enemy." This in turn "contributed to a dilution of our attempts to cover the many targets generated and has suppressed our utilization of offensive initiative."

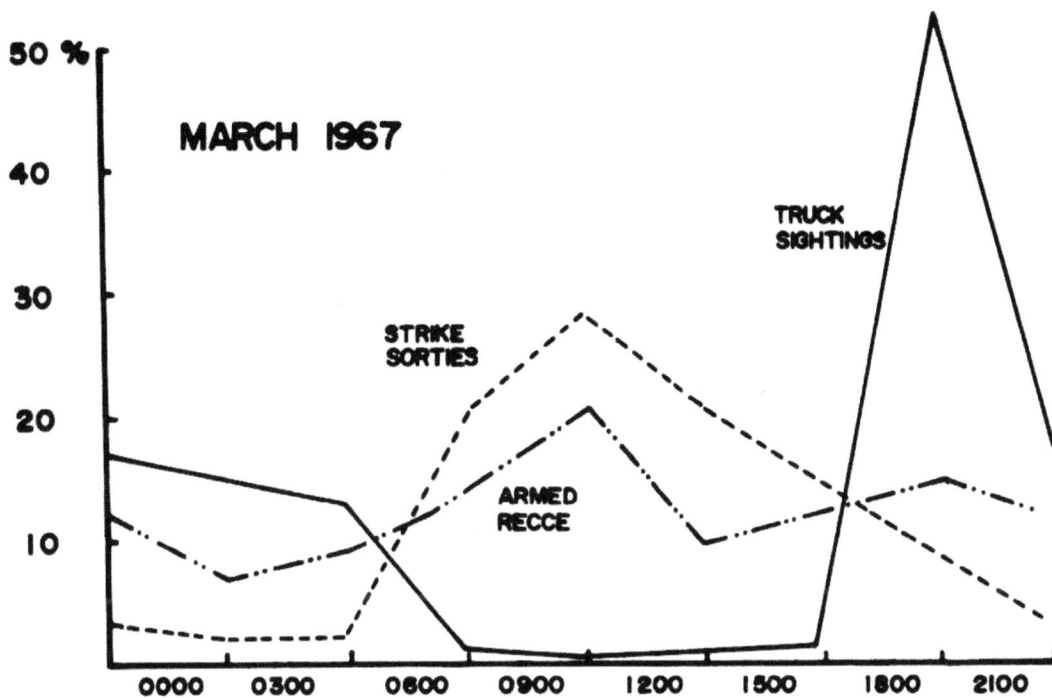

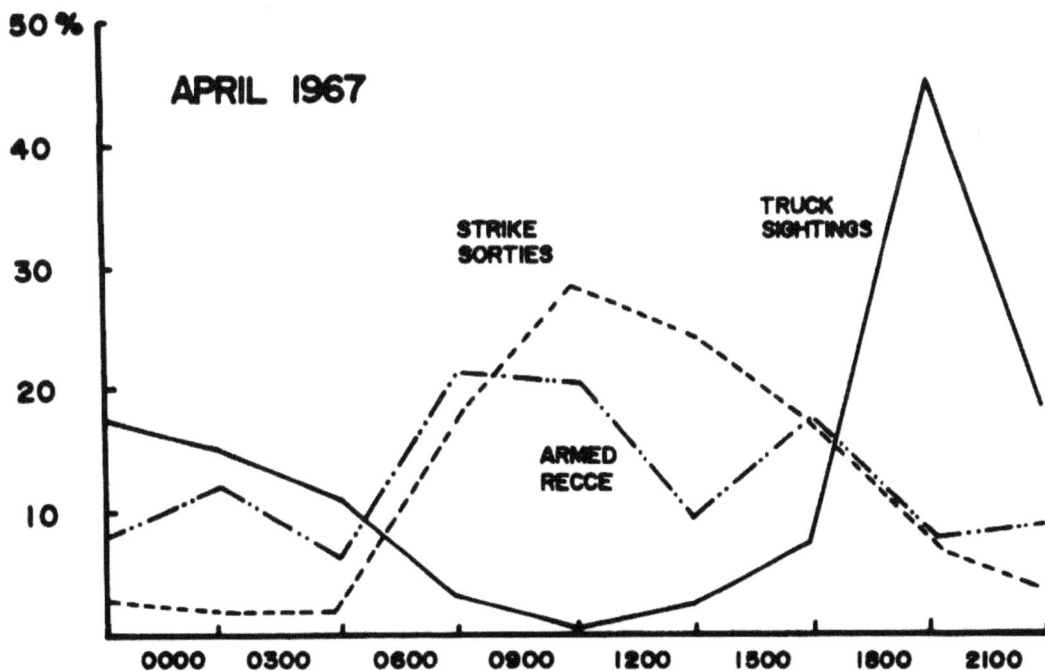

SORTIE TOT vs ROADWATCH TRUCK
MOVEMENT TIME in SOUTH LAOS

FIG. 18

The study proposed 16 hypothetical choke points in the Laotian and North Vietnamese panhandles, each to be cut and kept closed by four sorties every eight hours. The potential of this proposal appeared to have been overstated:[49/]

> "The LOCs in a geographical area are permanently inter-
> dicted to prevent ingress-egress of truck traffic within
> the area. This will enable a systematic effort to destroy
> almost all trucks 'trapped' within this geographical area
> and force the enemy to utilize, solely the slower and more
> costly (manpower) manual movement of supplies."

In outlining this proposal, it was also suggested the upcoming HUB operations be watched closely.

OPlan 483-67 outlined the concept of a "hub"--a major LOC junction where two or more road/river routes intersected. Closing a hub would cause trucks and supplies to pile up into lucrative targets. This refinement of the choke point concept proposed to keep the hub closed "by presence as well as ordnance," which meant it would rely on a 24-hour surveillance to prevent enemy road crews from opening the hub.[50/] Interestingly enough, the term "hub" gained enough currency to be routinely included in the 1968 ROLLING THUNDER Operation Order as any major junction of road/river routes.[51/]

From 13-21 March, HUB, also called Operation STOPWATCH, employed this concept at the junction of Routes 911 and 912, the roads, respectively, from the Mu Gia and Ban Karai Passes. By maintaining 24-hour surveillance with O-1 FACs in the daytime and BLINDBAT C-130s at night, 7AF would know when the HUB needed more strikes to keep it closed. The HUB remained open most nights. The following comment from the STEEL TIGER Task Force at Nakhon Phanom to 7AF captures some of the disappointment:^{52/}

> *"Understand there is some lack of confidence in HUB plan. We are not fully satisfied here, but also are not yet ready to say it is not working....SLTF is beginning to take a hold and possibly can tighten up on HUB execution by ABCCC. We have worked with ALLEY CAT and have him on track but CRICKET seems to need some assistance. Another weak area is in having strike acft available to strike sighted trucks most of the time."*

Figure 19 summarizes the hourly status of the operation and shows that only on the first night was the HUB closed.^{53/} A FAC who worked the HUB made two significant comments. First, the presence at night in the form of a C-130 flareship could not prevent repairs at night, though putting side-firing guns on the C-130 probably would have done the trick. Second, ground fire soon became severe in the area and a T-28 was eventually shot down by 37-mm fire. The FAC thought the failure to move the operation away from the AAA concentration was due to a lack of flexibility among the "people who do the planning and targeting."^{54/}

This last criticism implied 7AF could not keep completely abreast of the situation in STEEL TIGER from its headquarters in South Vietnam and that 7AF schedulers did not have an intimate "feel" for local conditions. Being at a distance did put 7AF at a disadvantage, sometimes causing the field units to begin messages with "people there at 7AF must realize...."^{55/} This was an old problem in control and for this reason, the ABCCCs orbited over Laos to provide a battlefield extension of the 7AF command post.

To further exploit the advantages of being in the immediate area of

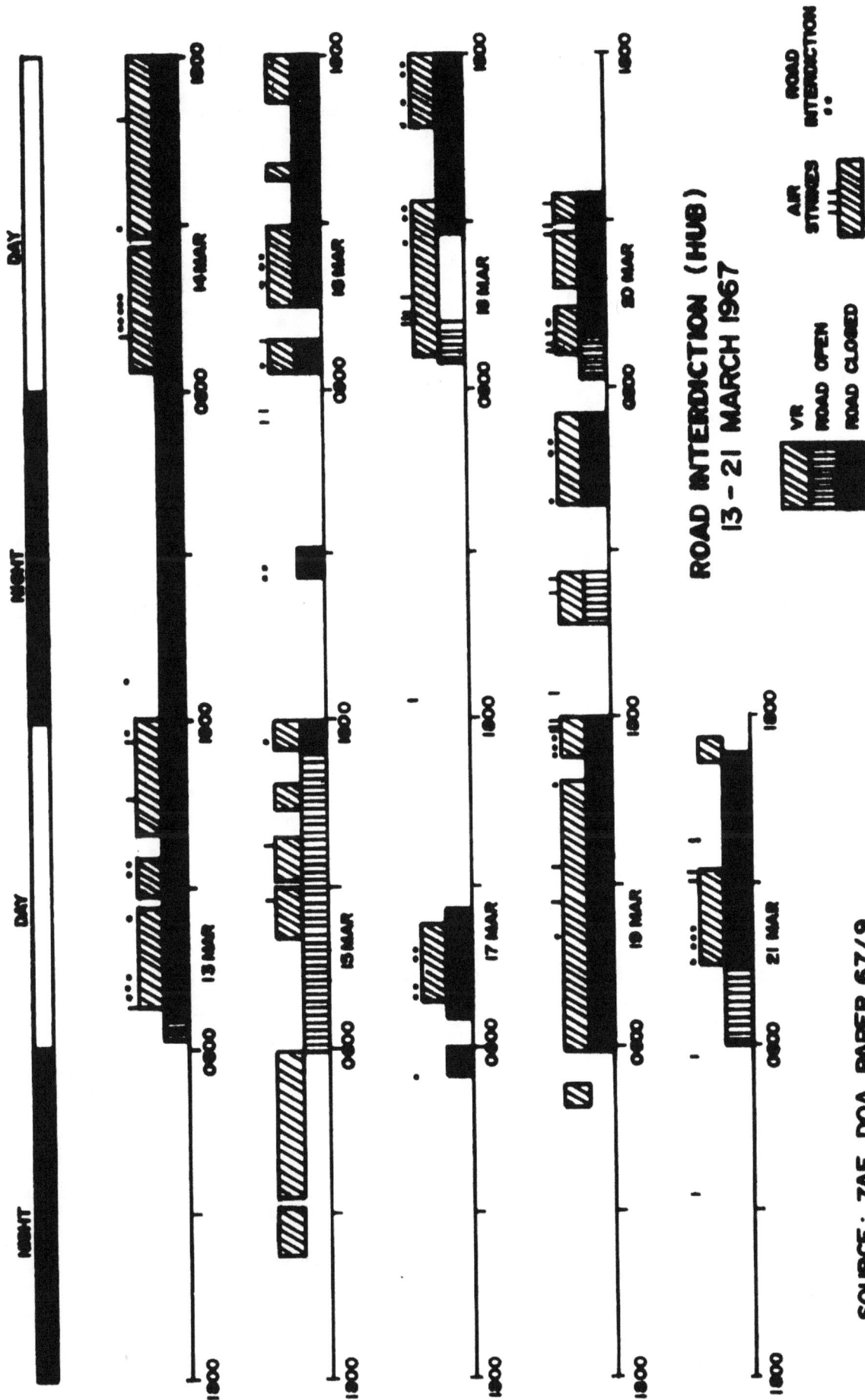

ROAD INTERDICTION (HUB)
13 – 21 MARCH 1967

SOURCE : 7AF DOA PAPER 67/9

FIG. 19

operation, 7AF created STEEL TIGER Task Force and stationed it at Nakhon Phanom across the Mekong from Laos. As planned, SLTF evolved into Task Force Alpha, which controlled the electronic sensor program in Laos, but initially it participated in the intensified interdiction campaign ordered by 7AF to run until the rainy season.

Just what authority SLTF had was controversial since its charter directed it to "effect control and supervision in conjunction with 7AF CP (DOCO) of all forces used in an offensive role in STEEL TIGER NORTH..."[56] The underlined portion was not in the 17 March 1967 original order, but was added on 10 May to clarify the relationship between SLTF and 7AF.[57] The nebulous position of SLTF can best be conveyed by quoting the original OpOrd 485-67 with the 10 May amendments underlined. Part (3)(d) was replaced by the expanded version indicated.

Commander, STEEL TIGER Force, will:

(1) Establish and maintain a facility adequate for mission accomplishment. Initially the STEEL TIGER Task Force will share the existing TUOC at Nakhon Phanom.

    (a) The STEEL TIGER Task Force Commander will exercise operational control of the out-country (Laos) TUOC functions.

(2) Monitor all frag orders and instruction issued by Headquarters 7AF and take necessary action to insure compliance.

(3) Provide an on-the-spot evaluation and render decisions necessary to achieve maximum utilization of offensive forces available.

    (a) Divert, cancel, and request accelerated sorties from resources based at Nakhon Phanom RTAFB, Thailand, keeping 7AF CP (DOCO) advised.

    (b) Request for additional strike or support forces not located at Nakhon Phanom will be through 7AF CP (DOCO).

(d) Diversion of strike aircraft to fleeting, perishable targets will be through ABCCC with concurrent notification to Seventh Air Force CP. (The 10 May amendment substituted the following: Diversion of strike aircraft other than those based at NKP or executed into SLTF area, will be through coordination with 7AF CP (DOCO) prior to request of ABCCC. Day and Night ABCCCs will be responsive to SLTF divert request strikes of fleeting lucrative targets, consistent with available resources and other immediate operational requirements. Where conflict is evident in use of forces, 7AF CP (DOCO) will resolve and direct accordingly.)

(4) Effect liaison and coordination with and between units under operational control of Commander, Seventh Air Force, as necessary.

(5) Correlate results/activities of day and night sorties and make recommendations to Headquarters, Seventh Air Force (DOC).

(6) Implement and control program/procedures as directed by the Commander, Seventh Air Force.

(7) Keep the Commander, Seventh Air Force, informed with timely reporting through DOC.

Since 7AF wrote the frag and supervised changes and additions, SLTF was essentially an intelligence collection and evaluation center having certain discretionary authority to commit forces after advising 7AF. One of its important functions was to receive the road watch Peacock reports and relay them, if timely, to the appropriate ABCCC.

STEEL TIGER Task Force became operational on 21 March at Nakhon Phanom with personnel TDY from 7AF and on loan from the 56th Air Commando Wing at that base. [58/] By early May, the Commander, 7AF/13AF, recommended SLTF be terminated due to the decline in truck traffic in the rainy season and because 7AF/13AF wanted its TDY intelligence personnel back. [59/] However, SLTF continued in token form through the summer and fall of 1967 until Task Force Alpha was formed.

Through April and May, 7AF waged a mixed campaign against trucks, truck parks, interdiction points, and storage areas. The best results came on 8 May, when U.S. aircraft got 112 secondary explosions and many secondary fires from an attack on a suspected ammunition dump near Route 922 heading for the A Shau Valley.[60] In May, the total Air Force strike sorties in STEEL TIGER dropped below 3,000, for the first time in four months, thus heralding the end of the 1966/1967 dry season campaign.[61] At the same time, the enemy hurried to get as much tonnage down the Trail as possible before the road became too muddy. Pilots reported seeing long convoys driving with their lights on even under attack.[62]

Meanwhile, along Route 110 near the Cambodian Border, several SHOCK operations were flown. These SHOCKs were conceived by the American Embassy in Vientiane to use tac air rather than B-52s to destroy supply sortage areas. These short operations (SHOCK I ran from 27-30 April and SHOCK II from 20-28 May) combined flareships, road watch teams, tac air, FACs, and Royal Laotian T-28s. In SHOCK II on Route 110, the RLAF T-28s flew 57 of the 204 attack sorties.[63]

1967 Wet Season

During the wet months from late May through October 1967, the enemy truck traffic dropped to very low levels, as did 7AF strike sorties. Enemy AAA moved back to RP I. By mid-May, pilots reported only sporadic firing along Routes 911/912 which only a month ago had been mostly nonpermissive.[64] With good weather in North Vietnam, 7AF concentrated on the expanding ROLLING THUNDER program and the railroad interdiction campaign. The June through September strike sortie totals for STEEL TIGER were 1,009, 919, 807, 1,262, respectively.

77

In four weeks of July, 350 of the 686 trucks sighted in STEEL TIGER were on Route 110 and this predominence continued until mid-October, with the only competition being from Route 922, another route that entered South Vietnam. From 3 July to 15 October, 43 percent of the 2,680 trucks sighted were on Route 110.[65] Besides being an all-weather road, Route 110 was paralleled in the Cambodian/Laotian Border area by the Tonle Kong/Se Kong River, which sampans found navigable in the wet months. The enemy used this river extensively to move men and supplies from Cambodia into southeastern Laos.[66] (Toward the end of the 1966/1967 dry season, large numbers of POL barrels were seen floating down the Se Kong between Ban Bac--about 90 miles north of the Cambodian Border--and Route 964.)[67] According to an NVA lieutenant who defected in April 1967, approximagely 1,200 tons of supplies a month--rice, medicine, sugar, POL--moved north from Cambodia at night. His unit, Military Post 5, responsible for the Sihanouk Trail, had about 60 motorized boats and 40 trucks (hampered by fuel shortages) and approximately 2,000 bicycles for wet season movement along Route 110.[68]

On 5 September, road watch teams reported 100 dead and wounded in an air attack on a truck park/troop bivouac near Route 110 and further, 60 dead and 30 wounded the next day by an attack on a troop concentration.[69]

1967/1968 Dry Season: Killing Trucks

Though interdiction strategy had always been much debated within 7AF and tested with varied tactics in numerous combinations, strong proponents emerged in 1968 on each side of the question: truck kills or choke points? During most of the 1967/1968 Laotian dry season, destroying trucks was preferred. Then toward April, the choke point as a tactic made a comeback in a preview of the choke point campaign in RP I. Of course, it was never an either-or-proposition but a matter of emphasis, and airstrikes continued to attack the total target system from moving trucks to storage areas, from truck parks to choke points.

In late October, heavy truck traffic began. In the five weeks from 9 October to 12 November, truck sightings on Route 911, the most heavily traveled road, increased from 13 in the first week to 547 in the fifth. Total weekly STEEL TIGER sightings according to one count recorded the following rise: 114, 190, 645, 938, and 1,104. In the last week of 1967, the total for STEEL TIGER reached 1,776, over ten times the rate of traffic in August and September.[70] (Fig. 20.)

This traffic surge, which by hindsight, can be related to the Tet Offensive, spurred truck killing activities. A further incentive was the inauguration of MUSCLE SHOALS (renamed IGLOO WHITE in June 1968), on 1 December, or more specifically, its antivehicle component called MUD RIVER. (See CHECO report, "IGLOO WHITE".) Seismic and acoustic sensors airdropped along enemy LOCs in the MUD RIVER area of STEEL TIGER NORTH detected truck traffic and forwarded the information to the airborne EC-121s for relay to the Infiltration Surveillance Center (ISC) at Task Force Alpha (TFA), which replaced STEEL TIGER Task Force at Nakhon Phanom. As conceived by its developers, TFA would digest real-time data and direct airstrikes on the trucks thus pinpointed. In line with this, a module of three sensor strings would successively detect, provide convoy time-distance, and monitor strike results.[71]

However, 7AF saw TFA not as a control agency, but as an intelligence center, and several operational limitations made it so. The difficulty of accurate sensor drops made it practical to work with single strings rather than three-string modules. Radio communications between TFA and MUD RIVER made an ABCCC desirable. Most importantly, there were usually more trucks found by the conventional FAC/road watch resources than could be handled or attacked. Rarely could FACs be spared to search for sensor-located targets passed by TFA to the ABCCC in the form of Spotlight Reports and such searches were not always rewarding. In January 1968, only 6 percent of more than 2,000 Spotlight Reports were investigated and confirmed. This situation reinforced 7AF's tendency to use MUSCLE SHOALS for intelligence analysis rather than moving target generation.[72/]

The traffic surge of late 1967--more trucks to attack--and the high level interest in the MUSCLE SHOALS system put a stress on truck kills. The November and December totals ran far above the previous year. In an End-of-Tour Report dated 28 November, the DI, 7AF, noted the repair of LOCs at a level "not previously attempted" and postulated that this confirmed "the desperate need" to supply troops in the battle of Dak To and elsewhere. The DI noted from 1 October to 21 November, 520 trucks were D/D and 2,859 secondaries were caused by airstrikes in STEEL TIGER, which was four times those of the previous corresponding period.[73/] Similarly, a message from the American Ambassador to Vientiane, Laos, to 7AF on 3 January 1968, expressed "great satisfaction with continuing high of truck kills" on the Ho Chi Minh Trail in December. The Ambassador thought "losses of this magnitude should significantly impair effectiveness" of the enemy LOCs.[74/]

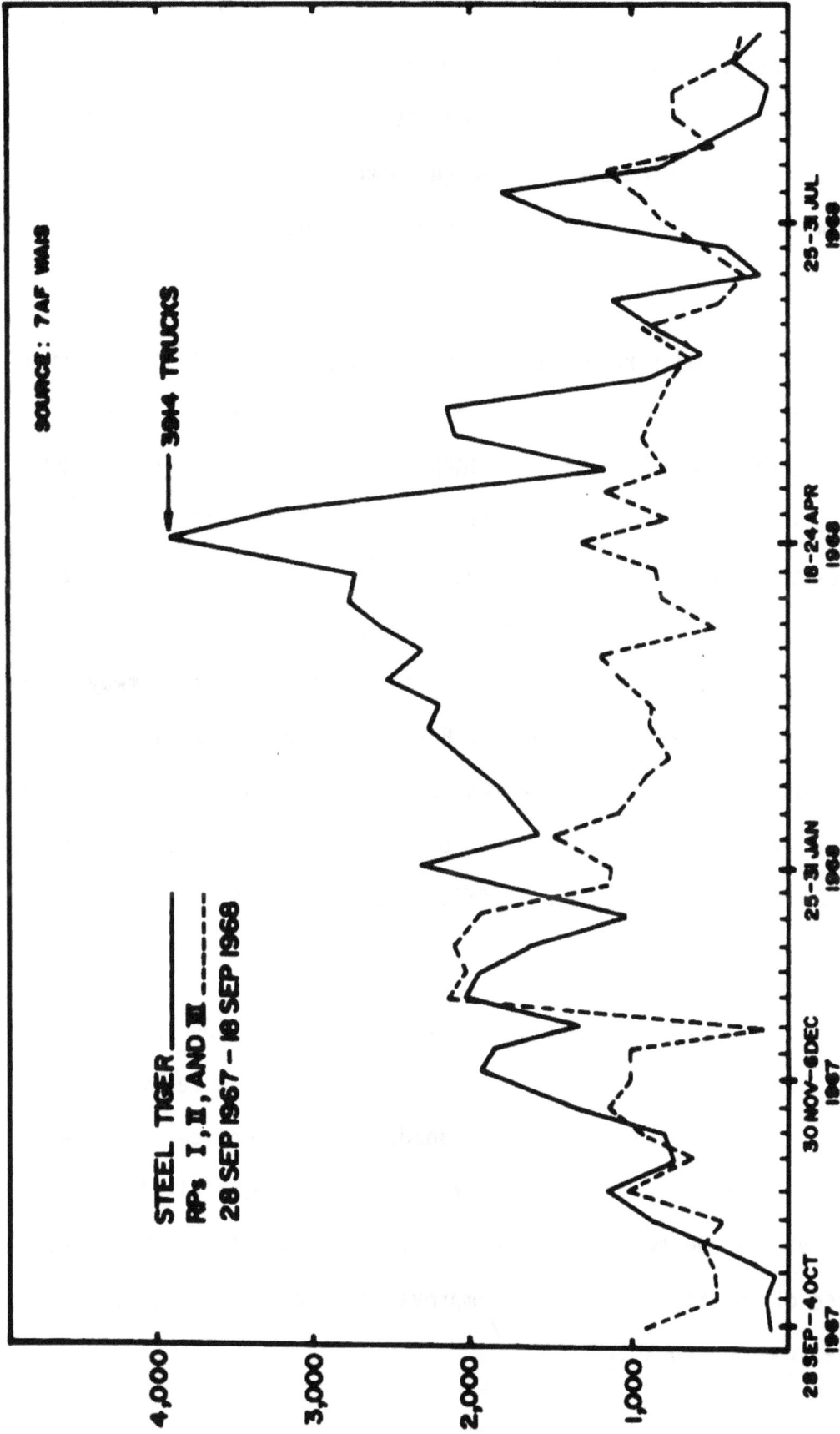

SOURCE : 7 AF WIS

STEEL TIGER _____
RPs I, II, AND III ....
28 SEP 1967 – 18 SEP 1968

3914 TRUCKS

4,000

3,000

2,000

1,000

28 SEP – 4 OCT
1967

30 NOV – 6 DEC
1967

25 – 31 JAN
1968

18 – 24 APR
1968

25 – 31 JUL
1968

WEEKLY TRUCK SIGHTINGS IN THE PANHANDLES
OF LAOS AND N. VIETNAM

FIG. 20

In target emphasis and weight of command interest, 7AF ran a truck kill-ing campaign in STEEL TIGER from December 1967 to May 1968, though in April several developments caused a shift toward choke points and truck parks. This section examines the dry season campaign as a whole, while the next section discusses several innovations of April.

From December 1967 through April 1968, a total of 42,621 trucks were sighted by all sources in STEEL TIGER, according to the 7AF Truck File. Of these, 78 percent were seen in STEEL TIGER NORTH and 22 percent in TIGER HOUND. Further, about 80 percent of the traffic in STEEL TIGER NORTH passed down the so-called Eastern Corridor, the road system from the Mu Gia Pass along Routes 23A/911/91 to the Tchepone area where it merged again with the Western Corridor. Route 912 from the Ban Karai Pass fed into this system about halfway down. The Western Corridor--or Route 23--down Routes 23A/23/91 had significant traffic in December, but little in later months despite its reputation for much heavier forest cover and greater security. One of the MUSCLE SHOALS contributions was sensors on Route 23 to verify low traffic levels and thus free FACs for more lucrative areas.[75]

During this five-month period, 7AF records showed 4,554 trucks destroyed and 1,295 heavily damaged in STEEL TIGER compared with the December 1966-April 1967 period of 652 destroyed and 419 damaged. Fully 78 percent of the 1967/1968 trucks destroyed were in Armed Reconnaissance Area Echo. This increase in trucks D/D between the two dry season campaigns--5,849 versus 1,071--was due to expanded use of the Starlight Scope, improved Air Force tactics, and especially the sizable jump in truck traffic.[76]

81

Because 7AF required FAC/MSQ control even in ROE Zones I and II, accomplishing truck kills required scheduling both FACs and strike aircraft in adequate numbers and at appropriate times. The FACs available included C-123s, C-130s, O-2s, and F-100Fs, the latter for day missions only. Because of vulnerability to AAA, the O-1 flew its last STEEL TIGER day flight on 13 December 1967, and its last night mission on 5 January 1968. The number of trucks observed per flying hour for night FACs was as follows: [77]

	Dec 67	Jan 68	Feb 68	Mar 68	Apr 68
C-123 SLN	8.5	7.0	4.3	8.0	9.8
C-130 SLN	1.9	2.4	1.5	1.4	3.2
C-130 TH	1.2	1.3	1.0	1.0	2.0
O-2 SLN	1.2	1.6	2.0	1.4	3.5
O-2 TH	.8	.4	.4	.5	1.1

Achieving better results in STEEL TIGER versus TIGER HOUND was in line with the approximately three times greater truck traffic in the northern area. The C-123 had the advantages of a better platform for the Starlight Scope than the O-2, enough personnel to record all sightings, and flying areas with large truck traffic. The fundamental fact of life in all STEEL TIGER was that FACs had to locate the target whether initially generated by sensors, road watch teams, strike pilots, or the FAC himself.

Nearly all truck sightings in STEEL TIGER came at night. PACAF calculated 98 percent; the sensors indicated 85 percent of the movement between the hours of 1500 and 0700. [78] The A-26, B-57, and T-28 were the primary truck killers. Together, the first two claimed 80 percent of the truck kills (D/D) in STEEL

82

TIGER North and 70 percent in TIGER HOUND, with 27 percent and 23 percent of the total strikes in each area, respectively. The A-26 generally gained more than 50 percent of the total truck kills but the B-57 was more effective. Kills per attack ran 1.78 for the B-57 and 1.20 for the A-26; kills per sortie ran 2.17 and 1.58 respectively. Since the B-57 flew nearly 45 percent of its sorties in TIGER HOUND versus only 8 percent for the A-26, the B-57 achieved more effective kill rates despite the inherent disadvantage of flying less in the truck-rich areas.[79/] These two aircraft had the advantage of using M-35 (670-lb.) and M-36 (900-lb.) incendiary bombs until the supply ran out in April 1968. The FACs and pilots thought the M-35s/36s the best antivehicle bombs. The F-4, because it carried external ordnance, did not use the high drag M-35s/36s.[80/] The B-57 truck kills dropped when the incendiary bombs were replaced by general purpose bombs sometimes supplemented by fire bombs.[81/]

Excluding the A-1E (a special case) and the A-26/B-57/T-28 truck killers, the other aircraft--mostly the F-4s and F-105s--made only 15 percent of their attacks on trucks, the balance being 49 percent on truck parks and storage areas, and 27 percent on roads. To illustrate this division of effort, the following statistics show the percentage of all strike aircraft in STEEL TIGER North from December through April, with the percentage of total strike effort given in parenthesis for each aircraft:[82/]

	A-26 (12.4) B-57 (14.4) T-28 (5.7)	A-1 (10.0)	F-4 (33.1) F-100 (.2) F-105 (24.2)
Trucks Parks/ Storage Areas	33.8%	64.5%	47.7%
Trucks	59.0%	25.7%	13.4%
Roads	6.0%	6.3%	27.6%
Bridges/Fords	1.1%	3.4%	11.3%
Total Attacks	5,170	1,705	12,564

This shows that the truck killers flew 59 percent of their attacks against trucks and 34 percent against truck parks and storage areas in STEEL TIGER North, while the jet fighters put 75 percent of their attacks on truck parks, storage areas, and roads.

Truck traffic, the most obvious measures of continued enemy activity, increased in January (to support Tet and Khe Sanh) and increased again from late February to the traditional peak in April, where one week had 2,760 reported truck sightings. Sensors gave the same general picture, except that no precipitous drop occurred in sensor tracks in May corresponding to the sharp fall in sightings.[83/] The early monsoon overcast restricted the FACs but did not stop the trucks. According to one 7AF estimate, one truck in ten was destroyed by direct attack while traversing STEEL TIGER.[84/] This led the DI, 7AF, to ask the value of killing trucks if 90 percent got through.[85/]

The MUSCLE SHOALS sensor system failed to enhance truck kills. By one estimate, 7AF had sufficient strike aircraft in STEEL TIGER to achieve an "aggregated potential kill" of 30 to 50 trucks a night. However, the nightly sightings ran between 100 and 500 trucks. In short, the FACs found so many trucks that the Spotlight reports proved superfluous in target generation. (From January to March, the 0-2 FACs found 1.13 sightings per one hour of searching. The FAC confirmation rate of Spotlight reports was quite low--18 percent in March of those investigated. The FAC search time over the area averaged 50 minutes. The Spotlights found 1.2 sightings per hour--no better results than the FAC on his own.)[86/]

Analyzing the effectiveness of MUSCLE SHOALS detection of truck parks proved difficult, but was attempted. Of 612 strikes against truck parks, 76 were against truck parks reported by MUSCLE SHOALS within the ten previous days and within 500 yards of the MUSCLE SHOALS coordinates. The 76 strikes had 53 secondaries, while the 612 had 397 secondaries. These were equivalent results.[87/] However, by April, sensors were being dropped into suspected truck parks and this technique worked well.

In the first four months, TFA passed to the ABCCC 99 percent of the Spotlight Reports from the Infiltration Surveillance Center--about 40 per night. In early April, 7AF had TFA begin screening reports and passing the most lucrative as judged by intelligence appraisal and operational considerations--about 39 percent of those passed by the ISC. The FAC confirmation rate of Spotlight Reports rose from 18 percent in March to 40 percent in April. However, the high density of trucks in April precluded crediting MUSCLE SHOALS with this improvement, though it must be acknowledged that, without screening, the ABCCC would have been unbelievably swamped with Spotlights.[88/] MUSCLE SHOALS provided better in-depth analysis of traffic trends and truck park locations than generation of real-time moving targets.

TURNPIKE, POINT GOLF, and Ban Laboy

As March and Operation NIAGARA ended together, the attention of MACV and 7AF turned to countering the traditional April surge in Laos. In MUSCLE SHOALS, the screening of Spotlight Reports began to upgrade the quality of targets found by sensors. Confirmations by FACs did rise to 40 percent from the March level of 18 percent.[89/] Another innovation placed three A-26s on alert at Nakhon Phanom to fly against truck convoys. It became apparent that the A-26 could get as many truck kills in its normal two and one-quarter-hour loiter time as by being sent on alert against confirmed targets. The conclusion was to keep short loiter time aircraft on alert.[90/] In late March, COMUSMACV directed the Acting Commander, 7AF, to intensify attacks against routes in southern TIGER HOUND. The resulting Project ATHENS proposed to interdict the junction of Routes 96 and 110.[91/] However, events overtook ATHENS when the 4th Infantry Division initiated TRUSCOTT WHITE in-country in the Tri-Border area; two major operations also began out-country in STEEL TIGER North.

On Route 911, north of its junction with 912, 7AF made Point Golf a choke point and scheduled a three-week operation which fragged 154 sorties (and dropped 1,042 bombs). The idea was to force traffic to come through the Ban Karai Pass, thus permitting a concentration of tac air. The Infiltration Surveillance Center calculated the following before and after truck counts above Golf, below Golf, and down the "bypass" of 912:[92/]

86

		16 Mar-2 Apr 68		3-20 Apr 68	
		North	South	North	South
North of Golf:	Rt 23A	549	126	800	91
	Rt 911A, B	100	92	473	341
South of Golf:	Rt 911C	241	400	245	261
Bypass of Golf:	Rt 912A, B	332	271	302	762

These and other data were cited as proving that heavy traffic above Point Golf returned north through the Mu Gia Pass and then came down through the Ban Karai Pass. Proponents of choke points took the Point Golf example as proof of the potential of this concept.

In mid-April, COMUSMACV acted on 7AF suggestions and authorized 30 B-52 sorties a day until 1 May against 7AF nominated targets in Laos. Operation TURNPIKE attacked truck parks and storage areas, especially along Routes 911 and 91B. Many park and storage areas were chosen for proximity to main traveled roads, allowing use of the tremendous ARC LIGHT firepower, a bonus in the road interdiction role. Targeting nominations were directed from the ISC to 7AF to MACV. ARC LIGHT could bomb large target areas such as enemy truck parks and storage areas more effectively than tac air. [93/]

According to the 7AF WAIS, TURNPIKE from 19 April to 10 June put 626 ARC LIGHT sorties on 107 target boxes with 13,772 tons of bombs. The BDA included 154 road cuts, 308 secondary explosions, and 117 secondary fires. A comparison of traffic before and after specific strikes often showed a noticeable decrease in traffic, though sometimes the traffic remained as high after as before strikes. A variation of this effect occurred in late May, when in-country operations drained away the B-52s and no ARC LIGHT appeared on some of the routes in MUD RIVER. Traffic rose above the record high of mid-April.[94]

One special problem in TURNPIKE was the lengthy validation times. According to 7AF records, which the U.S. Embassy in Vientiane disputed, MACV passed 88 initial requests for target validations of Vientiane in an average of 1.4 days; the Embassy required an average of 4.4 days to validate them. Since 7AF data suggested a six-ship strike, a 1x2-kilometer target box had a 30 percent chance of destroying or damaging equipment in the box. Accordingly, lucrative targets should have been attacked four or five times. However, 58 revalidation requests took 4.6 days in MACV and another 9.9 days in Vientiane. These delays hampered restriking many lucrative targets.[95]

Aside from hurting the enemy, the POINT GOLF and TURNPIKE operations had the important effect of encouraging those within 7AF who wanted to conduct further intensive choke point operations as more effective than attacking trucks. This led to the 30-day interdiction campaign in RP I.

It also led to the attempt in late September and early October to close the Ban Laboy Ford on Route 912. Despite the RP I campaign, sizable amounts of supplies reached the border through Route 137. Eight kilometers south of the Ban Karai Pass, the road crossed the Nam Tale River on an underwater rock causeway which the enemy had used for three years. Tac air managed to prevent large amounts of supplies from crossing the river; Intelligence personnel estimated 8,000 tons of supplies lay above Ban Laboy.[96]

Numerous fighter-bomber attacks had failed to destroy the causeway and

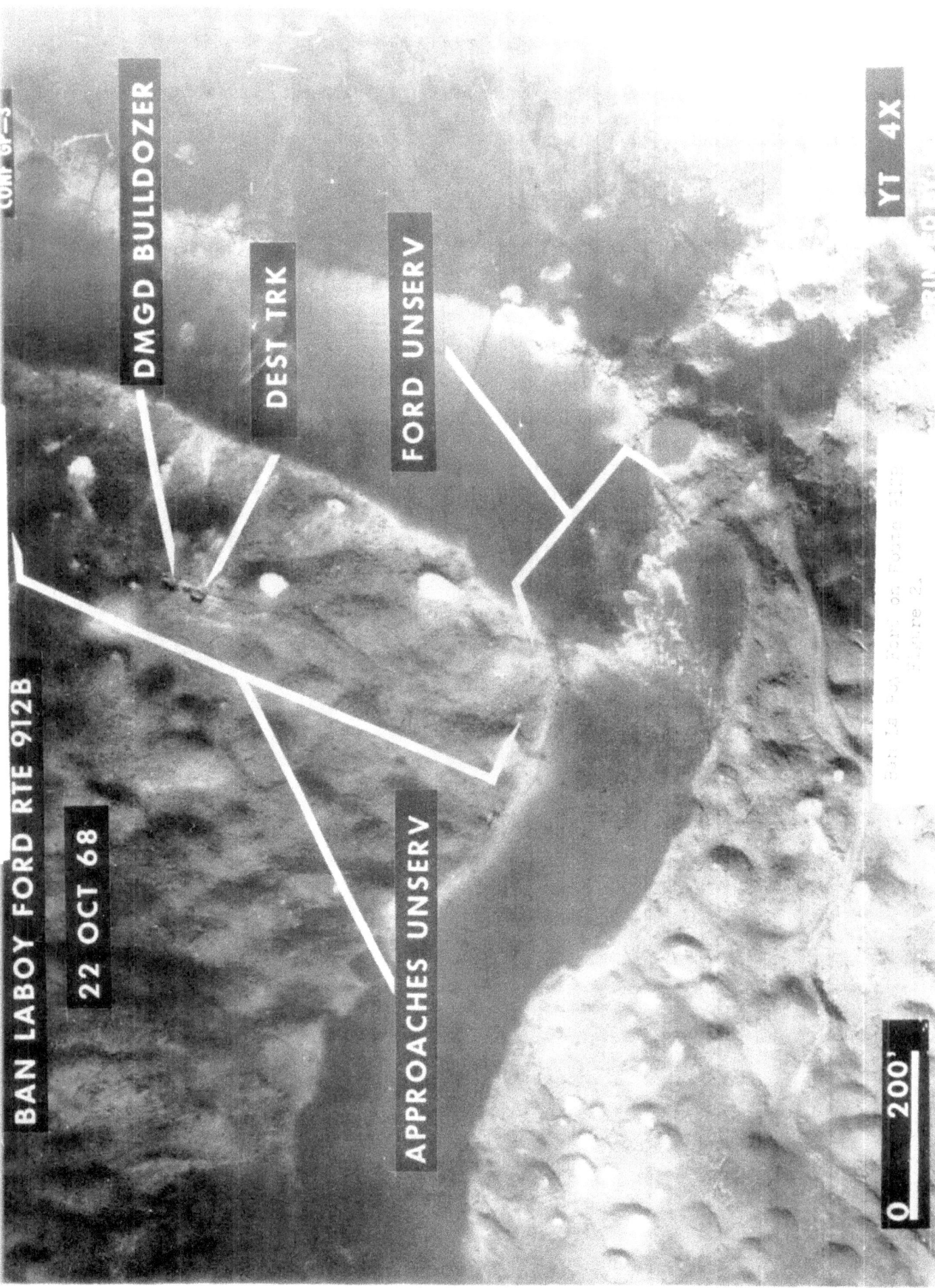

BAN LABOY FORD RTE 912B
22 OCT 68

DMGD BULLDOZER

DEST TRK

FORD UNSERV

APPROACHES UNSERV

YT 4X

0 200'

ARC LIGHT was forbidden by Vientiane due to an old PW camp reported in the area. Finally, the Embassy relented and on 18 September, about 30 B-52 sorties attacked, claiming 73 secondary explosions, some five to 20 times normal size. Then on 1 October, a six-ship mission scored a bull's-eye using a bomb train reduced from 4,500 feet to 760 feet. Two-thirds of the causeway was destroyed and the next day F-105s with 2,000-lb bombs finished the job. In the ensuing weeks, tac air kept the pressure on to prevent repairing or bypassing Ban Laboy. According to Intelligence, the enemy moved two engineer construction battalions into the area to cope with the bottleneck.[97/]

A DI briefing in 7AF judged the operation highly successful:[98/]

> *"Traffic flow detected by IGLOO WHITE sensors provide a
> further indication of the effectiveness of the campaign.
> In the three weeks preceding the 18 September strikes, an
> average of 175 trucks per week were detected shuttling the
> ford. During the ensuing weeks, shuttle activity decreased
> to less than 20 trucks per week. Visual observation, FAC,
> and photography confirm the total closure of the enemy's
> only major infiltration route through Laos into SVN."*

Ban Laboy and RP I were part of the successful choking operations in the months before the 1 November bombing halt that the 7AF DI called "one of the most successful interdiction campaigns in modern history."[99/]

CHAPTER V

INTERDICTION IN SOUTH VIETNAM

Introduction

Enemy supplies that survived the long haul south through North Vietnam and then through Laos still had to be positioned inside South Vietnam. This gave the air interdiction campaign a third chance to destroy the guns, ammunition, medicines, and electrical gear that had come so far at such great cost. The NVA moved their supplies across the Laotian border through four primary areas: Routes 9/926 near Khe Sanh, Route 922 into the A Shau Valley, Route 165 near Kham Duc, and Route 110 near Dak To. Seventh Air Force concentrated its in-country interdiction campaign on these areas.

Just as the Rules of Engagement put their imprint on operations in the Red River Valley and the Ho Chi Minh Trail, so they shaped the in-country war. All South Vietnam was open to allied ground operations; all parts of South Vietnam lay within numerous areas of operation (AO), each with its ground commander, and all ground commanders tended to regard airstrikes in their AO as supporting their operations and therefore close air support. Close air support was requested by a ground commander and passed to MACV and its Tactical Air Support Element (TASE), which passed the approved requests to 7AF for accomplishment. In short, the ground commanders designated the in-country targets. Since, as a practical matter, the ground units concentrated on ground operations, they rarely organized or implemented concentrated air interdiction campaigns. Consequently, what air interdiction occurred was done by scattered FACs flying border reconnaissance and back-country road surveillance. If they found a lucrative target such as a bridge or truck, they might get a few airstrikes. Vulnerable road segments and choke points were not apt to appear so lucrative to a ground commander intent on fixing and destroying enemy troops. Thus, the ground commanders called the shots and 7AF supplied the airpower. No significant in-country air interdiction took place.

In March 1967, I Field Force Vietnam (I FFV) proposed the establishment of Specified Strike Zones (SSZs) along the I-II and II-III Corps borders to use airstrikes and artillery to counter enemy use of the border areas as sanctuaries (due in part to border coordination problems within the U.S. command structure). 1/

From 24-30 April 1967, I FFV directed the Kylo Valley Interdiction Program southwest of Qui Nhon to attack, harass, and possibly destroy the 95th Regiment and 5th NVA Division. A SSZ was established, along with a Special "Reconnaissance/Intelligence Team" at the controlling DASC. According to the DASC Alpha Director, "This Operation marked the first occasion, in which a military target in South Vietnam has been virtually turned over to the 7AF for tac air interdiction." The 113 tac air sorties obtained a BDA of two KIA (BC), 26 military structures destroyed, three secondary fires, and five secondary explosions. Obviously, this was not a LOC interdiction campaign, but it had other elements that later appeared in the in-country interdiction campaign. 2/

In late 1967, the 7AF DI in-country targeting section conducted a two-month study on known or probable enemy infiltration routes from Cambodia and

Laos into South Vietnam. Specifically, 15 select points were chosen for intensive analysis looking toward a proposed LOC interdiction effort. However, it was the siege of Khe Sanh and enemy road construction that provided the real impetus for an in-country air interdiction campaign.

Khe Sanh: The Forerunner

In early 1968, the VC/NVA sprang their largest offensive of the war to date. Even as they launched the massive Tet Offensive, they also tightened their siege around Khe Sanh in the far northwest corner of I Corps. The MACV and 7AF commanders had foreseen the enemy threat against the camp and established a SLAM operation called NIAGARA, to begin on 22 January. The 7AF Commander as Deputy COMUSMACV for Air, was given the responsibility by COMUSMACV for coordinating and directing all tactical air resources in NIAGARA, except for Marine air in direct support of Marine units. This situation later blossomed into the single manager for tactical air issue. The essence of NIAGARA was that the 7AF Commander coordinated and directed the tac air and therefore had targeting authority. He established the NIAGARA Intelligence Control Center to generate and nominate targets to be struck and he controlled the strikes through an ABCCC. Two days after the SLAM began, the Marines attempted to deal with the coordination and control issue by designating the five coordination and control zones shown in Figure 1. As a generalization, the degree of positive control lessened in the areas farthest from the Khe Sanh friendly forces. Zones Delta and Echo were "free strike zones" permitting airstrikes without FAC or other positive control. (Fig. 22.) NIAGARA was an air operation against enemy troops, bunkers storage areas, and gun and mortar positions. Although interdiction was only a part of NIAGARA, the authority granted the 7AF Commander was

92

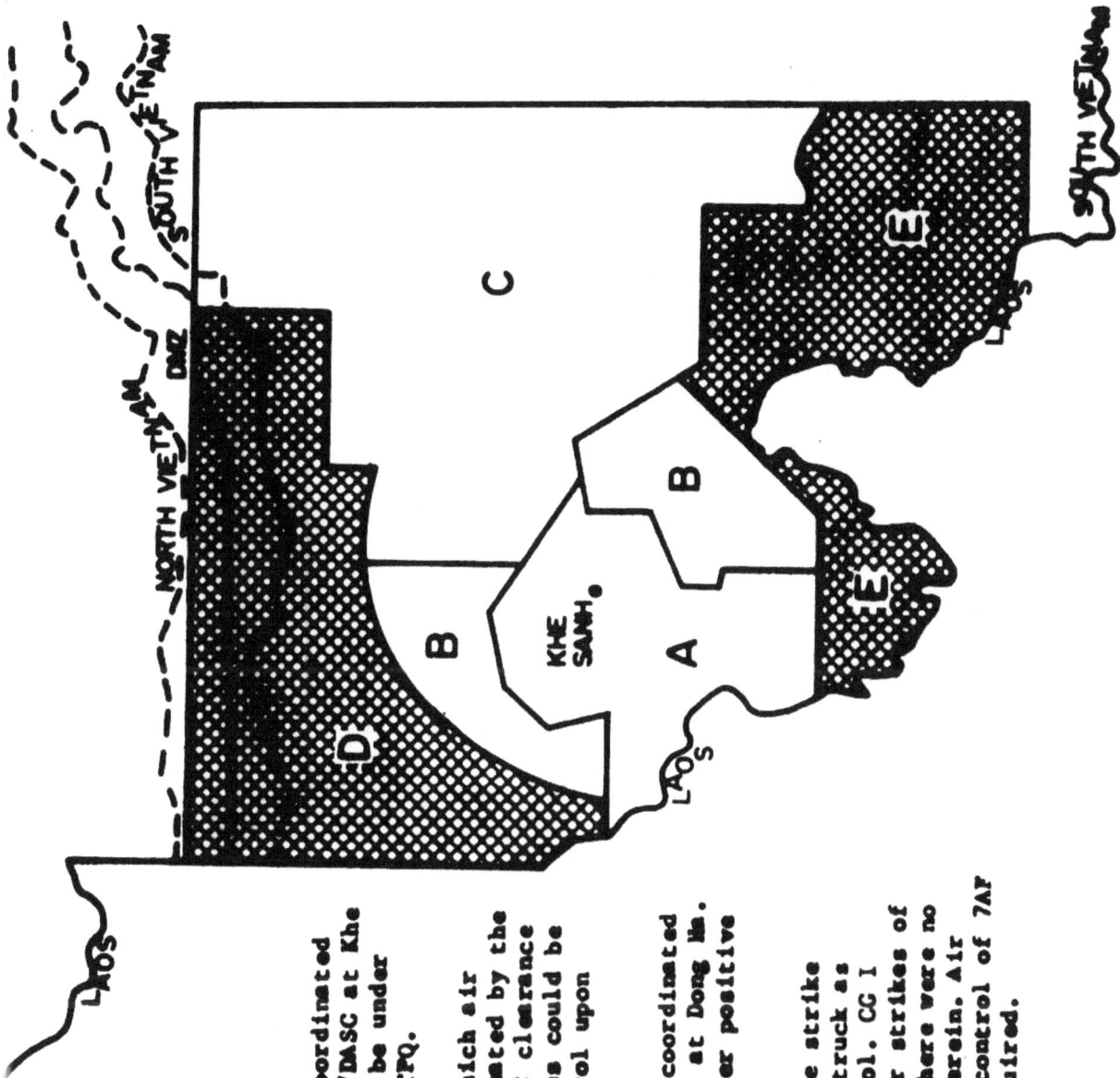

Zone Alpha: Restricted fire area coordinated and controlled by the Marine FSCC/DASC at Khe Sanh. Air support was required to be under positive control of FAC, MSQ, or TPQ.

Zone Bravo: A controlled area in which air strikes and artillery were coordinated by the Marine FSCC/DASC at Khe Sanh. DASC clearance was required for entry. Air strikes could be executed under flight leader control upon approval of FSCC/DASC Khe Sanh.

Zone Charlie: Restricted fire area coordinated and controlled by Marine FSCC/DASC at Dong Ha. Air support was required to be under positive control of FAC, MSQ, or TPQ.

Zone Delta and Echo: These were free strike zones. Military targets could be struck as required under flight leader control. CG I Corps granted blanket clearance for strikes of military targets in these areas. There were no known friendly forces operating therein. Air strikes in these zones were under control of 7AF ABCCC. FSCC/DASC Clearance not required.

NIAGARA STRIKE AND CONTROL ZONES IN SOUTH VIETNAM
FIG. 22

a real impetus toward an in-country interdiction campaign. It provided an in-country area where the Air Force could direct tactical air operations; it gave birth to an unprecedented in-country Air Force intelligence exploitation center. [3/]

Since normally MACV and ground commanders had nominated and authorized the targets in-country, 7AF had no compelling need for an elaborate in-country intelligence exploitation capability and, instead, had devoted much of its intelligence resource to the out-country war. Even here, an intensified campaign would at some time require establishment of intelligence and control task forces. In March 1967, the STEEL TIGER Task Force became operational at Nakhon Phanom, and in September 1967, a Special Intelligence Task Force was formed to collect intelligence and determine targets for a SLAM--Operation NEUTRALIZE--just north of the DMZ.

The NIAGARA Intelligence Control Center was located in the 12th Reconnaissance Intelligence Technical Squadron building next to 7AF headquarters. As stated in the 7AF Weekly Air Intelligence Summary: [4/]

> "The Control Center was organized to reflect the
> functional flow of intelligence information from
> acquisition by Seventh Air Force to the nomination
> of targets and the production of target materials.
> Through the use of maps, charts, photographs, and
> illustration boards, all the products and services
> of the intelligence collection and analysis systems
> were displayed in the Control Center. This per-
> mitted a rapid review of progress toward objectives.
> It also served as a position from which to manage
> effectively the diverse activities contributing
> to the development and maintenance of a tactical
> targeting system.

*"Management became a continuous process of review
directed toward improving the effectiveness of all
intelligence assets. This began with the collection
effort which obtained reports from interrogation
centers, reports of vehicle and personnel movements
from MUSCLE SHOALS system, operations reports from
combat units, data from special intelligence sources,
and imagery interpretation. The interrogation program, directed primarily at determining enemy troop
dispositions, plans and intentions, concentrated on
information from PWs and other persons familiar with
the NIAGARA area who could be interrogated. Combat
reports received from various military centers were
collated to give a composite picture of friendly and
enemy orders of battle and activities. But by far
the greatest input to the collection effort was
provided by imagery interpretation. This was accomplished by a specially augmented team of photo interpreters who exploited in depth all available reconnaissance products.*

*"Information from the various sources was correlated
to insure that the location and identification of
targets developed from one source was checked with
the data obtained from others. The central display
of all this information permitted real-time management of the entire effort, allowing collection assets,
or exploitation teams, to be directed to specific
problem areas on a minute by minute basis."*

The in-country 7AF directorate--SIERRA--was neither manned nor organized
to provide the necessary support. All except essential out-country intelligence
programs were temporarily suspended to devote a maximum effort to NIAGARA.
Manpower for the Control Center came from all 7AF intelligence staff sections
and was augmented by Army photo interpreters from MACV and personnel from Air
Force commands worldwide. At the height of its activity, the Control Center
had 213 personnel. By 27 January, the operation developed 300 daily targets
and by the end of March daily averaged 150 developed targets, of which 10 percent were nominated for airstrikes. In the total operation, the Control Center

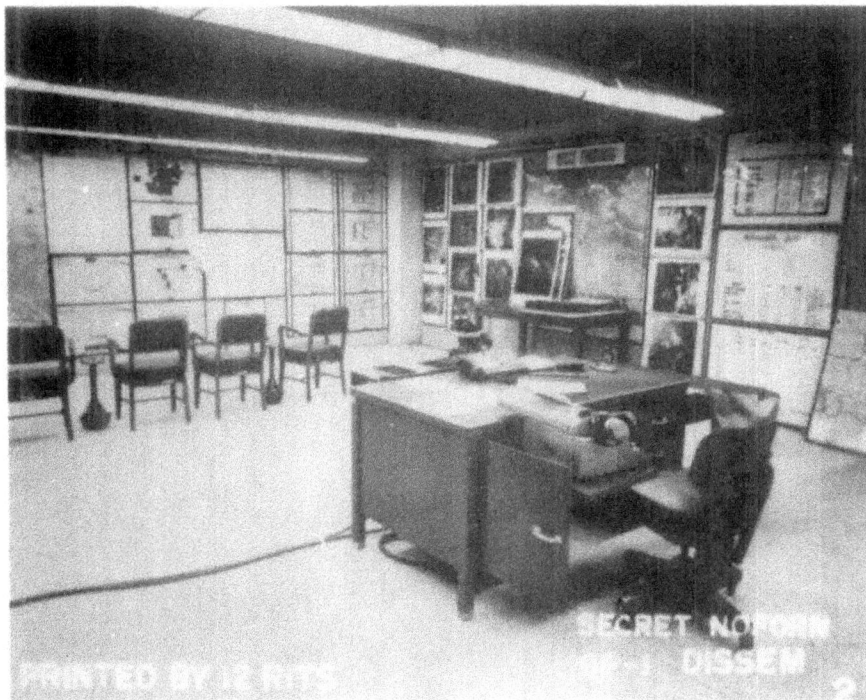

NIAGARA Control Room
Figure 23

in 70 days nominated 2,095 targets.[5/]

TURNPIKE In-Country

With the termination of NIAGARA on 31 March, 7AF had an effective intelligence exploitation center and a precedent for targeting and directing an
intensified in-country air campaign. At about this time, American ground
commanders, who had been concentrating on Khe Sanh and the Tet Offensive, turned
their attention to the sizable enemy road construction and infiltration effort.
Consequently, in the next few months Marine, Army, and Air Force interdiction
campaigns were conducted in the border areas where the Laotian road joined the
South Vietnamese national highway system.

The enemy road construction extended over several months. As early as
September 1967, the NVA moved heavy construction equipment onto Route 966 in Laos
and by 25 January 1968, the extended road crossed into South Vietnam.[6/] (Fig. 24.)
Also in early 1968, FACs discovered road construction farther south in the Tri-
Border Area.[7/] In March, other new or improved roads appeared near the A Shau
Valley and in northeastern III Corps.

COMUSMACV responded by directing 7AF to initiate interdiction campaigns.
On 9 March, he requested the 7AF Commander to place MUSCLE SHOALS sensors
into the Khe Sanh and A Shau Valley areas and several nearby enemy base areas.[8/]
It was clear that immediate action had to be taken to counter the enemy push,
and COMUSMACV, with the NIAGARA experience in mind, expected 7AF to play a
major role.

Later that month, he asked 7AF about putting gravel mines and MK-36

95

destructor mines into the A Shau Valley. The 7AF Directorate of Intelligence informally proposed a mixture of delay-fuzed bombs and MK-36s as the optimum, if such a program were to be implemented.[9] The Directorate of Operations rejected this proposal, due to the high MK-36 dud rate and the enemy's ability to defuze chemical delay fuzes. If an alternative were needed, DO suggested pinpoint interdiction of roads with large general purpose bombs and the use of the C-130 Gunship II at night and in low ceilings.[10]

On 23 March, 7AF took action to initiate an in-country campaign. A message was sent to the three northern DASCs requesting them to "take immediate action to contact the necessary agencies to obtain and approve areas along these routes [of enemy infiltration] where strikes can be put in under FAC control without further clearance."[11] On the staff coordination summary sheet, it was noted:[12]

> "The current in-country fragging method thru the TASE /Tactical Air Support Element of MACV/ is not responsible to stop the flow of supplies and troops in SVN. The TASE is not concerned with interdiction, but close air support."

Therefore, if DASCs could secure designation of special areas with blanket clearance, then an interdiction program could begin. The message also directed the appropriate FACs to fly night coverage of the routes in question.

A week later several divergent actions were taken by Seventh Air Force and the Third Marine Amphibious Force (III MAF). First, on 30 March 1968, III MAF responded to 7AF by promising to grant some area clearances by a subsequent message. But III MAF also cited MACV Directive 95-11 in which

"harassment and interdiction must be considered the same as close air support
at the request of the appropriate ground commander." The proposed 7AF campaign was termed "parallel" to past programs and not likely to sufficiently
restrict enemy supply. Then III MAF proposed a meeting of Corps, 7AF, and
Navy representatives to plan "an effective interdiction campaign."[13] Two
days later, 7AF received a III MAF message initiating the Marine Project
YELLOWBRICK to collect all-source intelligence on the mountain areas of the
four northern I Corps provinces.[14]

Also on 30 March 1968, COMUSMACV directed the Acting Commander, 7AF, to
impede and harass enemy equipment and supplies entering South Vietnam. To
interdict the Tri-Border area, 7AF created Project ATHENS to concentrate primarily on the Laotian junction of Routes 96 and 110.[15] However, ATHENS was
to have an in-country phase, a fact shown by a 6 April message from 7AF directing I DASC to divert any weathered out sorties as soon as possible to DASC
Alpha for employment in ATHENS.[16] In the A Shau Valley and Route 547 leading
east from the valley, 7AF established Projects GRAND CANYON and BUFFALO. (See
CHECO Report "Operation DELAWARE.")[17] Initially, the concept was to combine
strike and reconnaissance aircraft, B-52s, and gunships into an intensified
Air Force directed interdiction campaign. GRAND CANYON and BUFFALO began on
1 April 1968, but never became official interdiction operations because III MAF
did not grant the necessary clearance. However, 7AF monitored the areas and
conducted as much of a program as possible under the circumstances. The final
total sorties were:[18]

	GRAND CANYON	BUFFALO
7AF	187	215
SAC	300	75
Navy	2	0
Marines	38	26
	527	316

A partial BDA included 84 secondary explosions, 20 KBA, 98 roadcuts, and 11 trucks destroyed.[19/]

The lineage and relationships of the various projects and operations became very complicated in April. Seventh Air Force, under COMUSMACV's direction, had drafted a comprehensive coordinated Southwest Monsoon interdiction plan that spanned both in- and out-country LOCs.[20/] Here again NIAGARA provided the precedent for operations spanning the border. However, key areas of the in-country campaign did not receive needed clearance from ground commanders. In April, plans remained uncertain and in flux.

For instance, the I FFV and 4th Infantry Division jointly initiated RED FOX to interdict the roads inside South Vietnam in the Tri-Border area. The overall monitoring and interdiction program in the I FFV area was called TRUSCOTT WHITE and the code name RED FOX disappeared. This preempted the 7AF Project ATHENS in-country. The III MAF actions concerning the A Shau Valley (already mentioned) caused 7AF to inform COMUSMACV on 6 April 1968:[21/]

> *"MACV (TASE) informs this date that area clearances and free strike zones are not planned to be provided 7AF for conduct of in-country interdiction program along nominated routes.*
>
> *"Accordingly, 7AF will execute strikes on enemy LOCs in-country upon receipt of individual strike requests from MACV (TASE)."*

98

In short, 7AF could not direct an interdiction campaign without designated strike zones.

COMUSMACV then restated his desire for a 7AF campaign linking in- and out-country efforts in the SW Monsoon plan called Operation TURNPIKE (discussed previously). In a message to CINCPAC dated 18 April 1968, COMUSMACV mentioned the "recent unprecedented volume of truck traffic" in Laos and Route Package I and the new roads in South Vietnam, as requiring an integrated, sustained campaign. He described his concept:[22/]

> "The out-country tactical strike effort will be provided by out-country resources primarily. The in-country interdiction program will be provided 100 sorties per day from in-country resources. Approximately 70 sorties are presently being expended in this role on a preplanned basis within field force sortie allocations. However, in this program, it is intended that the effort will have continuity and be controlled by 7AF in coordination with field force commanders. Commanders will be requested to provide Specified Strike Zones for specified periods of time for implementation of this program."

On 26 April 1968, 7AF asked III MAF and the two field forces to designate Specified Strike Zones (SSZs) in accordance with MACV Directive 95-4. Seventh Air Force suggested the following roads be included in SSZs:[23/]

I Corps

. Route 547A - The new segment of 547 running east from the A Shau Valley.

. Route 548 - The road through the A Shau Valley.

. Route 922 - The road from Laos into the north end of the A Shau Valley.

. Route 548 Extended - The southern extension out of A Shau
  Valley toward Da Nang.

II Corps

. Route 110 - The road from Laos toward the Ben Het and
  Dak To Special Forces Camps.

. Plei Trap Valley - The road system turning south from
  Route 110 and threatening Kontum and Pleiku.

. Route 165 - The road from Laos joining the South Vietnamese National Highway 14, southwest of Kham Duc.

III Corps

. "New LOC" [Song Be Road]-The road running SSE in Phuoc
  Long Province.

IV Corps

. Seven Mountains Area.

Hopes in 7AF were high that an integrated in-country/out-country program
could be managed under TURNPIKE. Briefing maps were made showing the proposed
SSZs in relations to the out-country operations. However, the campaign never
jelled into a unified whole. Each area in the message cited eventually had
either an Air Force campaign or an interdiction program run by some ground unit.
A short history of each is given here (from north to south), with special
emphasis on the 4th Infantry Division's efforts to illustrate an Army-directed
air interdiction campaign.

The NIAGARA Intelligence Control Center, or its equivalent, did not exist
to provide these operations with the all-source intensive exploitation capability originally envisioned for the in-country campaign. When NIAGARA ended
on 31 March 1968, the TDY personnel began leaving and the 7AF DI staff turned

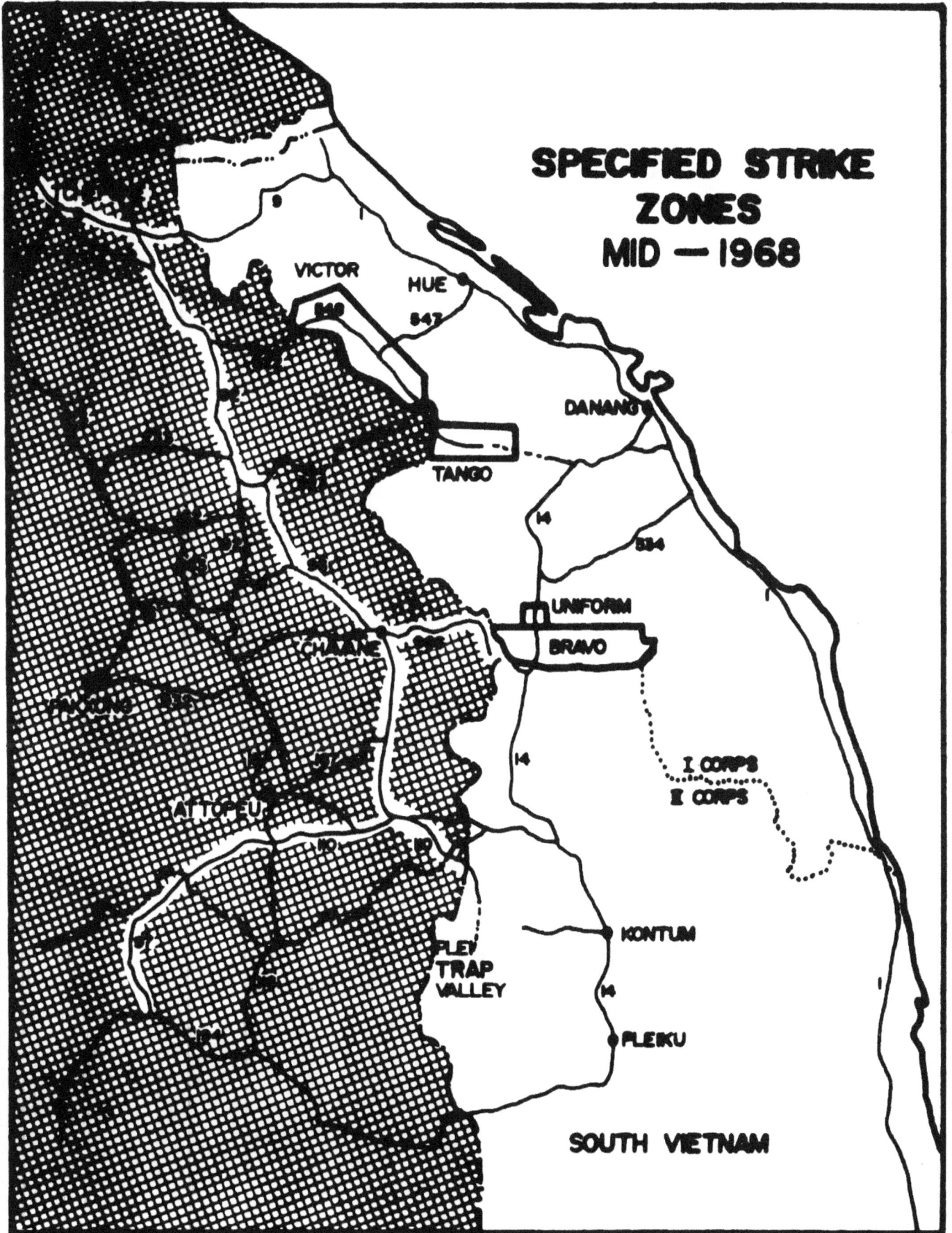

SPECIFIED STRIKE ZONES
MID — 1968

VICTOR

HUE

842

847

DANANG

TANGO

14

534

UNIFORM

BRAVO

14

I CORPS

II CORPS

KONTUM

FLEI
TRAP
VALLEY

14

PLEIKU

SOUTH VIETNAM

FIG. 24

to new projects such as TURNPIKE out-country and later a B-52 targeting project in Route Package I. The Intelligence Control Center had been created to meet an emergency of the first order and, when a comparable major in-country interdiction campaign failed to materialize immediately, the resources dissipated.

Specified Strike Zones

Victor. When the NVA began pulling back from Khe Sanh, COMUSMACV and III MAF were especially concerned that some enemy troops would move south through the A Shau Valley and then east toward Hue or Da Nang. Thus, COMUSMACV in March had requested sensors and explored the feasibility of putting MK-36s into the valley. By 1 April 1968, III MAF had established Project YELLOWBRICK and 7AF had its GRAND CANYON and BUFFALO, but still there were no SSZs. The two 7AF projects ended on 18 April, when U.S. troops heli-assaulted into the valley. Operation DELAWARE (19 April - 17 May) included sending the 1st Cavalry Division onto the valley floor and one brigade of the 101st Airborne Division along Route 547A. Neither division encountered sizable enemy combat units, but they did discover significant quantities of enemy supplies, including 60 destroyed or damaged trucks. DELAWARE may be viewed as an Army hit-and-run interdiction operation against an enemy rear base supply area.

On 31 May 1968, III MAF established SSZ Victor. That provided blanket military and political clearance for 7AF to frag strikes into the valley and surrounding mountains. The most notable strike was a B-52 hit on 30 July that caused a reported 300 secondaries. From 4 - 19 August 1968, the 101st Airborne conducted SOMERSET PLAIN on the valley floor and SSZ Victor was suspended. Interdicting the rather flat valley proved very difficult, though the more mountainous northern part offered some targets. The results were uncertain. On the whole, traffic was light. Summer and fall were wet seasons in the valley and to the west in Laos. Further, the interdiction campaign in Route Package I probably hindered resupply to areas such as the A Shau Valley. With the return of dry weather in mid-November, the enemy built a bypass around a vulnerable portion of the road in the northern part of the valley, and 7AF responded by establishing five interdiction points. Figure 25 shows one such point. According to 7AF, DI, day and night operations closed the valley.[24]

Tango. Upon request by 7AF DI, in early 1968, the I DASC directed FACs to closely observe the area west of Da Nang. In mid-March, FACs discovered a new road being built south out of the A Shau Valley which cut through a small portion of Laos and then turned east toward the coastal plain. By 9 April, the road was 25 kilometers into South Vietnam and linked to an old foot path that led to Da Nang. Construction was occasionally proceeding at more than two kilometers a day. Some 37-mm antiaircraft guns were confirmed.[25] This was a very alarming situation in light of the Tet Offensive and intelligence indicating an impending second offensive in I Corps. Along with this heightened interest, the U.S. forces pinned several names to the route: Yellow Brick Road, 548 Extended, Da Nang Expressway, and, officially, Route 614. A 7AF DI evaluation saw it as a potential attempt "to neutralize our own significant logistics capability at the major deep water port and airfield complex in I Corps."[26] The Marines conducted an interdiction campaign beginning in early April, one they eventually named CARIBOU TRAIL.[27] From the beginning, their Air Support Radar Teams (ASRT), providing automatic bombing control in bad weather and darkness,

INTERDICTION POINT 1 A SHAU VALLEY

A BULLDOZER

PRINTED BY 12 RTS

Interdiction Point 1 in the
A Shau Valley
Figure 25

could not reach Route 614. The I DASC suggested that 7AF or the Navy frag
COMBAT SKYSPOT to the area. [28/]

Operation DELAWARE to the north apparently disrupted enemy logistics
operations and brought construction to a halt. On 20 May, SSZ Tango was
authorized and two days later 7AF fragged its first strike. [29/] In July, enemy
activity quickened, though to improve the existing parts of Route 614 rather
than extend it. [30/] Infrared missions on 7 and 9 July discovered 70 and 52
emissions, respectively. [31/] A glimpse of the interdiction campaign came from
a message by HORN DASC at III MAF to 7AF on 15 August. HORN DASC explained
that ground fog hampered morning missions, and thunderstorms weathered out
late afternoon ones. Therefore, missions were to be scheduled from 1000 to
1300 hours. Further, the desired ordnance for closing roads was 750-pound GPs
with .025 delays and gravel and MK-36s. The DASC thought the Yellow Brick
road was being "rapidly developed." [32/]

According to DI, 7AF, "By August Route 614 was effectively interdicted." [33/]
On 26 September, an enlarged SSZ Tango incorporated the trail to the east. A
December evaluation by 7AF DI judged Route 614 interdicted: [34/]

> *"In summary, even though we have not been able total-*
> *ly to deny the enemy the use of Route 548, we have*
> *rendered his southern extension, Route 614, closed,*
> *unusable to vehicular traffic. As long as 614 remains*
> *closed, the enemy's logistics movements in I Corps*
> *will be greatly impeded."*

Bravo and Uniform. Beginning in September 1967, the NVA moved heavy construction equipment into the Chavane, Laos area to upgrade Route 966 to a 3.5 to 4.5

meter motorable road.[35/]   Route 966 crossed the border to join Route 14, South

Vietnam's second most important north-south road system. The in-country segment

between the border and Route 14 was first called Alpha Road and later Route 966A.

By early April 1968, Alpha Road was open, motorable, and heavily used by

vehicles to within two kilometers of Route 14.[36/]   Other intelligence revealed

uniformed NVA troops and cache points spaced along Route 14, and by late April,

convoys were moving along that road, threatening Dak Pek to the south and

Kham Duc to the northeast.[37/]

In late April 1968, the 1st Brigade, 4th Infantry Division, published an

OPlan to interdict Alpha Road at choke points using tac air, ARC LIGHT, gravel,

and chemicals. Alpha Road was beyond allied artillery range. The OPlan de-

tailed a six-day operation requiring 62 FAC-controlled sorties and 14 COMBAT

SKYSPOT sorties. The exact coordinates for 36 tac air sorties against AW

positions and six sorties against a bridge were written into the OPlan. Two

target boxes for gravel (XM-41) were also given.[38/]

Intelligence came mostly from Army resources, though the brigade's Air

Force FACs flew VR and the 460th Tactical Reconnaissance Wing provided photo

recon. Army SLAR, IR, VR, (with Army O-1s), and Snoopy (the "people sniffer")

generated the daily intelligence by which the brigade conducted its interdic-

tion of Alpha Road.

Results of the project were inconclusive. According to the Director,

DASC Alpha in Nha Trang, the operation had significant impact on enemy

movement:[39/]

> *"A relatively small but tremendously significant in-*
> *terdiction effort by fighter bombers was flown against*
> *roads in the far northwest corner of II Corps. This*
> *effectively prevented reinforcements from reaching the*
> *primary target area by cutting roads, destroying bridges,*
> *and laying aerial mines."*

Tac air attacked Alpha Road and Route 14 throughout May but, judging by daily reports, Alpha Road was never permanently closed. Early in May 1968, units of the 2d NVA Division moved east out of Laos and attacked and overran Kham Duc Special Forces Camp. On 12 May 1968, a spectacular air evacuation removed Allied Forces from the camp.[40/]

On 28 May, 20,480 pounds of CS-1 were dropped in 80-pound drums from a C-123, the first such use of the C-123 in South Vietnam. Intelligence reported a significant drop in enemy activity. On 1 June, another 17,920 pounds were also dropped on Alpha Road.[41/] For at least two weeks after the drops, there was no repair to the road at the site of the CS. The chemical warfare section of MACV evaluated the two drops:[42/]

> *"This operation, which constitutes the two largest*
> *CS bulk drops conducted in RVN, was successful. In*
> *future drops, consideration should be given to CS-2*
> *as the agent of choice. /CS-2 was considered twice*
> *as persistent as CS-1, but was not available in South*
> *Vietnam in June 1968/. The target weather must be*
> *considered (monsoon season reduces effectiveness)*
> *and the target should be such as to preclude any*
> *other means of /going/ into or out of the area."*

In late May, III MAF began its own interdiction program in the far south-west corner of I Corps, and on 28 May established MONGOOSE RUN to concentrate strikes within 200 meters of Route 14. (Fig. 26.) On 1 June 1968, a similar program, called MUSKRAT RAMBLE, was established on Route 534, which branched off Route 14.[43/] The Quang Tin Sector ALO developed and directed this program to interdict Routes 14 and 534, to establish "choke points," to attack resulting "area targets," and to discover any new enemy infiltration routes into and through Quang Tin Province.[44/] By mid-June the Alpha Road/Route 14 system was open and motorable to Kham Duc and being serviced by at least one NVN bulldozer.[45/] On 9 July, III MAF established SSZ Uniform and SSZ Bravo to permit the added weight of an Air Force interdiction effort.[46/]

Some scattered evidence exists on effectiveness of the several efforts. Between 13 and 26 July, 82 preplanned sorties in the area dropped more than 120 tons of ordnance and produced a BDA of 80 road cuts, 12 secondary fires, nine secondary explosions, and one truck destroyed. A PW report stated the interdiction had hampered road repair of Route 534.[47/] From mid-August through late December, the roads were little used due to rain and deterioration, though several sightings of tracked vehicles--possibly tanks--were reported in the An Hoa area halfway between Kham Duc and Da Nang.[48/] In September, the enemy mounted a heavy but unsuccessful attempt to overrun the Thuong Duc Special Forces Camp on Route 14, where that road entered the coastal plain. This latter attack gave the impression of an enemy linking his Laotian road net to Route 14 by April, moving down to capture Kham Duc in May, and finally reaching Thuong Duc by September 1968. However, from then until February, there was no major enemy offensive in the area, suggesting that the interdiction program had been successful.

TRUSCOTT WHITE. Begun in December 1967, construction to extend the Laotian

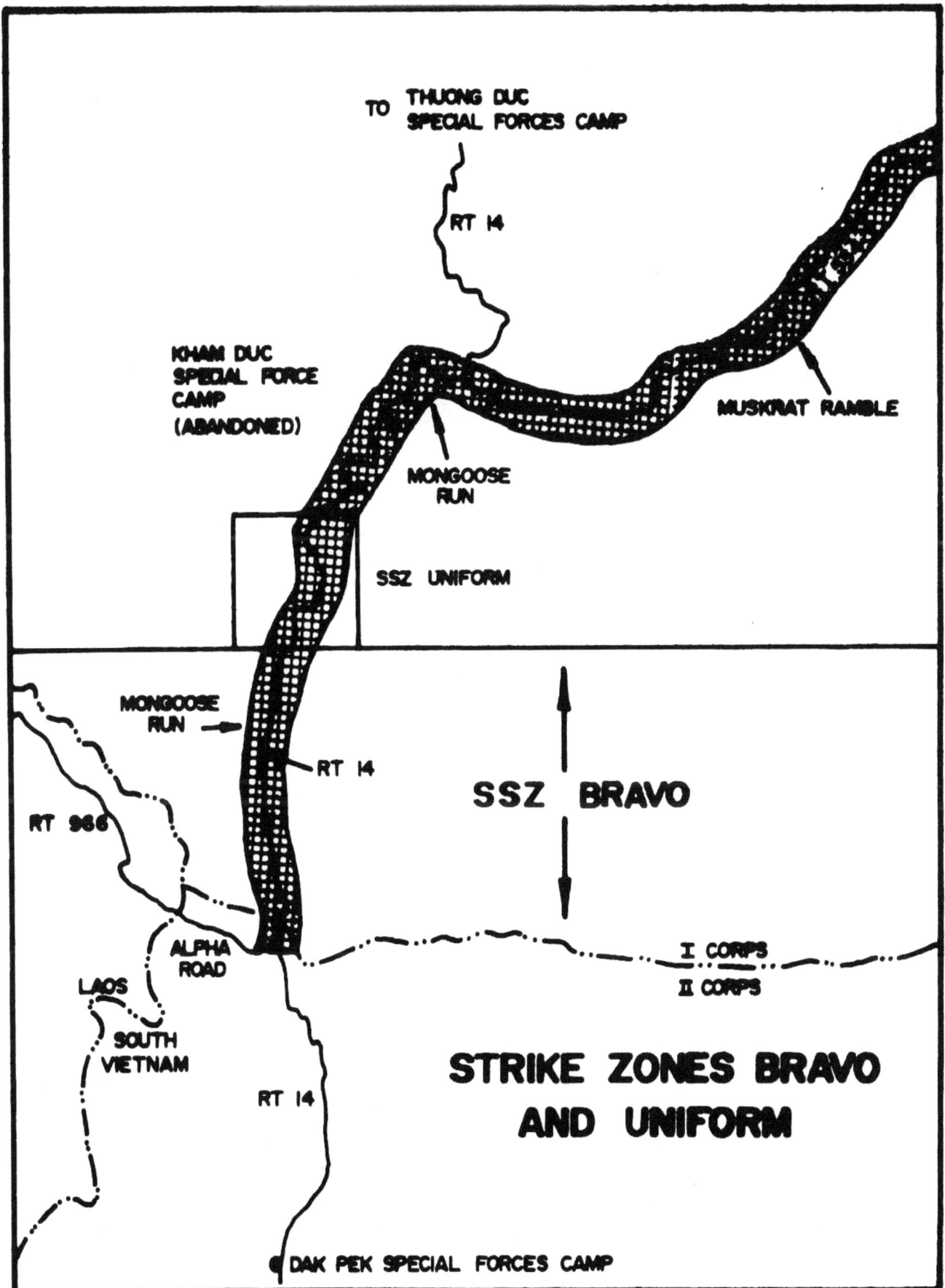

TO THUONG DUC
SPECIAL FORCES CAMP

RT 14

KHAM DUC
SPECIAL FORCE
CAMP
(ABANDONED)

MUSKRAT RAMBLE

MONGOOSE
RUN

SSZ UNIFORM

MONGOOSE
RUN →

RT 14

SSZ BRAVO

RT 966

ALPHA
ROAD

I CORPS

II CORPS

LAOS

SOUTH
VIETNAM

RT 14

STRIKE ZONES BRAVO
AND UNIFORM

DAK PEK SPECIAL FORCES CAMP

FIG. 26

Route 110 through Cambodia and into South Vietnam was completed by February
1968.$\underline{^{49/}}$ In late January 1968, the FACs of the 4th Infantry Division first
discovered new road construction in the Tri-Border area, which might eventually
permit enemy traffic to enter South Vietnam rapidly from Route 110 into
southern Laos. As enemy work crews pushed the network south toward the Plei
Trap Valley, the FACs made increasing references to the new construction in
their debriefings, but they seemed to generate little interest from higher
headquarters.$\underline{^{50/}}$ At this time, nearly all U.S. resources in-country were devoted to combating the enemy Tet Offensive and the siege of Khe Sanh.

The new enemy road construction in the Tri-Border area threatened Kontum
and Pleiku, the two largest cities in the Western Highlands. Once the road
in the Plei Trap Valley reached south to the Se San River, it would break onto
the populated plateau and connect with improved roads to Pleiku City. Other
branches of the new network were being built to join the government roads to
Dak To/Ben Het and Polei Klen SF Camp north and west of Kontum City. Thus the
enemy sought a motorable network with a north-south road in the Tri-Border/
Plei Trap Valley area and several branches thrusting east to attach themselves
to the South Vietnamese roads at three vital points.

In March, various allied intelligence systems produced increasing evidence
of the still rudimentary enemy network. Army Long-Range Reconnaissance Patrols
(LRRP) and airborne reconnaissance pilots intensified their efforts. On
9 March, a FAC located six trucks at the northern end of the north-south road
called Charlie Road (later redesignated Route 613). Three of the trucks were
destroyed, as were three more on 18 March, when an LRRP team observed nine trucks

in the same area. By the end of the month, the FACs and helicopters supporting the LRRPs were receiving 37-mm AAA fire. [51/] Through March 1968, the enemy used his improved roads to supply the 1st NVA Division in its eastward push against the Polei Kleng SF Camp, a drive stopped by the development of U.S. Fire Support Bases to shield the camp. [52/] By 1 April, I FFV was issuing a daily message on the status of NVA roads in II Corps, detailing enemy activities in the Tri-Border area and on Alpha Road in the extreme northwest corner of Kontum. [53/]

The threat to central Kontum Province caused MACV and the 4th Infantry Division to formulate plans to destroy the NVA forces and their LOCs. At the direction of MACV, the 4th Infantry Division wrote a very detailed operational plan to interdict the Charlie Road complex. Called TRUSCOTT WHITE, the stated mission of the operation was to conduct air, artillery, and chemical attacks on the enemy road network to deny use of the road and to destroy enemy installations, personnel, and equipment. [54/]

Published on 5 April 1968, the plan called for a three-phase operation. Phase I would interdict at the north end where the road entered from Cambodia. As the OPlan stated, "If the road can be cut in this area, all vehicle traffic can be effectively shut off." The interdiction effort centered around ARC LIGHT, with eight strikes envisioned, of which the OPlan specially detailed three target boxes to be struck not later than 15 April by a minimum of 18 B-52s (six per strike). These boxes centered on the point of entry from Cambodia. Other types of aircraft would drop gravel mines (XM-41) and drums of chemical agent (CS-1) on each choke point. Tac air would be used against AAA positions. [55/]

Phase II envisioned intensive air/artillery operations against hard targets and targets of opportunity. CBU-19A (CS) would be used against troop concentrations and targets of opportunity. These operations would continue into Phase III, which added the use of ARC LIGHT on targets developed throughout TRUSCOTT WHITE by the intensive air intelligence of VR, Red Haze (IR), SLAR, and photo recon. Toward the end of the second phase, three missions of eight UC-123s would defoliate Charlie Road.

Based on the assumption of a one month operation, the OPlan estimated 262 FAC-controlled tac air sorties and 108 COMBAT SKYSPOT sorties would be required. Eventually, 1,420 sorties were flown from 7 April to 29 June 1968.[56] Of these, the OPlan targeted fully 194 sorties, giving the exact coordinates.[57] This later caused trouble because the given coordinates were based on inaccurate and outdated maps. When the coordinates did not coincide with the target description, the FACs asked permission to shift to what they thought was the target. At first, the Division refused such permission and the FACs were forced to do some unauthorized adjusting to destroy the targets. There were no friendly troops in the area. Later, the Division allowed movements of up to 1,000 meters without prior approval but, according to one FAC, some tac air was wasted until the Division became more lenient about deviations from the fragged coordinates.[58]

If enemy inability to repair and use roads is a criterion for judging the effectiveness of the interdiction program, TRUSCOTT WHITE was successful in interdicting Route 613.[59] Construction nearly halted. According to one FAC, the evidence of night vehicle traffic ceased and the road became overgrown with grass. [60/] In May, the TRUSCOTT WHITE message from I FFV gave mostly negative reports on construction of the Route 613 complex, though bunkers, AAA positions, and troop movements continued to be reported. The original interdiction and road cuts remained through at least September 1968, and the wet Southwest Monsoon caused further deterioration. [61/]

In late April 1968, the 4th Infantry Division directed its 1st Brigade to develop an interdiction program against Bravo Road, the enemy extension toward Ben Het/Dak To, and against Alpha Road, the extension onto Route 14 between Dak Pek and Kham Duc SF Camps. Bravo was later redesignated the northern end of Route 613. A plan was published on 28 April as an annex to the Division's interdiction plan. Called the "Two-Road" plan, the brigade concept employed the same mixing of resources and ordnance as used on Charlie Road. The mission was to attack, destroy, and deny. Tac air destroyed lucrative bridge targets and cratered the roads at choke points. Artillery sought out hard targets and targets of opportunity. ARC LIGHT was directed on choke points and suspected enemy troop concentrations. Gravel and chemicals were dropped at choke points after the interdiction was completed. [62/]

The brigade ALO recommended two primary choke points on Bravo: a road cut with an overhang susceptible to slides and a marshy valley requiring corduroy. The majority of the ordnance went into these points and successfully blocked the roads, especially since the craters in the marshy area remained full of water. The ALO found ARC LIGHT ineffective for interdicting a road, because only a random bomb or two in the target box hit the narrow road. Artillery was at near maximum range and unable to find the road, though it was useful as

harassment and interdiction of probable enemy locations. For carrying out
road interdiction, the ALO had high praise for tac air, especially in destroying
the small bridges. His major criticism was the marked delay between the dis-
covery of road construction and the beginning of the interdiction program. In
his opinion, the NVA had possibly moved its primary traffic before the roads
were cut. 63/

In late May, the 325C NVA Division moved out of Cambodia to threaten
Ben Het, causing the 4th Infantry Division to create Task Force MATHEWS with
two brigades and an AO encompassing Dak Pek, Dak To, and the neighboring area
to the Cambodian/Laotian Border. This operation, running from 24 May to 12 June
1968, deserves mention because it became confused with TRUSTCOTT WHITE.
Actually, it was a routine ground operation against massed NVA troops, though
it did occur within the area monitored by TRUSCOTT WHITE. Operation MATHEWS
was notable for the use of ARC LIGHT in essentially a close air support role--
sometimes within 1,500 meters of friendly troops. Back in November 1967, the
the 4th Infantry Division had suffered very heavy losses in assaulting NVA
troops holding the hills south of Dak To. In MATHEWS, the U.S. troops stood
back and let B-52s in mass employment destroy the enemy west of Ben Het. 64/

In summary, TRUSCOTT WHITE was a joint Army/Air Force interdiction effort
to deny the enemy the use of roads in the Tri-Border area. Overall management
and responsibility lay with the 4th Infantry Division, since the new NVA roads
lay within the Division's AO. No SSZ was ever authorized in this area. Targeting of tac air was accomplished based primarily on Army-developed intelligence
using Army resources: LRRP teams and Army O-1s, SLAR, IR, and Snoopy Airborne

Personnel Detector. The Air Force FACs contributed significant VR reports but their primary duty was to direct tac air. The firepower to implement the interdiction was supplied almost entirely by the Air Force, but targeted by the Army.

Song Be. In III Corps at Tet 1968, the sudden convergence of the NVA and VC divisions toward Saigon and Bien Hoa pulled American troops from the border areas into the cities. At the same time, the 101st Airborne Division left northern III Corps to help drive the enemy from Hue. The enemy took advantage of this withdrawal to build or widen a road south from Base Area 351 toward War Zone D with the intent of resupplying his troops harassing Bien Hoa. By early April, this road, discovered by FACs in early March, could handle five-ton trucks in places. [65]

On 18 May, II FFV established SSZ Song Be, permitting a 7AF campaign which in two weeks drove the enemy road crews from the area. Following this, the U.S. Army and ARVN commanders responsible for the area agreed to a FAC-directed campaign to continue the minimal pressure necessary to keep the road unusable and to a wider effort against lucrative enemy targets in this isolated area. Using 7AF intelligence, visual reconnaissance, and intelligence from combat patrols, the FACs put in sorties fragged directly to themselves. From 19 May to 24 October, 285 scheduled sorties struck within the expanded specified area of the Song Be road. The partial BDA for this period from May to October 1968 included 110 secondary explosions, 119 secondary fires, 152 KBA, eight trucks damaged, 40 road cuts, and 18 gun positions destroyed and three damaged. A 7AF WAIS article stated: [66]

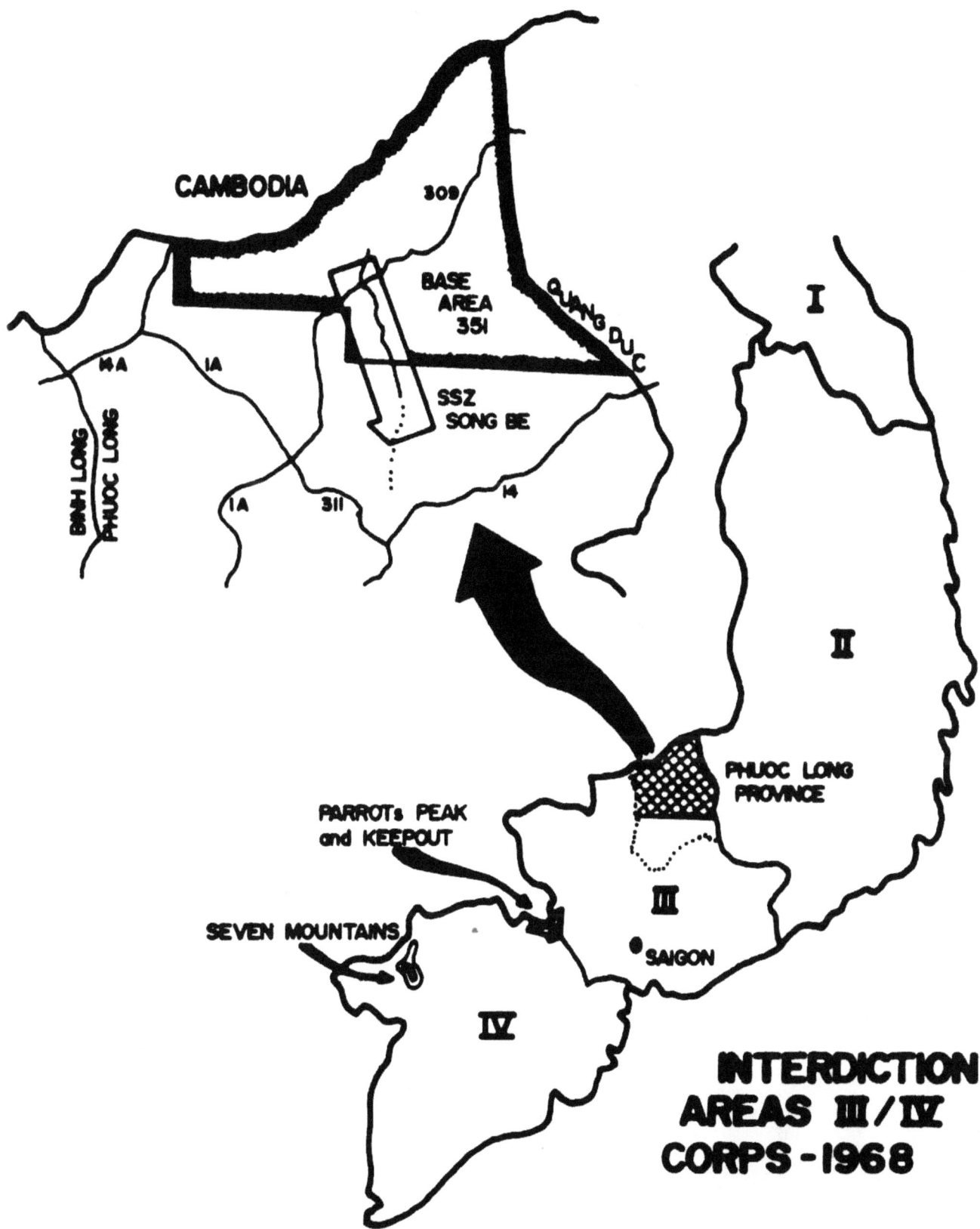

CAMBODIA

309

BASE AREA 351

QUANG DUC

14 A

1A

SSZ SONG BE

BINH LONG

PHUOC LONG

1A

311

14

I

II

PHUOC LONG PROVINCE

PARROTs PEAK and KEEPOUT

III

SEVEN MOUNTAINS

SAIGON

IV

INTERDICTION AREAS III/IV CORPS-1968

FIG. 27

"Because of close coordination between forward air controllers, U.S. Army and ARVN ground commanders, and operating units, operations and intelligence staff elements of Seventh Air Force Headquarters, strikes in the Song Be area have denied the enemy the use of the Song Be Road for logistical movement."

Conclusion

Aside from the formal 7AF-directed interdiction in the SSZs, Air Force resources engaged in interdiction efforts such as defoliation, B-52 strikes on storage areas, and visual reconnaissance by FACs. The FACs managed much LOC interdiction by working closely with the ground commanders to keep tabs on enemy activities and by requesting preplanned sorties through the tactical air support system. MONGOOSE RUN was one such FAC-directed effort; another was the summer campaign in the Seven Mountains stronghold of western IV Corps.

Air Force FACs and strike aircraft supported Army area denial operations such as KEEPOUT and Navy Riverine operations such as GIANT SLINGSHOT to intercept enemy supplies coming into III Corps by rivers from Cambodia. KEEPOUT I and II occurred in mid-February 1969 in a two-kilometer border strip around the Parrot's Beak to impede enemy supplies coming through the bulge of Cambodia pointing toward Saigon. By seeding trails and dry land with antipersonnel CBU-42B tripmines (WAAPM) and the waterways with MK-36 mines, II FFV hoped to disrupt the enemy's use of the Parrot's Beak as a supply and staging area.[67] KEEPOUT occurred in the 1968/1969 dry season after the cutoff date for this report, but it illustrated the growing use of sophisticated area denial weapons in an in-country interdiction role.

The impact of an interdiction effort along a wide front is difficult to measure. As supplies pile up behind an interdicted road, the enemy becomes desperate to find ways through, either via a bypass or by shifting his major operations to another area. On the other hand, the enemy may shift operations for reasons divorced from interdiction and may be able to push through a choke point. It becomes difficult to know if non-use of a road is due to the interdiction effort or an unrelated shift in enemy operations.

Two concluding generalizations deserve comment. First, 7AF was not able to establish a unified in-country/out-country interdiction campaign under TURN-PIKE and within both DO and DI, targeting and fragging were done separately for in-country and out-country. The classified "NOFORN" nature of the air war in Laos necessitated separating the Vietnamese and Laotian operations. This continued into 1969, although a suggestion advised making COMMANDO HUNT an in-country/out-country interdiction campaign. A working paper by 7AF in early August 1968 outlined the proposed in-country portion of COMMANDO HUNT.[68/]

> "Specified Strike Zones along the SVN/Laos Border
> identified by 7AF and approved by the U.S. ground
> commander and the SVN province chief will be
> integrated into the interdiction of Laos LOCs.
> Specified Strike Zones will be areas where strikes
> may be conducted without additional clearance ex-
> cept when 7AF TACS is notified of ground operations
> planned in the area. Targets within the SSZs will
> be attacked under control of COMMANDO HUNT FACs or
> SCARs. The need for close integration of Air Force
> and Army interdiction operations require complete
> coordination between 7AF TACC, ALOs, and U.S. Corps
> Commanders."

Attacks "under control of COMMANDO HUNT FACs or SCARs" never occurred. Rather, COMMANDO HUNT became the campaign in Laos and included no in-country SSZs.

Second, 7AF had no adequate in-country intelligence exploitation center to collect and evaluate all-source intelligence and BDA such as existed in NIAGARA. The In-Country Intelligence Directorate at the end of 1968 had about 32 to 34 personnel. Of these, three captains and four airmen were assigned to the In-country Targeting Branch to maintain the target base in-country, nominate targets and, among other duties, assess results achieved in two physically separate locations. This lack of a suitable exploitation center, capable of a sustained, concentrated, and sizable exploitation effort on enemy LOCs and base areas in-country was of special concern to the American director of the Tactical Air Control Center at 7AF. Brig. Gen. George W. McLaughlin asked for more photo reconnaissance to confirm BDA and develop targets.[69] By the end of July 1968, the in-country interdiction campaign received 30 sorties a day and General McLaughlin established portions of the DO afternoon briefing to cover that aspect of the in-country war. Problem areas were: (1) incomplete detailed target weather forecasts; (2) incomplete intelligence due to a lack of visual, sensor, or photo reconnaissance; (3) too few SSZs; (4) a lack of follow-up BDA reports; and (5) a dearth of feedback for schedulers.[70] In short, 7AF lacked an in-country all-source exploitation/control capability for an interdiction campaign.

CHAPTER VI

CONCLUSION

Measuring Interdiction Success

Air Force Manual 2-1 says interdiction campaigns "seldom achieve complete isolation of an area of conflict" but can "reduce the enemy's battlefield reserves to critical levels and seriously limit his capability to continue effective action."[1] The enemy's ability to mount offensives or counteroffensives conducted against him provided a readily available indication of whether battlefield reserves had sunk to critical levels. The official Air Force history of World War II used this criterion to evaluate Operation STRANGLE, the U.S. air interdiction campaign in Italy from March to May 1944:[2]

> "The first point to note is that the ultimate objective of STRANGLE, which was to make it impossible for the enemy to maintain his armies south of Rome, could not be achieved until the Allied armies in Italy forced him into a real battle. As Slessor put it, airpower 'can not by itself enforce a withdrawal by drying up the flow of essential supplies' when the enemy 'is not being forced to expend ammunition, fuel, vehicles, engineer stores, etc. at a high rate.' But as soon as the Germans were involved in a major fight it was immediately evident that STRANGLE had fully accomplished its purpose: the interdiction of supplies, the cutting of rail lines, and the destruction of motor vehicles had so crippled the enemy that he speedily used up his stores and motor transport, lost his mobility, and had no choice but to retreat. The effects of STRANGLE then turned an orderly withdrawal into a rout."

The railroad interdiction campaign in Korea, conducted by the Air Force from the fall of 1951 to mid-1952, received credit for curtailing the enemy's offensive capabilities, though it could not completely halt enemy resupply

116

during this period of a static front. According to USAF's history of the Korean War, this air interdiction kept the enemy resupply down:[3]

> "Viewed in terms of its stated purpose, the air interdiction did not fail. The enemy did bring his front-line logistical support up from the bankruptcy level of June 1951 to a sufficiency for what the Eighth Army estimated was necessary to sustain some 14 days' frontal offensive action in August 1952. With the ground front static, the Communists built up their supply levels by virtual osmosis, the accretion of small amounts in excess of daily consumption. Such seeping resupply could not be interdicted....Granting that the enemy did eventually provide himself with enough supplies to sustain a limited duration offensive, it must nevertheless be noted that the rail interdiction program did such extensive damage to the North Korean railway network as to guarantee that the Communists would not possess the major logistical support necessary for a sustained offensive which would be capable of driving UN forces from all of Korea."

Air interdiction faced a more complex situation in Southeast Asia than in Korea. Tropical jungles provided good cover for LOCs and storage areas for an enemy expert at maintaining long supply lines, and Cambodian sanctuaries gave the enemy forward base areas free from attack. His famous Viet Minh road to Dien Bien Phu in 1954 stretched 500 miles along all its switchbacks and had 800 Russian 2 1/2-ton trucks in the system. The few available French bombers could not stop the Viet Minh from hauling more than 8,000 tons of supplies, ammunition, and equipment to Dien Bien Phu.[4] In the Vietnam War, the North Vietnamese showed the same determination in moving supplies over extended LOCs. By skillfully exploiting natural and political advantages and accepting huge losses to U.S. interdiction, the NVA achieved partial success in getting enough supplies into South Vietnam to conduct several offensives.

In using enemy offensives as one indicator of how successful interdiction was in impeding supplies, it is necessary to review the pattern of enemy LOCs entering South Vietnam and the sources and destinations of the various types of supplies. By MACV/DIA estimate, the enemy needed 17 tons of munitions daily in-country to maintain a February 1968 level of fighting. This was only 8.6 percent of his estimated daily requirement of 197 tons of all kinds of supplies, of which food composed the bulk.[5]

The enemy had to import large amounts of food from North Vietnam and Cambodia into I, II, and III Corps to supplement local procurement. No large importation of food was necessary in IV Corps, the rice bowl of Vietnam. Cambodian rice was sent north to the Tri-Border area and east into III Corps, while much of the food for I Corps came down the Ho Chi Minh Trail. Munitions down the Ho Chi Minh Trail were just a part of the total tonnage and were used to support I Corps and northern II Corps. Munitions for III and IV Corps came through Cambodian ports such as Sihanoukville and Ream. The potential impact of Air Force interdiction on III and IV Corps was considerably less than that on I and II Corps.[6]

At Tet 1968, the enemy began his largest offensive of the war, a simultaneous attack on nearly all provincial capitals and U.S. bases in South Vietnam. In May and August, he conducted two more "General Offensives," each less intense and more geographically limited than the last. (Fig. 28.) Only rarely, such as at Hue during Tet and in Saigon during May, did the VC/NVA sustain attacks beyond a few days. Overwhelming Allied firepower from airstrikes and artillery made sustained enemy attacks suicidal. Several factors

118

contributed to the enemy's declining offensive capability: his severe troop losses, intensified air interdiction in RP-1 and Laos, American ground operations in in-country enemy rear base areas such as the A Shau Valley, and aggressive Allied exposure of in-country enemy caches. The contribution of interdiction was to disrupt and impede the flow of necessary supplies for these enemy offensives. In the three months prior to the Tet Offensive, the Air Force destroyed or damaged more than 2,400 trucks in STEEL TIGER alone. The U.S. Ambassador to Laos and the DI, 7AF, both noted with satisfaction the increase of truck kills by a factor of four or five over those in late 1966.[7] This increase is shown graphically in Figure 29. The 1968 TURNPIKE Campaign in Laos and the Summer Interdiction Campaign in RP-1 received major credit from another 7AF Intelligence Chief for denying the enemy necessary supplies for the Third Offensive in I Corps.[8] (Because sizable amounts of enemy supplies came through Cambodia, air interdiction could not affect enemy operations in III and IV Corps to the extent that it did in I and II Corps.)

Seventh Air Force did not expect and could not expect to stop the war with an interdiction campaign, but it could prevent the enemy's having a "free channel" of supply into South Vietnam. The preface of this report cited several 7AF plans on the objective of interdiction: to destroy, harass, disrupt, and impede enemy logistics. In the two years covered by this report, the enemy had at least 6,700 trucks destroyed and damaged in STEEL TIGER by airstrikes and 6,000 D/D in RP-1.[9] (App. I.) In five months in mid-1967, 7AF recorded more than 2,000 railroad cars destroyed or damaged around Hanoi.[10] To this attrition must be added the expense of hundreds of thousands of men

119

needed to keep thousands of miles of road and railroad in repair, build bypasses, repair bridges, man AAA defenses, and keep an inefficient shuttle system operating. It is doubtful if anyone can measure the many ways in which interdiction degraded the enemy logistics system and multiplied a myriad of inefficiencies. The enemy drove only at night; he took elaborate, time-consuming precautions to hide roads, storage areas, and truck parks; he lived under constant threat of attack. These and many other disruptions impeded his movement of supplies into South Vietnam.

In attempting to measure the results of interdiction, 7AF analysts developed several methods, some of which this report summarizes. To quantify the impact of interdiction, the analysts attempted to calculate the number of trucks on the Ho Chi Minh Trail, the number that got through, and the tonnage that entered South Vietnam. As an illustration of methodology, the calculations of one DI approach will be given.

On the basis of routine intelligence such as sensor reports, visual truck sightings, road watch reports, and captured documents of the NVA 559th Transportation Group, 7AF DI estimated that in April 1968, the enemy had 1,000 trucks in the Laotian/South Vietnamese system. Daily visual sightings averaged 233, one quarter of the estimated truck inventory. To balance attrition, more trucks moved south than north. One line of reasoning then calculated that 23 percent of the truck sightings were attacked and destroyed and another 3 percent of the total trucks were lost from accidents and wear and tear, for a total loss rate of 8.3 percent daily.[11/]

120

The DI analysts then determined from captured documents of the 559th Transportation Group that in dry weather it took supplies four days to move by truck to South Vietnam from the Mu Gia and Ban Karai Passes. By trial and error, they constructed a model by which, if 167 trucks entered the system at the passes, the 8.3 percent loss/attrition rate reduced the inventory over the four days to 153, 140, 128, and finally 117. If these trucks arriving in South Vietnam carried 3.5 tons, then 410 tons moved through the system. Assuming 100 tons were sent daily to support the soldiers and road crews along the Trail, 310 tons daily entered South Vietnam. This DI line of reasoning thus calculated a 29 percent net attrition in supplies in the dry season for the four-day trip down the Ho Chi Minh Trail. Any increase in transit time increased attrition by subjecting supplies to a greater likelihood of being destroyed.[12/]

Through-put must be weighed against enemy needs. A fluid relationship existed between through-put and enemy consumption, especially for munitions, medicines, and other supplies rapidly consumed during heavy fighting and not procurable within South Vietnam. The enemy might gear projected through-put to anticipated combat levels and reserve accumulations, while conversely, reserves permitted short-term consumption in excess of through-put. Since the intensity of fighting in-country bore directly on reserve levels and available through-put, the enemy could vary consumption by offering or avoiding battle. Likewise, the Allies could force more rapid use of enemy supplies by conducting offensives, a tactic the enemy countered by dispersing his troops or crossing into Laos and Cambodia.

Analysts working with the available statistics on enemy through-put and consumption for the period November 1967 to April 1968 arrived at totals not favorable to the enemy. There could be no doubt that the enemy's surge effort in late 1967 pushed through enough supplies to mount an offensive. Air interdiction took a heavy toll in trucks and tonnage, but did not prevent the offensive. Other evidence substantiates the enemy's supply capabilities. The 7AF Weekly Air Intelligence Summary of 4 May 1968 stated:[13]

> "Enemy forces in SVN require imports of approximately 85 tons per day from outside sources to conduct normal operations exclusive of those on the scale of TET. The enemy now appears to be bringing in supplies to the border areas at least double this requirement."

Concerning the concentrated air interdiction campaign waged in Laos at this time, a report by the 7AF Office of Operations Analysis (COA) said, "It is problematical whether interdiction in MUD RIVER is reducing the enemy's combat level below that which he had anticipated."[14]

The COA report cited the MACV/DIA estimate that, at the February 1968 level of fighting, the enemy's daily logistical requirements were 197 tons, of which munitions comprised only 17 tons.[15] Although much of the Class V (munitions) came from North Vietnam, sizable amounts of food were procured in South Vietnam and Cambodia. Comparing this estimate of enemy needs with the DI calculation of 310 tons through-put in April suggests sufficient supplies were getting down the Ho Chi Minh Trail.

The Tet and May Offensives ate deeply into supplies, while the summer rains in Laos curtailed use of the Ho Chi Minh Trail. For the enemy to mount a

ENEMY OFFENSIVES
(FRIENDLY AND ENEMY CASUALTIES COMBINED)

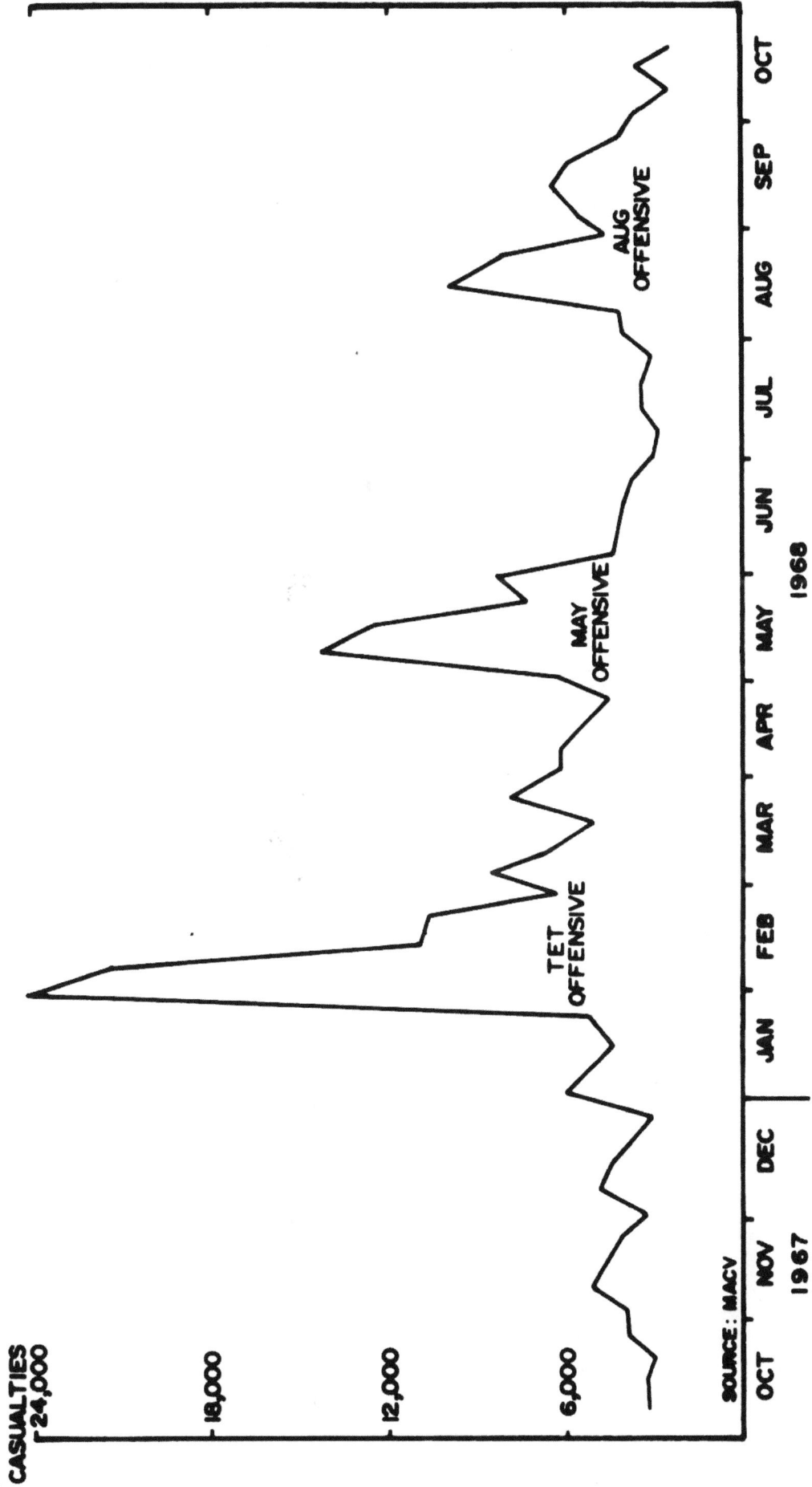

CASUALTIES
24,000

18,000

12,000

6,000

OCT   NOV   DEC   JAN   FEB   MAR   APR   MAY   JUN   JUL   AUG   SEP   OCT
1967   1968

TET OFFENSIVE

MAY OFFENSIVE

AUG OFFENSIVE

SOURCE: MACV

FIG. 28

Third Offensive, he would have to reach into his reserves built during the spring truck surge. However, in the opinion of the Operations Analysis Section of Headquarters, USAF, the enemy was unable to accumulate stockpiles in 1968, and was consuming supplies in South Vietnam "at about the same annual rate as he brings them in." [16/] (This estimate included 300 tons per month moving through the DMZ and did not include tonnage coming through Cambodia.) If the enemy did indeed live hand-to-mouth, then his supply posture in-country must have started at a robust level early in 1968, and gotten progressively weaker until the August Offensive was a mere ghost of Tet.

Trucks

The tactics of interdiction were of considerable interest within 7AF and an important topic of debate between proponents of truck kills and those favoring choke points. Trucks were attractive targets because they were tangible, unlike hidden truck parks or dirt roads. For instance, during the STEEL TIGER interdiction campaign from December 1967 to April 1968, one in four airstrikes attacked trucks, destroying an estimated 9,400 tons of supplies. Proponents of truck kills could rightly claim that this 9,400 tons would never reach South Vietnam. [17/]

Destroying a truck meant reducing enemy resupply capabilities and tallying a number of tons destroyed. The DIA conversion factor for BDA allowed 2.5 tons per truck destroyed and .625 tons per truck damaged. Sometimes DIA used a factor of three tons per destroyed truck. A secondary fire or secondary explosion, such as caused when a truck park was struck received credit for .125 tons destroyed. Statistics from 7AF indicated that in January 1968, attacks on 930

123

"truck type targets" destroyed 1,996 tons, while 2,099 attacks against truck parks and storage areas achieved credit for 468 tons destroyed. From these statistics, COA concluded:[18]

> "*This display illustrates, rather convincingly, the advantage of striking a truck in lieu of a truck park-storage area target. As can be seen, an attack against a truck yields about seven times the tonnage of supplies destroyed as does one against a truck park-storage area.*"

Using truck kills as a major measure of interdiction results raised the question of which aircraft were the most effective truck killers. In its simplest terms, the debate became "props versus jets." In late 1967, the Secretary of Defense proposed the replacement of two F-4 squadrons in Thailand with two A-1 squadrons, because the A-1s achieved 12.8 vehicles (trucks and watercraft) D/D per 100 sorties versus the F-4 rate of 1.5. The estimated cost per truck or watercraft ran $55,000 for an A-1 and $700,000 for the F-4.[19] COMUSMACV, 7AF, CINCPACAF, and CINCPAC successfully opposed the switch as restricting flexibility, reducing the ability to strike at the source of supply (Hanoi/Haiphong), and lessening the ability to operate in high AAA areas in Laos. The Secretary of Defense study itself acknowledged the limitations of the A-1 in a heavy AAA environment and stated the substitution of two A-1 squadrons would be at an additional cost of 18 planes and eight pilots lost over F-4 losses. Specifically answering the 12.8 to 1.5 kill ratio, CINCPACAF contended that:[20]

> "*Recent comparative analysis by 7AF, excluding such factors /as flak suppression, escort, and attacks*

124

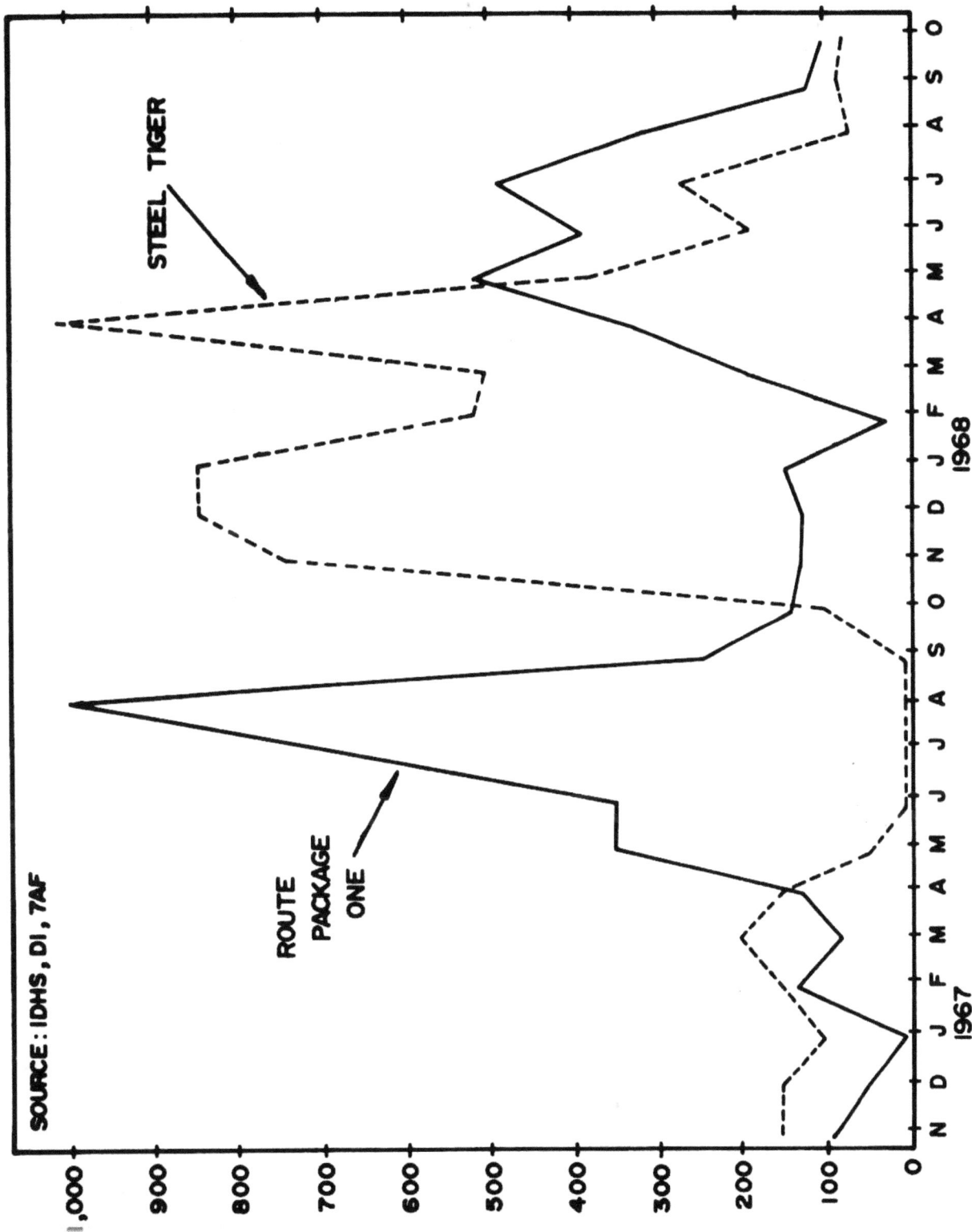

SOURCE: IDHS, DI, 7AF

STEEL TIGER

ROUTE
PACKAGE
ONE

1967   1968

TRUCKS DESTROYED/DAMAGED IN STEEL TIGER & ROUTE PACKAGE I

FIG. 29

*against fixed targets/ found that on a sortie
for sortie basis in a permissive air defense
environment, under conditions where jet forces
cannot maximize ordnance load to destroy trucks,
the propeller aircraft has demonstrated 2 to 1
capability over jets in destroying/damaging
trucks. However, on year around operation basis
requiring attacks in both Laos and Route Package
I where equal numbers of aircraft committed to
same mission, jet force kills more trucks than
propeller forces."*

In the months after the Secretary made this proposal, the dry season campaign in Laos from December 1967 to April 1968 produced further statistics on aircraft effectiveness. Based both on sorties flown and attacks made against trucks, the following results were achieved in STEEL TIGER North and TIGER HOUND. (The percentage distribution of truck kills between aircraft is given in parenthesis, first STEEL TIGER and then TIGER HOUND.) [21]

	Truck Kills per Sortie		Truck Kills per Attack	
	SL*	TH**	SL*	TH**
A-26 (45/5)	1.63	.88	1.24	.68
B-57 (38/65)	2.28	2.02	1.93	1.60
T-28 (7/1)	.93	2.00***	.84	2.00#
A-1 (4/10)	.93	1.08	.54	.61
F-4 (5/13)	.35	.37	.27	.30
F-105 (1/0)	.45	.09	.25	.08
F-100 (0/1)	.50#	.80	.50#	.28
A-37 (0/5)	N/A	.80	N/A	.80

*   STEEL TIGER
** TIGER HOUND
\# Very Small Sample

125

These figures substantiated the 7AF contention that attack for attack, the A-1 was only twice as effective. Further, the real truck killers were the A-26s and B-57s (a "slow mover" though jet-powered) because they carried the M-35/M-36 incendiary bombs, the best truck killing ordnance before the inventory essentially ran out in April 1968.

A 7AF statistical analysis of ordnance used against trucks substantiated that incendiary munitions were the most effective. Further, compared with the M-35, the M-36 with its greater penetrating capability and three times as many bomblets, was considerably more effective. However, the M-35 was more effective than the M-36 when used with a fragmentation munition. Other findings were that in December 1967 only 10 percent of the trucks sighted were destroyed despite 70 percent of them being struck. The M-117 750-lb. bomb had an effective radius of about 23 feet and the MK-82 500-lb. bomb of about 17 feet; therefore, these GP bombs "cannot be efficient for truck destruction." The GP bombs achieved 30 percent of the trucks D/D but were used in 42 percent of the strikes. Still other findings were that the A-26 and B-57 delivered the GP bombs most effectively; the M-117 and MK-82 differed little in truck kill effectiveness; napalm on the F-4 was "almost twice as effective as GP bombs," and the dual kill mechanisms (M-35 and MK-82 or the 250-lb. napalm and CBU-14) had "considerably more effectiveness than each separately."[22]

Besides attacking trucks, 7AF sought to reduce enemy supplies by bombing truck parks and storage areas. More than 47 percent of the total STEEL TIGER strikes from December 1967 to April 1968 were directed against truck parks and storage area. During January 1968, the estimated tons destroyed in

STEEL TIGER North per attack on trucks were 2.15 versus .22 tons per attack on storage area/truck parks.[23/] In the first four months, an average of 30 to 40 percent of the strike aircraft could not find trucks at night, and had to attack less lucrative targets such as truck parks and storage areas. According to a COA estimate, during early April 1968, STEEL TIGER was "aircraft limited" and "all aircraft flying into the area could find truck targets within their loiter times."[24/]

Choke Points

In 1968, the choke point concept became increasingly prominent in interdiction strategy under the guidance of the Deputy Chief of Staff/Intelligence. The idea was not new. In Korea, an interdiction plan against Main Supply Routes had been called CHOKE[25/] and in Southeast Asia, several choke point plans had been tried, most notably in North Vietnam in GATE GUARD (May 1966) and the railroad campaign (June and July 1967) and in Laos in the CRICKET Interdiction Points (October 1966) and HUB (March 1967.) Time graphs included in this report of the latter two projects show the points were not always kept closed. (Figs. 16, 19.) However, based on the TURNPIKE/Golf results in April 1968, the 7AF DI urged that "non-bypassable" choke points in RP-1 receive a greater percentage of resources than had ever before been devoted to RP-1 choke points.[26/] This was done beginning in July. In September 1968, 27 percent of the effort in RP-1 was directed against six choke points and closed them often enough to curtail traffic substantially.[27/]

The DI hailed the effort in RP-1 as "one of the most successful interdiction campaigns in modern history." He noted in an article in the 7AF WAIS that impeding the flow of trucks by the choke point method in RP-1 cost approximately $1,000 per ton, while a comparable reduction in throughput by killing trucks would cost $13,000 per ton.[28/] According to these computations, the choke point concept using 154 sorties daily in RP-1 caused a reduction that could be duplicated by the truck-killing method only with an additional 1,600 F-4 sorties daily.[29/] Appendix II reproduces the DI calculations.

A viewpoint on road cuts was expressed in the COA report on the 1967/1968 campaign in STEEL TIGER. The DIA estimates of LOC closure times allowed nine hours for a bridge destroyed or cratered, six hours for a ford destroyed or cratered, and three hours for a road destroyed or cratered. However, evidence from STEEL TIGER operations suggested the enemy repair of road cuts took 45 minutes, while downed ford/bridge targets closed the LOCs for about an hour. Data for January 1968 did show that attacks on roads closed the LOCs .75 hours per attack and bridge/fords .58 hours, on the average.[30/] (Analysts in 7AF DI questioned these statics and thought a "figure of three hours per closure was well-verified by FAC and photography.")[31/]

The COA report acknowledged the difficulty of equating destroyed supplies with LOC hour closures. In a model of the traffic patterns in STEEL TIGER North, COA simulated the impact of road interdiction operations and found it negligible:[32/]

> "Working with a simplified representation of the MUD
> RIVER lines of communication, it was determined that
> road interdiction efforts as executed prior to 1 April

> *did not perturb the enemy transportation system*
> *to any great extent. In the representation,*
> *perfect road cuts, scheduling aircraft presence*
> *in proportion to the amount of enemy activity,*
> *short turnaround times, and optimistic road cut*
> *times were assumed. With these assumptions, which*
> *in effect are based in favor of the interdictor,*
> *the enemy's utilization (truck hours) was only*
> *reduced 9%. This was a coordinated and planned*
> *interdiction combined with the above assumptions*
> *yet it had little effect on the enemy."*

It appears the interdiction COA found so wanting in impact, however, was the random cratering of roads, not the intensified concentration against "non-bypassable" choke points. The report warned against too much concentration of effort and favored the ideal of neither too much nor too little: [33/]

> *"With an interdiction program which attacks the road*
> *in a random manner, the resulting effect on the enemy*
> *may even be less effective than the simulation indicated.*
> *However, by following the doctrine as specified in AFM 2-1,*
> *a further exploitation of the concept of concentration of*
> *forces could possibly pay higher dividends in terms of*
> *disruption of the enemy LOC. Because of the facility with*
> *which concentration can be accomplished, care must be*
> *exercised to avoid application of surplus effort which*
> *represents needless dissipation of resources. Conversely,*
> *time, force, and opportunity may be wasted if, because of*
> *vacillating pressure, the effort falls short of the goal*
> *by even a relatively small margin. The employment of the*
> *interdiction forces should be undertaken with the expecta-*
> *tion of sustaining the operation until the desired effect*
> *is accomplished."*

The use of "non-bypassable" choke points was desirable if such points existed. The myriad of bypasses built around vulnerable road segments in Laos and around bridges in North Vietnam was eloquent testimony to the persistence of the enemy. The 1968 RP-1 campaign had its greatest impact during the rainy September-October months and was not forced to stand the test of the November-

April truck surge. In any case, the choke point concept was carried over into the COMMANDO HUNT campaign that began in November 1968. The 7AF DI had some words on choke points relative to the RP-1 campaign and the upcoming COMMANDO HUNT: [34]

> "One of the most significant questions raised by this campaign /RP-1/ is whether or not a similarly success-ful impedance of flow could be attained in Laos through-out the dry season. There are very few non-bypassable points within Laos. The lack of such points clearly cannot be compensated for by the use of sensors. Only the massed use of fighters and B-52s on a daily basis against points, such as Ban Laboy and occupied truck parks, can compensate for the disadvantage of terrain in Laos. Similarly, such efforts are seriously impaired by the lack of suitable munitions such as efficient truck killers and land mines. Not one successful land mine has been available for use during the past three years. Consequently, the extent to which the enemy's flow through Laos can be impeded is difficult to forecast."

Closing choke points or cratering roads proved expensive and uncertain with the ordnance available to 7AF. For example, DOA, 7AF, made a study on the circular error probability (CEP) of the M-117 (750-lb.) and M-118 (3,000-lb.) general purpose bombs dropped by the F-105. The CEP in RP-VI from 8,000 feet was 385 feet and from 9,000 feet, it was 469 feet. The overall CEP averaged 447 feet with 5.5 percent of the bombs within 50 feet of their target for direct hits. Aircraft position within a flight caused a deterioration in CEP from Lead at 351 feet to Number Four at 490 feet. Ordnance on targets with no AAA defenses had a CEP of 365 feet versus one of 538 feet for heavily defended targets. [35]

Specifically relating to road cuts, a 7AF analyst calculated that with a

130

load of six M-117 bombs, the probability of one bomb hitting within 11 feet of the center of a road 10 feet wide and 200 feet long in an area of permissive ground fire was .085 and in moderate ground fire such as RP-I, it was .043. Other calculations showed the MK-84 2,000-lb. bomb modified with the laser Paveway guidance system had a CEP of 20 feet, excluding malfunctions and a reliability of 70 percent. A comparison of these two weapons and the AGM-12C (comparable in explosive power to the M-117) found the Paveway by far the most cost effective, and the AGM-12C second. According to the 7AF analysts, to cut a road within a 200-foot segment with the M-117 under moderated ground fire would take 23.2 sorties.[36/]

Once the road cut was made, 7AF did not have adequate long-term area denial weapons to prevent rapid enemy repairs. Mention has already been made of DIA's credit of three hour's closure for a road cut and how 7AF calculations suggest a closure time of under one hour would be more realistic. Area denial weapons such as gravel (XM-41), Dragon Tooth, delay-fused bombs, and MK-36s were used often and in several combinations but with generally unsatisfactory or unknown results. The enemy cleared the gravel mines by flipping them out of the immediate area with sticks.[37/] An analysis of the effectiveness of the MK-36 Destructor mine (the MK-82 500-lb. with a Navy magnetic fuze) from November 1967 to January 1968 provided these indefinite findings:[38/]

> "There appears to be no immediate change in truck
> traffic volume when the Destructor is seeded at
> Ferry crossings; instead, changes in traffic volume
> and pattern become apparent after several weeks.
>
> "There is very strong evidence that the MK-36 mine
> had a statistically significant effect on the routing

131

of traffic when used in large numbers along major waterways. However, statistical significance does not necessarily imply favorable cost effectiveness."

The effectiveness of the MK-36 on land was much more uncertain than at fords and ferries, because the mine was designed for waterways. In 1968, the subjective feeling grew within 7AF that the MK-36 was indeed a valuable land-effective weapon and should be used more. [39]

Summary

This report presented statistics and summations about the main interdiction programs. A blanket judgment on the success of two years of interdiction in Southeast Asia is premature and would be based on fragmentary evidence. Debate on the impact of bombing Germany in World War II continues after nearly thirty years despite access to both Allied and Axis archives. The task of analyzing and correlating the documentary sources in Vietnam has hardly begun.

The amount of enemy supplies destroyed by air interdiction was immense, yet aggressive U.S. Army/Marine operations continued to discover record-sized caches within South Vietnam. From November 1966 to October 1968, the enemy had an estimated 12,800 trucks destroyed and damaged in STEEL TIGER and RP-1, yet the truck traffic in late 1968 broke all records for comparable periods. [40] In short, the enemy paid the cost of trucks and manpower to keep his LOCs open.

The experiences over the two years covered by this report suggest several observations worthy of future detailed study. Probably the weakest link in interdiction was comparatively inaccurate ordnance delivery systems and the lack of effective area denial munitions, a situation similar to the Korean experience. Not only were road cuts costly in bombs and sorties, but area denial weapons available in these two years were of little assistance in preventing rapid enemy road/railroad repairs. The rate of kills against moving trucks was understandably low, but the use of "multiple kill" loads mixing explosive and incendiary ordnance and the use of gunships were obvious potential solutions.

The IGLOO WHITE sensor system and the in-country interdiction program spotlighted another prerequisite of effective interdiction--the need for a better intelligence exploitation capability. Raw intelligence must be assimilated, correlated, and acted upon in as near to real-time as possible. Manning in 7AF was not adequate for this task. CHECO report "Tactical Reconnaissance Photography Request/Distribution" discusses some of the 7AF problems regarding manning.

A broad and fundamental topic deserving in depth analysis concerns the air campaign in RP-V and VI and its impact on air operations in RP-1. The opinion was essentially unanimous in PACOM from CINCPAC down to 7AF that striking supplies at their source, such as Hanoi and Haiphong, was more effective than trying to interdict LOCs strung along 500 miles of road and railroad. Further, the major weight of effort went into RP-VI. CINCPACAF described the results while talking about the F-4 versus the A-1: 41/

> *"In order to take advantage of the marginal weather which prevails over the northern areas for extensive periods, we are forced to schedule maximum efforts into these areas, realizing in advance that it is highly probable*

*that they will divert. These diverts are planned
to make up a portion of the attack forces in Route
Package I and Laos. However, because these aircraft are weaponeered for maximum effectiveness
against hard targets and because they normally can
only stay in Laos for short periods (15 minutes),
their effectiveness against trucks is reduced. This
accounts for some of the relatively poor results when
these attacks are compared with the A-1 which is
weaponeered and scheduled for this one purpose. We
accept this poor truck killing configuration in order
to retain the most effective effort against the primary targets in the north and to maintain maximum
presence over the LOCs in Laos."*

The issue of priorities is not questioned here; rather, the point is made that
the sizable diverts from RP-VI heightened the tendency to run a random campaign
of attrition in RP-1 and STEEL TIGER. This report discussed how armed reconnaissance and FAC-directed operations, in the absence of guidelines to the
contrary, tend to attack the immediately available targets of opportunity as
they become avilable. Compared to this broad attrition of enemy logistics,
the more intensive campaigns were much more limited in geographical area or
type of target. The bombing halt in April 1968 above 19° North provides a
dividing line between the heartland campaign and the operations dedicated to
RP-1. The successful results of the latter (with perhaps a third more sorties),
concentrating large resources on choke points, at least raises the question of
the effectiveness of attrition versus intensive, more sharply focused campaigns.

134

FOOTNOTES*

FOREWORD

1. (U)   Interview, John K. Galbraith, Former Ambassador, Jun 68.

2. (U)   Article, Stewart Alsop, Political Analyst, "The Lessons of Vietnam," _Newsweek_, 17 Feb 69, pg 40, Asian Edition.

3. (TS)   Msg, 7AF to All "Bravo" Addressees, "Interim 7AF OPlan 483-67, "Air Campaign for SL North," 9 Mar 67.

4. (TS/NF)   7AF OPlan 100-68, "ROLLING THUNDER," 15 Dec 67.

5. (TS/NF)   7AF Oplan 512-68, "NE Monsoon Campaign," 15 Sep 67;
   (TS/NF)   7AF OPlan 433-68, "BARREL ROLL/STEEL TIGER," Sep 67.

6. (S/NF)   Command Status Rprt, 7AF, Mar 69, pg B.3.

CHAPTER I

1. (TS)   Testimony, Gen Earle G. Wheeler, CJCS, U.S. Senate Preparedness Investigating Subcommittee, "Conduct and Effectiveness of the Air War Against NVN," 16 Aug 67, pp 334, 405. (Hereafter cited: Senate Hearings, 16 Aug 67.)

2.   _Ibid_, pg 285.

3.   _Ibid_, pg 336.

4. (S/NF)   WAIS, 7AF, 27 Jan 68, pg 53.

5. (TS)   Senate Hearings, 16 Aug 67, pg 285.

6. (S/NF)   WAIS, 7AF, 27 Jan 68, pg 53.

7. (S/NF)   Weekly Intelligence Digest, PACOM, "The Means to Resist - Supply Lines to North Vietnam", 18 Agu 67, pp 2-7.

8. (TS)   Msg, CINCPACFLT to CINCPAC, "ROLLING THUNDER Targeting Concept Review," 8 Jan 67.

9. (S/NF)   Intelligence Digest, PACOM, "New Road Construction in North Vietnam," 3 Mar 67, pp 7-9.

10. (S/NF)   Study, DIOW, 7AF, "Infiltration of Communist Supplies into South Vietnam and North Vietnam," 27 Sep 68, pg 4. (Hereafter cited:

*Extracts from TOP SECRET Documents have a classification no higher than SECRET.

DIOW Study.)

11. (S/NF)   WAIS, 7AF, 18 Jan 69, pp 2-4.

12. (S/NF)   DIOW Study, pg 6.

13. (TS/NF) Summary of Air Operations, PACAF, Oct 66, pg 3.33.

14. (S/NF)   RAND Study, G. C. Reinhardt and E. H. Sharkey, "Air Interdiction
             in Southeast Asia," Nov 67, pg 10.

15. (TS/NF) CHECO Report, "Hq PACAF, DOTEC, "Interdiction in SEA 1965 - 1966,"
             pg 38.

16. (TS)   Hist Rprt, MACV, 1967, pg 37.

17. (S/NF)   Weekly Intelligence Digest, PACOM, "Enemy Routes and Facilities
             in Laos," 20 Oct 67, pp 2-20.

18. (C)   Rprt, DI, 432d TRW, "Procedures for Operation of Trucks on the
             Ho Chi Minh Trail," 2 May 67. (Hereafter cited: 432d TRW Rprt.)

19.   Ibid.

20. (S/NF)   WAIS, 7AF, 5 Mar 67, pg 39;
    (S/NF)   WAIS, 7AF, 16 Apr 67, pg 40;
    (S/NF)   WAIS, 7AF, 28 Oct 67, pg 42.

21. (C)   432d TRW Rprt.

22. (S/NF)   Intelligence Digest, PACOM, "Enemy Road Construction in the Laos
             Panhandle," 30 Aug 68, pg 9.

23. (S/NF)   WAIS, 7AF, 27 Apr 68, pg 7.

24. (C)   Rprt, Combined Document Exploitation Center, "Organization and
             Activities of the 559th VC Transportation Gp," 29 May 68.

25.   Ibid.

26. (S/NF)   WAIS, 7AF, 16 Apr 67, pg 33;
    (S/NF)   WAIS, 7AF, 14 Dec 68, pg 47.

27. (S/NF)   WAIS, 7AF, 24 Jul 67, pg 50;
    (S/NF)   WAIS, 7AF, 30 Jul 67, pg 45.

28. (S/NF)   WAIS, 7AF, 21 Dec 66, pg 25.

29. (S/NF)   WAIS, 7AF, 9 Apr 67, pg 38.

30. (S/NF)   WAIS, 7AF, 21 May 67, pg 43.

31. (S/NF)   WAIS, 7AF, 27 Jan 68, pp 54-55.

32. (S/NF)   WAIS, 7AF, 7 Sep 68, pg 53.

33. (S/NF)   WAIS, 7AF, 14 Sep 68, pg 48.

34. (S/NF)   Weekly Intel Digest, PACOM, "Cambodia's Logistical Support of Communist Forces," 28 Jul 67, pg 13.

35. (S/NF)   Weekly Intel Digest, PACOM, "Disposition of Foreign Military Aid to Cambodia," 9 Jun 67, pg 4.

36. (S/NF)   WAIS, 7AF, 13 Jan 68, pg 50;
    (S/NF)   WAIS, 7AF, 16 Mar 68, pp 52-53;
    (S/NF)   WAIS, 7AF, 14 Dec 68, pg 48.

37. (S/NF)   Weekly Intel Digest, PACOM, "Cambodia--Back Door to SVN," 23 Nov 68, pg 6.

38. (S/NF)   Weekly Intel Digest, PACOM, "Cambodia's Logistical Support of Communist Forces," 28 Jul 67, pp 13-17;
    (S/NF)   Weekly Intel Digest, PACOM, "The Se Song River," 30 Jun 67, pp 8-10.

39. (S/NF)   WAIS, 7AF, 23 Nov 68, pp 39-40.

40.   Ibid, pg 14.

41. (S/NF)   Weekly Intel Digest, PACOM, "The VC/NVA Supply System," 26 May 67, pp 8-10.

CHAPTER II

1. (TS/NF)   CHECO Rprt, Hq PACAF, DOTEC, "YANKEE TEAM," 8 Mar 66, pp 2, 6.

2. (TS/NF)   CHECO Rprt, Hq PACAF, DOTEC, "Escalation of the War in SEA, Jul - Dec 64," undated, pg 202.

3. (TS/NF)   CHECO Rprt, Hq PACAF, DOTEC, "Interdiction in SEA, 1965-1966," 25 May 67, pg 8. (Hereafter cited: "Interdiction in SEA, 1965-1966.)

4. (TS/NF)   CHECO Rprt, Hq PACAF, DOTEC, "USAF Operations from Thailand, 1964-1965," 10 Aug 66, pp 70-71.

5. (TS/NF)   "Interdiction in SEA, 1965-1966."

6. Ibid, pp 15, 17-19.

7. (U)   Rprt, Det 14, 1st Wea Gp, "Some Applications of Monsoonal Synoptic
            Models, Part I - SW Monsoon," Apr 68, pp 3, 9-10.

8. (S/NF) WAIS, DIP, 7AF, "The NE Monsoon," 28 Sep 68, pp 3-6.

9. (TS)   CHECO Rprt, Hq PACAF, DOTEC, "ROLLING THUNDER," 28 Mar 66, pp 14-19.

10. (TS/NF) Ibid, p 43.

11. (TS/NF) CHECO Rprt, Hq PACAF, DOTEC, "ROLLING THUNDER, Jul 65-Dec 65,"
            15 Jul 67, pg 8.

12.   Ibid, pp 20, 23.

13.   Ibid, pg 31.

14. (TS/NF) CHECO Rprt, Hq PACAF, DOTEC, "TIGER HOUND, 6 Sep 66, pp 4-7.

15.   Ibid, pg 10.

16. (TS/NF) CHECO Rprt, Hq PACAF, DOTEC, "Interdiction in SEA, 1965-1966,"
            25 May 67, pg 50.

17.   Ibid, pp 51-59.

18. (TS/NF) CHECO Rprt, Hq PACAF, DOTEC, "ROLLING THUNDER, Jul 65-Dec 66,"
            15 Jul 67, pg 24.

19.   Ibid, pp 39-42.

20. (TS/NF) CHECO Rprt, Hq PACAF, DOTEC, "Interdiction in SEA, 1965-1966,"
            25 May 67, pp 59-60.

21.   Ibid, pg 67;
    (TS/NF) CHECO Rprt, Hq PACAF, DOTEC, "Operation TALLY HO," 21 Nov 66,
            pp 35-36.

22. (TS/NF) "Interdiction in SEA, 1965-1966," pg 70.

23.   Ibid, pg 69.

                            CHAPTER III

1. (C)   OPREP-5, 7AF, Nov 66-Oct 68.

2. (TS)   Senate Hearings, SecDef, Robert S. McNamara, 25 Aug 67, pg 646.
            (Hereafter cited: Senate Hearings, 25 Aug 67.)

3.   *Ibid*, pg 652.

4.   (TS)   Senate Hearings, 16 Aug 67, pp 283-284.

5.   *Ibid*, pg 338.

6.   *Ibid*.

7.   (TS)   Senate Hearings, 25 Aug 67, pg 645.

8.   *Ibid*, pg 681

9.   (TS)   Rprt, PACAF, "Summary of Air Operations," Jul 66, pg 11;
      (TS)   Rprt, PACAF, "Summary of Air Operations," Nov 66, pp 1.1-2.

10.   *Ibid*.

11.   *Ibid*, Sep 66, pg 1.1;
      (TS)   CHECO Rprt, Hq PACAF, DOTEC, "Control of Airstrikes, 1961-1966,"
            1 Mar 67, pp 97-98.

12.   (C)   OPREP-5, 7AF, Nov 66-Mar 68.

13.   (TS)   Rprt, PACAF, "Summary of Air Operations," Nov 66, pg 1.3.

14.   (S/NF) Rprt, PACAF, "Effects of Air Operations, SEA, Annual Review,
            1966," undated, pg 10. (Hereafter cited: Annual Review, 1966.)

15.   (S/NF) Rprt, PACAF, "Effects of Air Operations, SEA, Jan 67," undated,
            pp 16-19.

16.   *Ibid*, pp 19, 21.

17.   *Ibid*, Feb 67, pg 21.

18.   *Ibid*, Apr 67, pp 12-16, 21.

19.   (TS)   Rprt, PACAF, "Summary of Air Operations," Mar 67, pg 2.

20.   (TS)   Senate Hearings, 16 Aug 67, pg 349.

21.   (TS)   Rprt, PACAF, "Summary of Air Operations," Feb 67, pg 4.3.

22.   (TS)   Msg, CINCPACAF to CINCPAC, "ROLLING THUNDER," 10 Jan 67.

23.   (TS)   Msg, CINCPACFLT to CINCPAC, "ROLLING THUNDER Targeting Concept
            Review," 8 Jan 67.

24.   *Ibid*.

25.   Memo for General Dunham, Lt Gen William W. Momyer, Comdr, 7AF, 11 Mar 67.

26.   Form 4, Lt Col Howard F. Lorenz, Chief, Combat Plans Div, 7AF, "Concise Treatment of the SW Monsoon Plan (COBRA)," 30 Jan 67.

27.   Ibid.

28.   Ibid.

29.   Form 4, Lt Col Howard F. Lorenz, Chief, Combat Plans Div, 7AF, "Operation COBRA Plan for SW Monsoon Season," 17 Jul 67.

30.   Ibid.

31.   Rprt, PACAF, "Summary of Air Operations, Apr 67, pg 1.5; Rprt, PACAF, "Summary of Air Operations, May 67, pg 1.1.

32.   Annual Review, 1966, pg 10.

33.   Ibid, Apr 67, pp 12-13, 48.

34.   Ibid, May 67, pg 26-30.

35.   Ibid, pp 56-58.

36.   Ibid, Jun 67, pg 21.

37.   Rprt, PACAF, "Summary of Air Operations," Jun 67, pg 2.

38.   Ibid, pg 1.9.

39.   Ibid.

40.   Rprt, PACAF, "Effects of Air Operations, SEA, Jun 67," undated, pp 1-2.

41.   Intelligence Digest, PACOM, "North Vietnam's Ability to Regenerate Destroyed RR Facilities (S)," 28 Jul 67, pp 13-20.

42.   Intel Digest, PACOM, "Alternate NVN River Crossing Techniques," 29 Sep 67, pp 13-19.

43.   Ibid, pg 19.

44.   Rprt, PACAF, "Summary of Air Operations," Oct 67, pg 7,C.1.

45.   Ibid.

46. (S/NF)   Rprt, PACAF, "Effects of Air Ops, SEA, May 57," undated, pg 52;
    (S/NF)   Rprt, PACAF, "Effects of Air Ops, SEA, Jun 57," undated, pg 43.

47.   Ibid, Jun 67, pg 43.

48. (TS)   Rprt, PACAF, "Summary of Air Ops," Jul 67, pg 1.3.

49.   Ibid, pg 1.2.

50.   Ibid, Aug 67, pg 1.2.

51. (S/NF)   Ibid, Feb 67, pg 1.3.

52. (S/NF)   WAIS, DIP, 7AF, "Air Ops Against NVN," 2 Nov 68, pg 20.

53. (S)   Ltr, Maj Gen Gordon F. Blood, DCS/Ops, 7AF, to CS, MACV, subj:
             7AF 30-Day Interdiction Plan for RP I," 18 Jul 68.

54. (S)   Briefing, DITO, 7AF, "USN Interdiction Program, NVN," 8 Aug 68;
    (TS/NF) Ltr, CINCPACFLT to CINCPAC, subj: Interdiction Operations,
             20 May 68.

55. (TS)   Msg, JCS to CINCPAC, "ARC LIGHT," 15 Jul 68;
    (S)   Form 4, Capt Paul F. Foley, DOA, 7AF, "Proposed Article on
             Intensified Interdiction in RP I and TALLY HO," 20 Sep 68.

56. (S)   Ltr, Col Benton K. Partin, Dir, DOA, 7AF, to Brig Gen Robert J.
             Holbury, DOC, 7AF, subj: Evaluation of 30-Day Intensified
             Interdiction Effort in RP-I and TALLY HO," 29 Sep 68, pg 1.

57. (S)   Form 4, Capt Paul F. Foley, DOA, 7AF, "Proposed Article on
             Intensified Interdiction in RP I and TALLY HO," 20 Sep 68, pg 6.

58. (S/NF)   WAIS, 7AF.

                              CHAPTER IV

1. (TS)   OpOrd 433-66, 7AF, "BARREL ROLL/STEEL TIGER," 10 Jun 66, Annex B.

2.   Ibid.

3. (TS)   Rprt, PACAF, "Summary of Air Ops SEA," Nov 66, pg 2.7.

4. (TS/NF)   CHECO Rprt, Hq PACAF, DOTEC, "USAF Air Ops from Thailand, 1 Jan 67-
             1 Jul 68," 24 Aug 68, pp 48-49.

5. (TS)   Rprt, PACAF, "Summary of Air Operations SEA," Jan 68, pg 2.5.

6.   Ibid, Mar 67, pg 2.2.

7.   Ibid.
    (TS)   OpOrd 433-68, 7AF, "BARREL ROLL/STEEL TIGER," Sep 67.

8. (TS)   Rprt, PACAF, "Summary of Air Operations SEA," Apr 67, pg 7.C.2.

9. (TS)   Msg, CINCPACFLT to CINCPAC, "ROLLING THUNDER Targeting Concept Review," 8 Jan 67.

10. (S)   Paper 67/2, DOA, 7AF, Maj Y. W. Ow, "Some Thoughts on Road Interdiction Strategy," 1 Feb 67, pg 2.

11. (S/NF) WAIS, 7AF, 5 Dec 67, pp 6-7, 11.

12. (TS)   Rprt, PACAF, "Summary of Air Ops SEA," Dec 66, pg 2.A.9.

13.   Ibid, Jan 67, pg 1;
         Ibid, Mar 67, pg 2.2.

14.   Ibid, Oct 66, pg 2.4.

15. (S/NF) WAIS, 7AF, 28 Nov 66, pg 11;
    (S/NF) WAIS, 7AF, 26 Dec 66, pg 19.

16. (TS)   Rprt, PACAF, "Summary of Air Ops, SEA," Dec 66, pg 2.7.

17.   Ibid.

18. (S)   Paper 67/2, DOA, 7AF, Maj Y. W. Ow, "Some Thoughts on Road Interdiction Strategy," 1 Feb 67, pg 2.

19. (TS/   Paper 67/9, DOA, 7AF, Maj Y. W. Ow, "Documentation and Analysis
    AFEO) of SL Interdiction Ops, Nov 66 - May 67," 1 Jul 67, pg 27.

20. (TS)   Rprt, PACAF, "Summary of Air Ops, SEA," jan 67, pg 2.

21. (TS/NF) CHECO Rprt, Hq PACAF, DOTEC, "Air Operations in the DMZ Area, 1966," 15 Feb 67, pp 19-20. (Hereafter cited: "Air Ops in DMZ Area.")

22. (TS/NF) CHECO Rprt, Hq PACAF, DOTEC, "Air War in the DMZ, Jan-Aug 67," 20 May 68, pg 59. (Hereafter cited: "Air War in the DMZ.")

23.   Ibid.

24. (TS)   Rprt, PACAF, "Summary of Air Ops, SEA," Oct 66, pg 2.6.

25.   Ibid, Feb 67, pg 2.6.

26.   _Ibid_, pg 2.6.

27.   _Ibid_, pg 2.8.

28. (TS/NF) "Air War in the DMZ," pg 61.

29.   _Ibid_, pp 61-62.

30. (S)   Msg, SecDef to JCS, "B-52 Operations in SEA," 2 Mar 67.

31.   _Ibid_.

32. (S)   Memo for Record, Brig Gen Willard Pearson, USA, J3-MACV, "CIIC Meeting," 25 Mar 67.

33. (TS)   Rprt, PACAF, "Summary of Air Ops, SEA," Mar 67, pg 2.13.

34. (S/NF) WAIS, 7AF, 19 Mar 67, pp 23-29.

35. (TS)   Msg, COMUSMACV to CINCPAC, "B-52 Interdiction Test Program in Laos (S)," 12 Mar 67.

36. (S/NF) WAIS, 7AF, 18 Nov 67, pg 31.

37. (S)   Rprt, 23d TASS, "Monthly Activity Report," 5 Feb 67;
    (TS)   Rprt, PACAF, "Summary of Air Ops, SEA," Jan 67, pg 2.

38. (S)   Msg, 634 (TUOC) to 7AF, "Daily Operations Wrap Up," 14 Jan 67.

39. (S)   Rprt, 23d TASS, "Monthly Activity Rprt," 5 Feb 67.

40. (S)   Working Paper 16-67, CINCPAC, Charles E. Thompson and Lehman L. Henry, "Evaluation of Laos interdiction Program Oct 65 through Jun 67," 5 Sep 67, pg 2. (Hereafter cited: Working Paper 16-67.)

41. (S)   Msg, 7AF/13AF to AIRA, Vientiane, "20 Feb Truck Kill under 'Commando Bases' Operations in Mu Gia Pass Area," 25 Feb 67.

42. (S)   Msg, 7AF/13AF to 7AF, "Peacock Reports," 16-20 Apr 67.

43. (S)   Msg, 7AF/13AF to 7AF, "Peacock Report, Nr 30, Covering 0001-2400Z 1 May 67," 3 May 67.

44. (S)   Working Paper 16-67, pp 39-40.

45. (S/NF) Paper 67/7, DOA, 7AF, Maj Y. W. Ow, "An Examination of SL Truck Operations," 24 Mar 67, pp 1-2.

46. (S/NF) WAIS, 7AF, 16 Dec 67, pg 24.

47. (TS)   Msg, 7AF to All "Bravo" Addressees, "Interim 7AF OPlan 483-67, Air Campaign for SL North," 9 Mar 67.

48. (S)   Paper 67/2, DOA, 7AF, Maj Y. W. Ow, "Some Thoughts on Road Interdiction Strategy," 1 Feb 67, pg 2.

49.   Ibid, pg 1.

50. (TS)   Msg, 7AF to All "Bravo" Addressees, "Interim 7AF OPlan 483-67, Air Campaign for SL North," 9 Mar 67.

51. (TS/NF)   OpOrd 100-68, 7AF, "ROLLING THUNDER," 15 Dec 67, pg B.1.3.

52. (S)   Msg, TUOC, SLTF to 7AF, "STEEL TIGER Task Force Status Rprt, Nr 3," 23 Mar 67.

53. (TS/   Paper 67/9, DOA, 7AF, Maj Y. W. Ow, "Documentation and Analysis
    AFEO)   of SL Interdiction Operations, Nov 66-May 67," 1 Jul 67.

54. (S)   End of Tour Rprt, Maj Gerald K. Taylor, FAC, 23d TASS, 12 Jun 67.

55. (S)   Msg, TUOC, SLTF to 7AF, "SLTF Status Rprt, Nr 3," 23 Mar 67.

56. (S/NF)   OpOrd 485-67, 7AF, 17 Mar 67.

57. (S)   Msg, 7AF to PACAF and Others, "Change Nr 1 to 7AF OpOrd 485-67," 10 May 67.

58. (S)   Msg, TUOC, NKP to 7AF, "SLTF Status Rprt," 20 Mar 67;
    (S)   Msg, TUOC, NKP to 7AF, "SLTF Status Rprt Nr 2," 22 Mar 67;
    (S/NF)   Msg, Dep Comdr, 7AF/13AF to 7AF, "Manning Assistance SLTF", 11 Apr 67.

59. (S)   Msg, Dep Comdr, 7AF/13AF to 7AF, "SLTF," 8 May 67.

60. (TS)   Rprt, PACAF, "Summary of Air Operations SEA," May 67, pg 5.

61. (C)   OPREP 5, 7AF, Jan-May 67.

62. (S)   Msg, 432d TRW to 7AF, "Enemy Truck Tactics," 13 May 67.

63. (TS/NF)   "Air War in the DMZ";
    (TS)   Rprt, PACAF, "Summary of Air Ops SEA," May 67, pg 2.7.

64. (S)   Msg, 432d TRW to 7AF, "Enemy Truck Tactics," 13 May 67.

65. (TS)   Rprt, PACAF, "Summary of Air Ops SEA," Jul-Oct 67.

66. (S/NF)   Weekly Intel Digest, PACOM, "The Se Kong River," 30 Jun 67, pp 8-10.

67. (TS)   Rprt, PACAF, "Summary of Air Ops SEA," Jul 67, pg 2.8.

68.   Ibid, May 67, pg 2.9.

69. (S/NF) WAIS, 7AF, 23 Sep 67, pg 46.

70. (TS)   Rprt, PACAF, "Summary of Air Ops SEA," Aug-Dec 67.

71. (TS)   CHECO Rprt, Hq PACAF, DOTEC, "IGLOO WHITE," 31 Jul 68, pp 1-12.

72.   Ibid, pp 12, 30-32.

73. (S/NF) End of Tour Rprt, Brig Gen Jammie M. Philpott, DI, 7AF, 27 Nov 6/,
            pg 14.

74. (S)   Msg, AMEMB, Vientiane, to 7AF, "December Truck Kills in Panhandle,"
            3 Jan 68.

75. (S/NF) Rprt 68-1, COA Staff, 7AF, "Air Interdiction - Laos (S),"
            1 Jul 68, pp 10, 11, B.5, D.3. (Hereafter cited: COA Report
            68-1.)

76.   Ibid, pp 5, B.36.

77.   Ibid, pg B.35.

78. (TS)   Rprt, PACAF, "Summary of Air Operations SEA," Apr 68, pg 2.8.

79. (S/NF) COA Report 68-1, pp B.37, B.55.

80. (S)   Memo 68-5, COA, 7AF, Ronald P. Black, "Air Interdiction in
            MID RIVER," 16 May 68, pg 40.

81. (S/NF) COA Report 68-1, pg B.57.

82.   Ibid, pp B.29-32.

83. (S)   Paper 68/1-5, COA Staff, 7AF, "SL (Laos) Monthly Interdiction
            Analysis (IGLOO WHITE)," 1 Jul 68, Exhibit 14.

84. (S/NF) COA Report 68-1, pg 3.

85. (TS/   Interview, Brig Gen George J. Keegan, Jr., DI, 7AF, 2 Dec 68.
    AFEO)

86. (S/NF) COA Report 68-1, pg 14.

87.   Ibid, pg 12.

88.   Ibid, pg 12.

89.   Ibid, pg 16.

90.   Ibid, pg D.59;
     (S)   Memo, Dr Robert N. Schwartz, COA, 7AF to Maj Gen Gordon F. Blood,
           DO, 7AF, "MUSCLE SHOALS Utilization in SL, 2 Apr 68 to 7 Apr 68,"
           12 Apr 68, pg 6.

91. (S)   Msg, 7AF to PACAF, "Operations in SVN," 5 Apr 68.

92. (S/NF) COA Report 68-1, pg 29.

93. (S/NF) WAIS, 7AF, "ARC LIGHT and TURNPIKE," 22 Jun 68, pp 7-11;
     (S)   Msg, COMUSMACV to CINCPAC, "7AF SW Monsoon Interdiction Plan,"
           18 Apr 68;
     (S)   Ltr, Brig Gen George J. Keegan, Jr., DI, 7AF, to Maj Gen George B.
           Simler, Dir of Ops, Hq USAF (Intelligence and Interdiction),
           19 Jul 68.

94. (S/NF) COA Report 68-1, pg D.62.

95. (S/NF) Ltr, Maj Leslie G. Thompson, DITTT, 7AF to DIT, 7AF, subj: ARC
           LIGHT Validation Procedures Conference, 24 Sep 68, undated.

96. (S/NF) WAIS, 7AF, "7AF Summer Interdiction Program," Brig Gen George J.
           Keegan, Jr., DI, 7AF, 7 Dec 68, pg 8.

97.   Ibid, pg 9.

98. (C)   Briefing, DI, 7AF, "7AF 1968 Summer Interdiction Campaign,"
           undated.

99. (S/NF) WAIS, Brig Gen George J. Keegan, Jr., DI, 7AF, "7AF Summer
           Interdiction Program," 7 Dec 68, pg 14;
     (TS/ Interview, Brig Gen George J. Keegan, Jr., DI, 7AF, 2 Dec 68.
     AFEO)

                              CHAPTER V

1. (S)   Msg, I FFV to COMUSMACV, "Specified Strike Zone," 27 Mar 67.

2. (S/NF) After Action Rprt, Col Melvin H. Bryant, Dir, DASC Alpha, "Kylo
          Valley Interdiction Program," 22 May 67.

3. (S/NF) CHECO Rprt, Hq PACAF, DOTEC, "Khe Sanh (Operation NIAGARA),"
          13 Sep 68, pg 79.

4. (S/NF) WAIS, 7AF, 11 May 68, pp 8-9.

5. (S/NF)   Ibid.

6. (S/NF)   Intelligence Digest, PACOM, "Enemy Road Construction in the Laos Panhandle," 30 Aug 68, pg 12;
    (S/NF)   WAIS, 7AF, 27 Jan 68, pg 20.

7. (S)   CHECO Rprt, Hq PACAF, DOTEC, "TRUSCOTT WHITE," 11 Dec 68, pg 2.

8. (TS)   Memo for Record, Gen William W. Momyer, Comdr, 7AF, "CIIB Meeting," 9 Mar 68.

9. (S)   Form 4, Capt Robert Nofsinger, Jr., DIS, 7AF, "Interdiction of Route 548 (C)," 19 Mar 68.

10. (S)   Form 4, Col H. H. Moreland, TACP, 7AF, "Interdiction of Route 548 (C)," undated.

11. (S)   Msg, 7AF to I DASC and Others, "Interdiction in SVN," 23 Mar 68.

12. (S)   Form 4, Col H. H. Moreland, TACP, 7AF, "Fragging Method," 23 Mar 68.

13. (S)   Msg, III MAF to COMUSMACV, "Interdiction of Enemy LOC," 30 Mar 68.

14. (S)   Msg, III MAF to 7AF and Others, "Priority Intelligence Collection Plan for the Annamite Mountain Area of Central I CTZ," 1 Apr 68.

15. (S)   Msg, 7AF to PACAF, "Operations in SVN," 5 Apr 68.

16. (S)   Msg, 7AF to I DASC and DASC Alpha, "I Corps Diverts for Athens," 6 Apr 68.

17. (S)   CHECO Rprt, Hq PACAF, DOTEC, "Operation DELAWARE," 19 Apr - 17 May 1968," 2 Sep 68.

18. (S)   Msg, 7AF to PACAF, "LOC Intelligence Summary of Results through 1600Z 23 Apr 68," 24 Apr 68.

19.   Ibid.

20. (S)   Msg, COMUSMACV to CINCPAC, "7AF SW Monsoon Interdiction Plan" 18 Apr 68;
    (S)   Msg, 7AF to III MAF and Others, "Air Interdiction Campaign," 26 Apr 68.

21. (S)   Msg, 7AF to COMUSMACV, "7AF Interdiction of Enemy LOCs in SVN," 6 Apr 68.

22. (S)   Msg, COMUSMACV to CINCPAC, "7AF SW Monsoon Interdiction Plan," 18 Apr 68.

23. (S)   Msg, 7AF to III MAF, "Air Interdiction Campaign," 26 Apr 68.

24. (S/NF)   WAIS, 7AF, "Interdiction Program in I Corps," pp 2-4;
    (S/NF)   WAIS, 7AF, Interdiction in A Shau Valley," pp 2-4.

25. (S/NF)   WAIS, 4 May 68, pg 9.

26. (C/NF)   Vietnam Intelligence Summary (VIS), 7AF, "New Roads in South
             Vietnam," 13-19 Apr 68, pp 38-39.

27. (S)   Msg, III MAF to COMUSMACV, "Air Interdiction Route 548/548
             Extended," 16 Apr 68.

28. (S)   Msg, I DASC to 7AF, "Yellowbrick," 14 Apr 68.

29. (S/NF)   WAIS, 7AF, "Interdiction Program in I Corps," pp 2-4.

30. (C/NF)   VIS, 7AF, "I Corps," 6-12 Jul 68, pg 6.

31.   Ibid, pg 6.

32. (C)   Msg, HORN DASC to 7AF, "Interdiction Targets", 15 Aug 68.

33. (S/NF)   WAIS, 7AF, "Interdiction Program in I Corps," 14 Dec 68, pg 4.

34.   Ibid.

35. (S/NF)   Intelligence Digest, PACOM, 30 Aug 68, pg 12.

36. (C)   Msg, I FFV to COMUSMACV, "NVA Roads," 13 Apr 68.

37.   Ibid.

38. (S)   OPlan 7-68, 4th Inf Div, 28 Apr 68, Annex G.

39. (S)   Ltr, Lt Col Robert M. Lowry, Jr., Dir DASC Alpha to TACD, 7AF,
             subj: Dak To to Air Offensive Narrative Report, 28 Jun 68,
             pg 2.

40. (C)   Operations Report, 4th Inf Div, "Lessons Learned," 31 Jul 68,
             pg 2;
    (C)   CHECO Rprt, Hq PACAF, DOTEC, "KHAM DUC," 8 Jul 68.

41. (C)   Operations Rprt, 4th Inf Div, "Lessons Learned," 31 Jul 68, pg 18.

42. (C)   Report, COC-7, MACV, "CS Drum Drops," undated.

43. (S/NF)   WAIS, 7AF, "Southern I Corps Interdiction," 21 Dec 68, pp 2-4.

44. (C/NF)   VIS, 7AF, "I Corps," 27 Jul - 3 Aug 68, pg 9.

45. (C/NF)   VIS, 7AF, "Status of Enemy LOCs in SVN," 22-28 Jun 68, pg 37.

46. (S/NF)   WAIS, 7AF, "Southern I Corps Interdiction," 21 Dec 68, pp 2-4.

47. (C/NF)   VIS, 7AF, "I Corps," 27 Jul - 3 Aug 68, pg 9.

48.   Ibid, pg 6.

49. (S/NF)   Intelligence Digest, PACOM, "Enemy Road Construction in the
             Laos Panhandle," 30 Aug 68, pg 12.

50. (C)   Interview, Maj Eugene Carnahan, FAC, 21st TASS, Pleiku, by
             Lt Col Robert A. MacDonough, 7AF, DOAC, undated. (Hereafter
             cited: Major Carnahan Interview.)

51. (S)   OPlan 7-68, 4th Inf Div, 5 Apr 68, App. 1.

52. (C)   Operations Report, 4th Inf Div, "Lessons Learned," 31 Jul 68,
             pg 2.

53. (C)   Msg, I FFV to COMUSMACV, "Activation of Operational Nickname,"
             8 Apr 68.

54. (C)   Msg, I FFV to COMUSMACV, "NVA Roads," 1 Apr 68.

55. (S)   OPlan 7-68, 4th Inf Div., 5 Apr 68, Annex B.

56. (S)   Ltr, Lt Col Robert M. Lowry, Jr., Dir, DASC Alpha to TACD, 7AF,
             subj: Dak To Air Offensive Narrative Report, 28 Jun 68, pg 5.
             (Hereafter cited: Lt Col R. M. Lowry, Jr. Letter.)

57. (S)   OPlan 7-68, 4th Inf Div, 5 Apr 68, Tab A to App 1.

58. (C)   Major Carnahan Interview;
    (C)   Interview, Maj Michael Burke, ALO, 1st Bde/4th Inf Div, by
             Lt Col Robert A. MacDonough, 7AF, DOAC, undated. (Hereafter
             cited: Major Burke Interview.)

59. (S)   Lt Col R. M. Lowry, Jr. Letter, pg 3.

60. (C)   Major Carnahan Interview.

61. (C)   VIS, 7AF, "Status of Enemy LOCs in SVN," 22-28 Jun 68, pg 38;
             Ibid, 31 Aug - 6 Sep 68, pg 52.

62. (S)   OPlan 7-68, 4th Inf Div, 28 Apr 68, Annex G.

63. (C)   Major Burke Interview.

64. (C)   Operations Report, 4th Inf Div, "Lessons Learned," 31 Jul 68, Incl 6.

65. (S/NF) WAIS, 7AF, 4 May 68, pg 12.

66. (S/NF) WAIS, 7AF, "Song Be Interdiction Program," 30 Nov 68, pp 2-5.

67. (S)   Ltr, Lt Col George K. Barson, ALO, II FFV, to 7AF, subj: Combat Operations After Action Report, 25 Feb 69.

68. (S)   Working Paper, "COMMANDO HUNT Integrated Interdiction Plan for the Northeast Monsoon Season 68-69," 7AF, 3 Aug 68.

69. (C)   Memo, Brig Gen George W. McLaughlin, TACC, 7AF to TACP, "Interdiction Program," 5 Jul 68.

70. (U)   Ltr, TACPS to DOA, "Interdiction Program," 21 Aug 68.

CHAPTER VI

1. (U)   AFM 2-1, "Tactical Air Operations--Counterair, Interdiction, and CAS," 14 Jun 65, pg 15.

2. (U)   Book, Westley Frank Craven and James Lea Cate, Editors, "The Army Air Force in WW II, (Chicago: Univ. of Chicago Press), 1951, Vol II, pg 395.

3. (U)   USAF Historical Study Nr 72, Hist Div, Air Univ, "USAF Operations in the Korean Conflict, 1 Nov 1950-30 Jun 1952," 1953, pg 162;
   (U)   Book, Matthew B. Ridgway, "The Korean War" (Garden City, N.Y.: Doubleday and Co.,) 1967, pp 75-6, 191, 245.

4. (S/NF) WAIS, 7AF, "New Roads in SVN," 4 May 68, pp 12-14.

5. (S)   COA Memo 68-5, Ronald P. Black, COA, 7AF, "Air Interdiction in MUD RIVER," 16 May 68, pg 12. (Hereafter cited: COA Memo 68-5.)

6. (TS/NF) Hist Rprt, MACV, 1967, Vol I, pp 34-43;
   (TS/NF) Hist Rprt, MACV, 1968, Vol I, pp 56-58.

7. (S)   Msg, AMEMB, Vientiane to 7AF, "Dec Truck Kills in Panhandle," 3 Jan 68;
   (S/NF) End of Tour Rprt, Brig Gen Jammie M. Philpott, DI, 7AF, 27 Nov 67, pg 14.

8. (S/NF) WAIS, 7AF, "7AF Summer Interdiction Program," 7 Dec 68, pg 14.

9. (S/NF)   Computer Printout, IDHS, DI, 7AF, 18 May 69.

10. (TS)   Rprt, PACAF, "Summary of Air Operations," Oct 67, pg 7.C.1.

11. (S)   Form 4, Lt Col R. D. Moe, DITO, 7AF, "Anti-Truck Infiltration,"
             6 Sep 68 with Attach: "Computation of the Rate of Infiltration
             through Laos."

12.   Ibid.

13. (S/NF)   WAIS, 7AF, "New Roads in SVN," 4 May 68, pg 14.

14. (S)   COA Memo 68-5, pg 56.

15.   Ibid, pg 12.

16. (S/NF)   Rprt, Hq USAF, "Measures of the 1968 Out-country Bombing Campaign
             in Southeast Asia," Ops Analysis, Dec 68, pg 21.

17. (S/NF)   COA Report 68-1, pg B.43.

18. (S)   COA Memo 68-5, pg 26.

19. (TS/   CHECO Rprt, Hq PACAF, DOTEC, "USAF Operations from Thailand,
    AFEO)   1 January 67 to 1 July 68," 20 Nov 68, pp 78-82.

20.   Ibid, pg 81.

21. (S/NF)   COA Report 68-1, pp 39-40.

22. (S)   DOA Paper 68-2A, Col B. K. Partin, DOA, 7AF, "Effective Ordnance
             for Destroying Trucks by Direct Air Attack," 25 Mar 68.

23. (S)   COA Memo 68-5, pg 27.

24. (S/NF)   COA Report 68-1, pg 3.

25. (U)   USAF Historical Study Nr 127, Hist Div, Air Univ, "USAF Operations
             in the Korean Conflict, 1 July 1952-27 July 1953," 1 Jul 56,
             pg 113.

26. (TS/   Interview, Brig Gen George J. Keegan, Jr., DI, 7AF, 2 Dec 68.
    AFEO)

27. (C)   Form 4, Col Robert E. Pater, Chief, TIGER HOUND/TALLY HO Div,
             7AF, "Interdiction Effort," 14 Oct 68.

28. (S/NF)   WAIS, 7AF, Brig Gen George J. Keegan, Jr., "7AF Summer Interdic-
             tion Program,: 7 Dec 68, pp 13-14.

29. (S)   Working Paper, DI, 7AF, "LOC Interdiction versus Truck Killing,"
             4 Oct 68.

30. (S/NF)   COA Report 68-1, pg D. 28-29.

31. (S/NF)   Ltr, Col Leonard P. Bull, DIT, 7AF, subj: Comments on Project
             CHECO Report, USAF Air Interdiction in SEA, Nov 66-Oct 68,
             5 Jul 69.

32. (S/NF)   COA Report 68-1, pg 28.

33.   Ibid.

34. (S/NF)   WAIS, 7AF, Brig Gen George J. Keegan, Jr., "7AF Summer Inter-
             diction Program," 7 Dec 68, pp 13-14.

35. (S)   DOA Paper 68-4A, Maj Bernard Appel and Capt Phillip R. Meinert,
             "Bombing Accuracy in a Combat Environment--SEA, Aug 67 - Jan 68,"
             undated, pp 1-2.

36. (S)   DOA Paper 68-13, "An Effectiveness Comparison of the M-117, the
             AGM-12C, and Paveway for Road Interdiction," 30 Oct 68;
    (U)   USAF Historical Study Nr 72, Hist Div, Air Univ, "USAF Opera-
             tions in the Korean Conflict, 1 Nov 1950-30 Jun 1952, 1 Jul 55,
             pg 141.

37. (S)   Msg, CINCUSARPAC to CINCPAC, "Analysis of MUSCLE SHOALS Weekly
             OPREP-5 (4-11 Apr 68)," 27 Apr 68.

38. (S)   DOA Paper 68-3, "An Evaluation of MK-36 Destruction Seeding in
             RP I, Nov 67-Jan 68," Apr 68, pg 1.

39. (S/NF)   WAIS, 7AF, Brig Gen George J. Keegan, Jr., "7AF Summer Interdic-
             tion Program," 7 Dec 68, pp 6-7.

40. (S/NF)   Computer Printout, IDHS, 7AF, 18 May 69.

41. (TS/   CHECO Rprt, Hq PACAF, DOTEC, "USAF Operations from Thailand,
    AFEO)   1 Jan 67-1 Jul 68," 20 Nov 68, pg 80.

APPENDIX I

TRUCKS DESTROYED/DAMAGED IN STEEL TIGER AND ROUTE PACKAGE I

	STEEL TIGER		ROUTE PACKAGE I		TOTAL	
	Dest	Dam	Dest	Dam	Dest	Dam
Nov 66	87	70	64	27	151	97
Dec	86	71	25	26	111	97
Jan 67	44	60	2	3	46	63
Feb	72	83	78	58	150	141
Mar	128	81	39	46	167	127
Apr	57	103	79	59	136	162
May	28	25	297	57	325	82
Jun	5	2	291	76	296	78
Jul	6	0	517	102	523	102
Aug	12	5	785	214	797	219
Sep	11	2	215	37	226	39
Oct	84	21	71	41	155	62
Nov	585	162	81	22	666	184
Dec	660	193	39	64	699	257
Jan 68	701	147	62	63	763	210
Feb	452	74	24	13	476	87
Mar	412	100	106	92	518	192
Apr	889	131	162	173	1,051	304
May	330	63	264	263	594	326
Jun	170	29	195	198	365	227
Jul	269	13	283	212	552	225
Aug	75	3	142	173	217	176
Sep	79	14	45	85	124	99
Oct	68	21	42	67	110	88
	5,310	1,473	3,908	2,171	9,218	3,644

APPENDIX II

LOC INTERDICTION VERSUS TRUCK KILLING*

9. (S) <u>Through-put Computation</u> (14-20 Jul 68):

Number of Sightings: 508/day

Total Number of Trucks: 2,032

Travel Time: 2 days

Bombing Loss Rate: 23% of trucks sighted

Note: The loss rate has been extrapolated from the Laotian dry season results where it was computed that 23% of the truckloads of supplies were destroyed or truckload equivalents were damaged or experienced secondary fires or explosions.

The loss rate due to truck replacement, accidents, major breakdowns, etc., is estimated at 2% of operable trucks. The loss rate due to spoilage or accidental destruction in storage is 1% of operable trucks.

Loss Rate:		Trucks:
Bombing: 23% of 508	=	116
Replacement: 2% of 2,032	=	41
Spoilage: 1% of 2,032	=	<u>20</u>
		177

These 177 trucks per day represent 8.7% of the total truck fleet in RP I. The number of trucks southbound is then 50% of 2,032 plus 8.7% of 2,032 or 1,192 trucks. Of these, 1,192 trucks, 8.7% will be lost daily or 104 southbound trucks.

Letter A = number of trucks input daily

S = number of southbound trucks

L = % loss of operable trucks

*Extract, Working Paper, Lt Col R. D. Moe, DITO, 7AF, 4 Oct 68, 14 pages.

Then $A = \dfrac{S}{2-L} = \dfrac{1,192}{2 - .087} = 623$ trucks

Working our Through-put Problem:

Input	623
Day 1 Loss	-54
End of Day 1	569
Day 2 Loss	-50
Through-put	519

Therefore, there were a total of 519 trucks passing into South Vietnam or Laos daily. If each truck carried 3.5 tons of supplies, there
were a total of 1,816 tons of military supplies exiting RP I daily. The
net attrition of the 623 input southbound trucks would be 104 trucks or
16.7% of the input.

10. (S) <u>Through-put Computation</u> (28 Aug-3 Sep):

Number of Sightings: 151/day

Total Number of Trucks: 604

Travel Time: 2 days

Bombing Loss Rate: 23% of trucks sighted

Replacement and Accidents: 2% of operable trucks

Spoilage: 1% of operable trucks

Loss Rate:		Trucks:
Bombing: 23% of 151	=	35
Replacement: 2% of 604	=	12
Spoilage: 1% of 604	=	6
Total Loss:		53 trucks

These 53 trucks represent 8.8% of the 604 total trucks in RP I. The total
number of trucks southbound is then 50% plus 8.8% of 604 or 355 trucks.
Each day 8.8% or 31 of the southbound trucks will be lost. Substituting
in our formula for through-put:

$A = \dfrac{S}{2-L} = \dfrac{355}{2 - .088} = 185$ trucks

Working the Through-put Problem:

Input	185
Day 1 Loss	-16
End of Day 1	169
Day 2 Loss	-15
Throughput	154

Therefore, there were a total of 154 trucks passing into the DMZ of South Vietnam or into Laos daily. If each truck carries 3.5 tons of supplies, a total of 529 tons of supplies were exiting RP I daily. This represents a difference of 1,287 tons of supplies per day between the first week and the last week of the period sampled, a decrease that can be ascribed to the intensified Summer Interdiction Campaign during which we concentrated on retarding the flow of traffic at a few key choke points. The net attrition over the two-day period of travel was 17% of the input.

11. Commutation of the Truck-Killing Equivalence of Choke Point Interdiction:

During the Summer Interdiction Campaign of 1968, a special effort was made to slow the flow of enemy trucks and supplies through a few key choke points. It was reasoned that throttling of the truck traffic would allow more chances to strike trucks congested behind choke points, permit the slowed trucks to be struck more often by lengthening their trip time, and reduce significantly the throughput of supplies. Choke points were re-struck at night with soft ordnance to harass and discourage road repair efforts. As the season progressed, there was a noticeable decrease in truck traffic due to road closures for extended periods of time. The level of truck activity fell from a high of 508 total sightings in the first week to a low of 151 sightings in the last week, a 70% decrease. We propose to show the number of trucks that would have to be destroyed to give an equivalent 70% reduction in traffic. To do this we will compute an input figure by computing backward from the through-put figure achieved in the last week to the southbound trucks sighted in the first week. We will as-sume 61% of the trucks are southbound as in the last dry season in Laos. If we destroyed trucks at the high rate necessary in this hypothetical problem, there would be a rapid reduction of the total number of trucks.

Assumptions:	Trucks:
Trucks Sightings:	504/day
Total Trucks:	2,032
Southbound (61% of 2,032):	1,240/day
Through-put:	154/day

156

The problem is one of iteration of the loss rate and input values until the throughput is 154 trucks and the sum of the input value and the number of trucks remaining at the end of the first day equals the southbound trucks. By trial and error we found that:

Input	871	58% of 871	=	505	
Day 1 Loss	-505	58% of 366	=	212	
End of Day 1	366	Total Loss	=	717	trucks/day
Day 2 Loss	-212				
Through-put	154				

Note that 871 + 366 = 1,237 and the through-put = 154 trucks. With round off error this is as close as we can approach the desired solution. A loss rate of 58% per day was computed. The total number of trucks lost per day throughout the entire area was 717. The net attrition of the input of 871 trucks was 82.3% over a two-day period.

12. (S) Since we know the number of trucks that would be lost each day with the normal application of force; i.e., without the extra emphasis on impeding the truck flow, it only remains to compute the difference between the daily truck loss figured in paragraph 10 (104 trucks) and the truck loss equivalent to impeding the flow computed in paragraph 11 (717). Therefore the truck-killing equivalence of the interdiction of traffic flow is 717 - 104 = 613 southbound trucks per day.

13. (S) Now 613 trucks/day is the number of trucks per day we would have to kill to reduce truck traffic from a level of 508 sightings per day to 151 sightings per day. If we assume an increase in F-4E sorties sufficient to destroy this number of additional trucks, we would have to apply 2.6 times 613 or approximately 1,600 additional sorties. As a matter of fact, it is unlikely that this high sortie level could be applied effectively in RP I because of air traffic congestion, limitations of control facilities, and limitations in the visual acquisition of trucks by FAC or strike aircraft.

14. (S) Assuming we could effectively apply this number of sorties in a truck-killing role, how much would it cost when compared with the cost of impeding flow at key choke points? Remember we have reduced the through-put from 519 truckloads in the period 14-20 July to 154 truckloads in the period 28 August-3 September or 365 truckloads.

Cost of Aircraft: $2,600,000

Operating Cost of Aircraft: $614/hour

Sortie Length: Mixed F-4 & F-105 Forces: 2:00
                F-4 Forces: 1:40

Cost of Munitions: $5,000/aircraft

Sortie Rate (Normal Force): 154/day

Sortie Rate (Truck-Killing Force): 1,600 Additional/Day

Aircraft Loss Rate: 0.0014/Sortie

Aircraft Losses (Normal Force): 7

Aircraft Losses (Truck-Killing Force): 114

Normal Force (Interdiction)

Cost of Aircraft Losses:	$356,800/Day
Operating Cost:	$189,112/Day
Munitions Cost:	$770,000/Day
Total	$ 1,315,912/Day

Truck-Killing Force (Additional Cost)

Cost of Aircraft Losses:	$ 5,824,000/Day
Operating Cost:	$ 1,640,000/Day
Munitions Cost:	$ 8,000,000/Day
Plus Normal Cost:	$ 1,315,912
	$ 16,779,912

365 truckloads reduction in through-put = 1,278 tons.

Cost per ton of reduction in through-put:

Interdiction Force: $ 1,030/Ton

Truck-Killing Force: $13,130/Ton

Conclusion: It is 13 times as expensive to reduce through-put from 519 trucks to 154 trucks by killing trucks than by interdiction of a few key choke points, if it is indeed feasible at all to attempt to do it by killing trucks. Percentage kills usually decrease with increasing truck numbers.

The fact remains that any truck-killing campaign which fails to reduce the rate of flow of traffic along LOCs is expensive, ineffective, and impractical. Conversely, the Summer Interdiction Campaign of 1968 in RP I showed that cutting roads and harassing road repair crews at a few key traffic choke points can effect large reductions in enemy through-put supplies. Interdiction of choke points is more effective and costs less than truck-killing alone.

GLOSSARY

AAA	Antiaircraft Artillery
AA/AW	Antiaircraft/Automatic Weapons
ABCCC	Airborne Battlefield Command and Control Center
AGL	Above Ground Level
ALO	Air Liaison Officer
AO	Area of Operation
ARVN	Army of Republic of Vietnam
ASRT	Air Support Radar Team
BC	Body Count
BDA	Battle Damage Assessment
CDEC	Combined Document Exploitation Center
CEP	Circular Error Probability
CINCPAC	Commander-in-Chief, Pacific Command
CINCPACAF	Commander-in-Chief, Pacific Air Forces
CINCPACFLT	Commander-in-Chief, U.S. Pacific Fleet
CINCUSARPAC	Commander-in-Chief, U.S. Army, Pacific
CJCS	Chairman, Joint Chiefs of Staff
COMUSMACV	Commander, U.S. Military Assistance Command
DASC	Direct Air Support Center
D/D	Destroyed/Damaged
DMZ	Demilitarized Zone
FAC	Forward Air Controller
GP	General Purpose
HF	Hornet Force
IR	Infrared
ISC	Infiltration Surveillance Center
JCS	Joint Chiefs of Staff
KBA	Killed by Air
KIA	Killed in Action
LOC	Line of Communication
LRRP	Long-Range Reconnaissance Patrol
MACV	Military Assistance Command, Vietnam
mm	Milimeter

OPlan	Operations Plan
OpOrd	Operations Order
PACAF	Pacific Air Forces
PACOM	Pacific Command
POL	Petroleum, Oil, and Lubricants
PW	Prisoner of War
RLAF	Royal Laotian Air Force
ROE	Rules of Engagement
RP	Route Package
RT	ROLLING THUNDER
SAC	Strategic Air Command
SAM	Surface-to-Air Missile
SCAR	Strike Control and Reconnaissance
SEA	Southeast Asia
SL	STEEL TIGER
SLAM	Search, Locate, Annihilate, Monitor
SLAR	Side-Looking Airborne Radar
SLN	STEEL TIGER NORTH
SLTF	STEEL TIGER Task Force
SSZ	Specified Strike Zone
ST	Shining Brass Team
SVN	South Vietnam
Tac	Tactical
TACAN	Tactical Air Navigation
TACC	Tactical Air Control Center
TASE	Tactical Air Support Element
TFA	Task Force Alpha
TH	TIGER HOUND
TUOC	Tactical Unit Operations Center
UN	United Nations
USN	U.S. Navy
VC	Viet Cong
VNAF	Vietnamese Air Force
VR	Visual Reconnaissance
WAAPM	Wide Area Antipersonnel Mine
WAIS	Weekly Air Intelligence Summary

161

www.ingramcontent.com/pod-product-compliance
Lightning Source LLC
Chambersburg PA
CBHW082354270326
41935CB00013B/1615